TACTICAL ESPIONAGE ACTION

METAL GEAR SOLID 3
SNAKE EATER

TABLE OF CONTENTS

INTRODUCTION

We at BradyGAMES are proud to bring you this guide. From the moment we began playing, we knew right away that we were working on a very special game. And that feeling carried through all the way to the ending credits. We have constructed this guide with the hope that it helps you become a *Metal Gear Solid 3: Snake Eater* expert, and furthermore, we hope it does justice to this great game.

The strategy contained in this guide, namely in the walkthrough chapters that lead you through the missions, focuses on providing tips and tactics for taking down guards that stand between you and your next objective. If an enemy discovers you in this game, it's not the end of the world. Thanks to Snake's damage resistance and regenerative abilities, he can survive nearly any combat situation.

Therefore, it's possible to *sneak* through the game or *blast* through the game, whichever you prefer. We tried to focus on sneaking through, because Snake generally consumes less health that way, and we feel it's in keeping with the spirit of the game. There is no single "right" way to play this game. Still, we endeavored to provide a method that allows you to maintain a rich item and ammunition supply, just in case someone spots you and things get crazy. Please use this guide with these concepts in mind, and enjoy this fantastic game!

INTRODUCTION

CHARACTERS

SYSTEM

WEAPONS

ITEMS

FOOD

CURE

PROLOGUE: VIRTUOUS MISSION

OPERATION SNAKE EATER

SNAKE VS. MONKEY

BONUSES & EASTER EGGS

KEROTAN LOCATIONS

INTERVIEWS

METAL GEAR SOLID COMIC

CHARACTERS

NAKED SNAKE

A man who formally introduced himself as "John Doe" and went also by the nickname "Jack." The operative assigned the codename Naked Snake during the historic operation "Virtuous Mission" reputedly cared little for the trappings of identity. Long before he would lead the U.S. to victory in the Cold War, his chief concern in life was the mission, and for many years he lived only to complete his objective. This was one of many disciplines he learned during his training under The Boss, the woman whose combat talents led the Allies to victory in World War II, also known as the mother of today's Special Forces.

The exact depths of the relationship between Naked Snake and The Boss remain unclear, but what is known is that they met ten years prior to Virtuous Mission and drifted apart perhaps five years after their meeting. Together they created the martial arts-inspired fighting style known as Close Quarters Combat, or CQC. A mixture of martial arts combined with handgun and knife techniques, CQC is a means of disarming and disabling an opponent in as few moves as possible.

Naked Snake utilized these legendary skills during the failed Virtuous Mission and the successive Operation Snake Eater. Though the circumstances of how he was able to complete the mission remain unknown, he was subsequently awarded the title of "Big Boss" and went on to establish the Special Forces Unit FOXHound. In later years he would betray his country and President to obtain the stolen weapon Metal Gear in an attempt to establish the soldier-ruled regime of "Outer Heaven" in Zanzibar Land. Many psychologists have attempted to puzzle together the roots of his demoralization and eventual treason, and some point to the vague events of Operation Snake Eater. Understanding this complex historic character may be more than most could hope for.

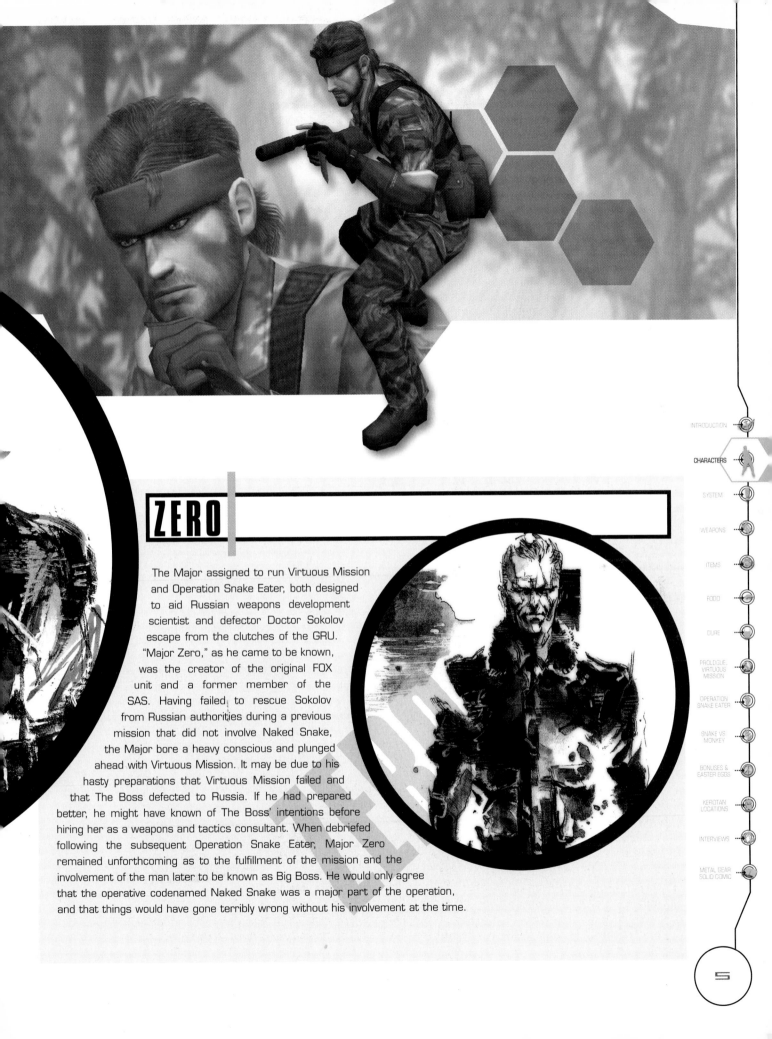

ZERO

The Major assigned to run Virtuous Mission and Operation Snake Eater, both designed to aid Russian weapons development scientist and defector Doctor Sokolov escape from the clutches of the GRU. "Major Zero," as he came to be known, was the creator of the original FOX unit and a former member of the SAS. Having failed to rescue Sokolov from Russian authorities during a previous mission that did not involve Naked Snake, the Major bore a heavy conscious and plunged ahead with Virtuous Mission. It may be due to his hasty preparations that Virtuous Mission failed and that The Boss defected to Russia. If he had prepared better, he might have known of The Boss' intentions before hiring her as a weapons and tactics consultant. When debriefed following the subsequent Operation Snake Eater, Major Zero remained unforthcoming as to the fulfillment of the mission and the involvement of the man later to be known as Big Boss. He would only agree that the operative codenamed Naked Snake was a major part of the operation, and that things would have gone terribly wrong without his involvement at the time.

PARA-MEDIC

A field surgeon and doctor assigned to provide scientific support on Virtuous Mission and Operation Snake Eater, Para-Medic would later go on to achieve great work in the field of genetic research and development. As to her involvement in the fabled mission that took place in Tselinoyarsk all those years ago, she remained fairly tight-lipped throughout her career. She has become a master of changing the subject to her favorite topic, movies and film. Extremely knowledgeable on all forms of biology, it is thought perhaps she provided information to field operatives on long-term missions as to the possible edibility of fruits and animals in the wildlife.

NIKOLAI STEPANOVICH SOKOLOV

A Russian weapons research scientist and attempted defector, Sokolov was the subject of the rescue attempt entitled Virtuous Mission and the subsequent campaign called Operation Snake Eater. Due to his disappearance during or after Snake Eater, many historians point out that he was likely assigned a new identity. Sokolov is, after all, credited with the infamous Shagohod project, a precursor to today's Metal Gears. Though his reason for wanting to defect remains unclear, one can surmise that perhaps he became disillusioned about the nature of his work and wished to cease weapons production in light of the supposed lethality of the Shagohod. However, since the United States intended to utilize Sokolov in its own weapons research and development, what he hoped to gain by defecting could not be determined.

EVA

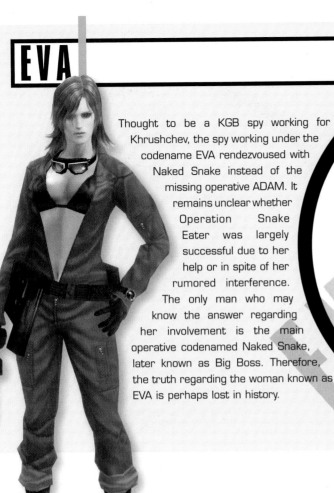

Thought to be a KGB spy working for Khrushchev, the spy working under the codename EVA rendezvoused with Naked Snake instead of the missing operative ADAM. It remains unclear whether Operation Snake Eater was largely successful due to her help or in spite of her rumored interference. The only man who may know the answer regarding her involvement is the main operative codenamed Naked Snake, later known as Big Boss. Therefore, the truth regarding the woman known as EVA is perhaps lost in history.

SIGINT

An electronics researcher and inventor assigned to act as technical support on Operation Snake Eater, Sigint is credited with creating many of the technologically advanced weapons and equipment today known as "spy gadgets." During Operation Snake Eater he purportedly provided weapons and vehicle data to field operatives, and may have provided strategic assessments for combat situations due to his highly analytical and problem solving skills.

OCELOT

The commander of the Ocelot Unit that served the renegade Russian Colonel Volgin of the GRU was well known for his amazing learning and adaptive capabilities. Able to employ advanced combat skills within mere hours of seeing them in action, the Ocelot commander was unmatched in his unit. For this reason, the GRU treated Ocelot as second in command to Volgin, despite the presence of other higher-ranking officials within the specialized army. In his later life, the man who would become known as "Revolver Ocelot" eventually joined the Special Forces unit FOXHound, the team created by Big Boss. However, most historians point out that if Ocelot was a soldier under Volgin in the GRU, then he may have at one time confronted or even fought Naked Snake, later known as Big Boss. Certain files leaked from the Shadow Moses Island incident and Nastasha Romanenko's controversial book indicate Ocelot's involvement in FOXHound's rebellion and the ensuing hostage situation that took place in Alaska. He was later involved in the sabotage and sinking of an oil tanker that was actually carrying an advanced prototype Metal Gear through Hudson Bay. Ocelot's actions indicate the possibility that he could be a double agent, calling his true loyalty and motivations into question.

VOLGIN

Colonel and commander of the Russian GRU, which led an uprising against Khrushchev in the early '60s, Volgin bore the codename "Thunderbolt" due to his reported ability to channel and control electric energy. Volgin built and presided over the impenetrable fortress Groznyj Grad, named for Ivan Groznyj, or "Ivan the Terrible." The Shagohod weapons system was allegedly being developed inside his fortress when Doctor Sokolov attempted to defect. As a result, Volgin tightened security on all scientific staff, meaning that any who attempted to escape were killed. Volgin's penchant for sadism knew no boundaries. His favorite method of dispatching unfortunate personnel he deemed traitorous or expendable was to beat them into bloody pulp with his fists. A powerful and beastly man, Volgin often uttered the Japanese phrase "Kuwabara, Kuwabara" before or after performing psychotic, vicious acts of cruelty. There is no exact translation in the English language for this phrase, but in Volgin's usage he most likely meant to say "The horror..." perhaps promising death and destruction to his enemies.

THE PAIN

Cobra Unit hornet soldier "The Pain" was a master bee tamer and hornet specialist supposedly capable of commanding entire swarms of stinging hornets to do his bidding and attack his enemies. A former comrade of The Boss, The Pain was one of several fearsome Cobra Unit commandos involved in the events of Operation Snake Eater. The Pain ostensibly developed his rare gift by allowing thousands of hornets to sting him for months at a time, until the hive came to believe that he was in fact another hornet himself. His intense willingness to suffer pain for his art enticed The Boss to recruit him for the Cobra Unit during the last world war.

THE FEAR

Cobra Unit spider soldier "The Fear" was appropriately named, due to his frightening appearance and abilities. The Fear dislocated limbs at will to enhance his strange ability to climb rough surfaces like a spider. The dislocation allowed The Fear to leap great distances and to crawl across the ground at lightning-fast speeds. A formidable wilderness hunter, The Fear preferred to use a crossbow gun to "sting" his opponents with toxic poisons extracted from the world's deadliest insects.

THE END

A veteran of dozens of wars, The End spent most of his latter days in a kind of preventative hibernation, staving off his own natural death until he finally found a battle worthy of his life. A superior marksman and sniper, The End employed camouflage techniques that made him invisible even the brightest, most exposed areas. His sole companion in life was a squawking parrot, which woke The End just in time for battle.

THE FURY

An astronaut on secret Soviet rocket missions, The Fury reportedly fought with all the anger and rage he felt regarding the warlike state of the world. Equipping a heavy spacesuit and the most powerful flamethrower ever made, The Fury would unleash his flames of wrath upon his enemies, consuming them in purifying fires he wished would consume the whole world, wiping mankind's slate clean.

THE SORROW

A former Cobra Unit spirit medium soldier, The Sorrow could evidently speak to dead men on the battlefield to determine enemy positions and armaments. His tap into the spirit world also provided him a means to see slightly into the future, and to read the minds of interrogation subjects. However, The Sorrow was reportedly killed years before Operation Snake Eater. Therefore, there is no way he could have been part of The Boss's defection and the GRU uprising...could he?

THE BOSS

Little is actually recorded in any of the files regarding the woman known by the revered title, "The Boss." This is mainly due to the top secret, cloak and dagger nature of most of the missions in which she participated. What all of the files do state in resonance is that she was largely responsible for the victory of the Allies in World War II, and that she went on to become the creator and "mother" of the Special Forces. Yet for reasons entirely unknown to the U.S. government, The Boss betrayed the country she had served for over 20 years and two wars, defecting to the U.S.S.R. during Virtuous Mission. She was blamed and accused of launching and detonating two "Davy Crockett" class portable nuclear warheads in Russian territory. The reasons for her sudden and erratic behavior were unknown to all, save the other participants in Operation Snake Eater and her beloved hand-picked Cobra Unit, also known as the "Sons of The Boss."

The Boss was a fearsome soldier who employed a unique short-range combat style she created herself called Close Quarters Combat, or CQC. She developed this disarming and disabling technique with the aid of the former student who was eventually assigned to Virtuous Mission. The operative known by the codename Naked Snake was also betrayed by The Boss' defection, and this may be the reason he took on the subsequent Operation Snake Eater designed to seek out and eliminate The Boss and her Cobra Unit.

SYSTEM

This chapter covers game control and mechanics in *Metal Gear Solid 3: Snake Eater*. Side activities, such as changing camouflage, feeding Snake, and curing injuries, must be performed often, and they are not covered in-depth in the walkthrough. This section provides additional tips to help you master the game. This chapter is one of the most important in the book, so please refer to this section whenever you have a question about controlling the game.

CONTROLS

STALKING/LOOK DIRECTIONAL PAD

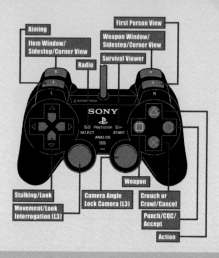

Press the directional buttons to make the character walk in the corresponding direction. When the directional buttons are used to move Snake, he moves with extreme caution and stealth. This is known as "Stalking," and it allows Snake to sneak up behind enemies with little margin for error. However, Stalking consumes Stamina more rapidly, and so it is recommended for only short periods immediately before attempting to grab an enemy. While holding the First Person View button **R1**, use the Directional Pad to look left or right, up or down, respectively.

MOVEMENT/LOOK LEFT ANALOG STICK

Move the Left Analog Stick to guide the character in the corresponding direction. Moving the Left Analog Stick upward guides the character toward the top of the screen, moving the Left Analog Stick to the right directs the character east, and so on. The degree to which the stick is pressed determines the character's movement speed. Move the stick only slightly to walk, or move it all the way to run.

INTERROGATION L3 BUTTON (DEPRESS LEFT ANALOG STICK)

When an enemy character has been grabbed in CQC, depress the Left Analog Stick and release the ● button to interrogate the person. Under duress, soldiers sometimes reveal traps to watch out for, hidden item locations, or other special information that can come in handy. But avoid being gullible, because *sometimes soldiers lie!* To interrogate a soldier multiple times, release and quickly re-press L3 to extract more information. Many enemies have more than one piece of information to divulge.

RADIO SELECT

Snake is not alone on this mission. Press SELECT to bring up the Radio menu. Start communicating with helpful, informative and entertaining support characters by manually setting the frequency or by choosing a stored contact from the Memory Window. More information regarding the Radio function is provided further on in this chapter. When the radio emits a ringing sound and the **[CALL]** message appears onscreen, press SELECT to receive the incoming transmission.

SURVIVAL VIEWER START

Press START to open the Survival Viewer. This menu allows for the changing of camouflage, the storage or retrieval of items from the Backpack, the eating of food, and the treatment of wounds and illnesses. A Map of the area can also be viewed. The Survival Viewer is described in greater detail later in this chapter.

CAMERA ANGLE RIGHT ANALOG STICK

While in normal, top-down view, move the Right Analog Stick in any direction to widen and shift the camera. Use this function to see better in the direction Snake is headed without having to enter First Person View every few steps.

LOCK CAMERA R3 BUTTON (DEPRESS RIGHT ANALOG STICK)

While in the standard top-down view, move the Right Analog Stick in any direction to widen and adjust the camera angle. When the camera is set to an angle that should be beneficial for a while, depress the Right Analog Stick to lock the camera angle. The camera follows Snake at the angle you have locked while he moves. To unlock the camera angle, depress the Right Analog Stick again, or enter First Person View, or press Snake's back up against a wall.

ACTION △ BUTTON

Press △ to perform various context-sensitive actions, depending on where Snake is standing and whether he is wearing a disguise. Actions are described in greater detail later in this chapter.

WEAPON □ BUTTON

Press □ to use a weapon equipped in Snake's hand. The function of the button depends on the weapon equipped. Check the description of each weapon in the Weapons chapter to determine how to control and fire each specific weapon.

PUNCH, CQC, ACCEPT MENU SELECTION ○ BUTTON

Press ○ to punch an enemy. By pressing the button continuously, Snake can execute a punch-punch-kick combination designed to throw enemies off balance and knock their feet out from under them. Extend this combination by performing two punches, pausing briefly, and then performing two more punches, followed by a kick or more punches. When in close proximity to an enemy, press and hold ○ to grab him and execute CQC moves, as described later in this chapter.

CROUCH OR CRAWL, CANCEL TO PREVIOUS MENU SCREEN ⊗ BUTTON

Press ⊗ to go from standing to a crouched position. Snake is less visible when he's crouched, allowing him to hide behind boxes and low obstructions. Press and hold ⊗ to go from standing to a prone position lying flat on the ground. While flattened, Snake is at his most invisible. Weapons can be aimed more steadily when lying down, and Snake can crawl into vent shafts or small tunnels to avoid enemy detection. When Snake crawls into tall grass or small passages, he automatically enters "intrusion view," which is a form of First Person View where Snake can still move and crawl forward.

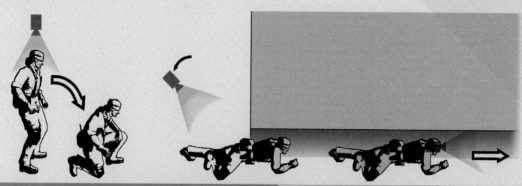

FIRST PERSON VIEW [R1] BUTTON

Press and hold [R1] to enter First Person View. The camera perspective switches to look through Snake's eyes. In First Person View, Snake is unable to move, but he can crouch or lie prone and aim weapons with greater precision. Use First Person View frequently to examine the environment ahead of Snake and identify possible dangers.

AIMING [L1] BUTTON

When shooting at an enemy, hold [L1] to lock Snake's aim on the target. Snake is then free to move around the area while firing at the enemy, as long as the angle does not become too severe. While in First Person View, hold [L1] to aim down the barrel of a weapon for greater targeting accuracy. If the weapon is fitted with a scope, press [L1] to peer through the scope and target an enemy accurately at long range.

WEAPON WINDOW/SIDESTEP/CORNER VIEW [R2] BUTTON

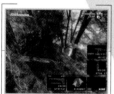

Press and hold [R2] to open the Weapon Window. All the weapons Snake currently has out of his Backpack are displayed. Move the Left Analog Stick or press the directional buttons to cycle left or right through the available weapons. When the desired weapon icon is positioned in the lower right corner of the screen, release [R2] to equip the weapon. While the Weapon Window is open, press ◯ to attach or remove a suppressor to an applicable weapon, or press △ to change an assault rifle's rate of fire.

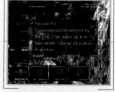

When Snake's back is pressed against a wall or tree, hold [R2] to sidestep quietly to the right along the surface. When pressed against a surface at the corner, hold [R2] to make Snake lean out and peak around the corner for a better view of the area beyond. Be careful to avoid discovery when leaning out.

ITEM WINDOW/SIDESTEP/CORNER VIEW [L2] BUTTON

Press and hold [L2] to open the Item Window. All the items Snake currently has out of his Backpack are displayed. Move the Left Analog Stick or press the directional buttons to cycle left or right through the available items. When the desired item's icon is positioned in the lower left corner of the screen, release [L2] to equip or activate the item. Items that run on battery power drain energy continuously until unequipped.

When Snake's back is pressed against a wall or tree, hold [L2] to sidestep quietly to the left along the surface. When pressed against a surface at the corner, hold [L2] to make Snake lean out and peak around the corner for a better view of the area beyond.

ONSCREEN DISPLAY

1. LIFE GAUGE

A gauge indicating the amount of life Snake has remaining. Damage inflicted by enemies reduces the gauge. If the gauge empties completely, Snake dies and the game ends.

2. WOUND METER

When a section of the Life Gauge turns red after an injury, Snake is wounded and requires medical treatment. Life regenerates extremely slowly or not at all as long as Snake remains wounded.

3. STAMINA GAUGE

A measure of Snake's remaining strength. As Snake performs actions and expends energy, the Stamina Gauge decreases. Decreased Stamina reduces combat performance and health regeneration, among other things. Eat nutritious foods to recover Stamina.

4. BOSS LIFE GAUGE

During special battles against unique enemies, the opponent's Life Gauge appears onscreen under Snake's. Attack the enemy until his or her life gauge empties to win the battle.

5. BOSS STAMINA

Indicates the amount of strength and energy remaining for a unique enemy. By performing certain attacks and actions, bosses also expend Stamina. When Stamina decreases badly, they become incapable of performing certain attacks. Some bosses may eat or pray to recover Stamina.

6. CAMOUFLAGE

Lists the Face Paint and Camouflage uniform that Snake is currently wearing.

7. CAMO INDEX

A percentage rating that indicates how well Snake is utilizing camouflage to blend into the environment. The Camo Index also increases when Snake stands still, when he crouches, and especially when he lies prone on the ground.

8. ITEM WINDOW

Displays an icon indicating the gadget or device currently active, in use, or on standby for use as needed.

9. WEAPON WINDOW

Displays an icon indicating the weapon currently equipped in Snake's hand and ready to use by pressing the ● button.

CARDINAL DIRECTIONS

Both within the game and in this guidebook, directions instruct you to head north, south, east or west. In the normal overhead view, north is always at the top of the screen, south is at the bottom, east is to the right, and west is left. Most stages of the game require Snake to head north in order to proceed.

FUN WITH CINEMATICS

Press START or ✕ to skip through dialog scenes and action sequences you have seen before. While a real-time scene is playing, meaning that 3D characters are "acting" onscreen, press △ and move the Left Analog Stick to zoom in on details of the character's faces and the environment.

LIFE

Snake's remaining life is displayed in the Life Gauge in the upper left corner of the screen. Damage from enemy or animal attacks reduces Snake's amount of life. When the Life Gauge becomes completely empty, Snake dies and fails the mission.

Life regenerates slowly as long as Snake does not take additional damage, and as long as he is not injured, sick, poisoned or in need of medical treatment. Snake's Stamina affects the rate at which he naturally recovers life. When Snake's Stamina is full, life regenerates quickly. But when Stamina is low, life recovers very slowly. Snake also recovers more quickly when he remains motionless in a crouching or prone position.

Life can also be regained by using Life Medicines. Search game environments to find Life Medicines and use them in emergency situations to prevent Snake from dying unnecessarily. Equip Life Medicines in the Item Window to allow Snake to use them automatically if the life gauge becomes completely empty during an enemy attack. Life Medicines restore only tiny amounts of health, so use the opportunity to retreat from battle and lie down to regain some health.

Snake can "rest" while the console is off. Life recovers gradually while wounds and illnesses naturally heal. The longer the console is left off, the more Snake recovers in all respects. However, keep in mind that food may rot and turn foul if the console is off too long.

INTRODUCTION

CHARACTERS

SYSTEM

WEAPONS

ITEMS

FOOD

CURE

PROLOGUE: VIRTUOUS MISSION

OPERATION SNAKE EATER

SNAKE VS. MONKEY

BONUSES & EASTER EGGS

KEROTAN LOCATIONS

INTERVIEWS

METAL GEAR SOLID COMIC

STAMINA

Snake's Stamina level determines how well he performs on the battlefield. When the Stamina Gauge is full, Snake recovers from minor damage quickly and can aim a weapon very steadily. When Stamina is depleting, Snake's aim begins to waver and his health recovers more gradually. The filled length of the Stamina Gauge also determines how long Snake can hang from a ledge before dropping, or how long he can hold his breath underwater without suffering damage. When Snake's Stamina becomes very low, his stomach growls. Enemies in the vicinity may hear his stomach noise and become alerted.

Stamina is expended gradually by moving and attacking. Actions such as climbing trees or ladders, stalking, crawling, swimming, or hanging from branches and ledges consume large amounts of Stamina. CQC and punch-kick combinations also consume large amounts of Stamina. The amount of weight Snake is carrying in weapons and items combined determines the rate at which Snake loses Stamina through his actions. To reduce Stamina consumption, store unnecessary items in the Backpack.

The only way to regain or maintain good Stamina is by eating food. Snake must hunt for various edible fruits, mushrooms and wild animals and eat them to regain his strength. Otherwise, his performance begins to suffer and the mission becomes harder to complete.

SURVIVAL VIEWER

Press START to open the Survival Viewer whenever Snake needs to eat food, withdraw weapons and equipment from his Backpack, check the map, perform medical procedures, or change camouflage to a pattern more suitable to the environment. While the Survival Viewer is open, press **R1** to view Snake. Move the Left Analog Stick to rotate Snake, and move the Right Analog Stick to tilt him. The functions of the Survival Viewer are explained below.

CAMOUFLAGE

Face paint
Select face paint.

When Snake's camouflage index is extremely low, open the Survival Viewer and enter the Camouflage screen to change Snake into more appropriate attire. Make sure that Snake is standing in the area that the Camouflage should suit before trying on new uniforms. The camo selection process may be easier if Snake lies prone on the ground before opening the Survival Viewer. If you want to blend into a wall or tree trunk, press Snake's back against those areas and open the Survival Viewer to pick the best attire.

Rain drop
Effective in the rain.

Camouflage is divided into two categories: Face Paint and Camouflage uniforms. First find the uniform that suits Snake's current environment best, and then choose appropriate face paint to match.

Woodland
For use in forested areas.

When choosing new Camouflage, the effectiveness of uniforms or face paints in the current environment is displayed as a positive or a negative. Equip Camouflage pieces with a positive to raise Snake's Camo Index, increasing his chances of being able to hide in plain sight. The higher the Camo Index percentage, the more likely Snake will be able to evade being seen.

CAMOUFLAGE

	NAME	LOCATION	DESCRIPTION
	Black	Obtain Backpack	Black battle uniform. Effective in the dark.
	Chocolate Chip	Bolshaya Past South	Camo pattern designed to provide cover in the desert. Named for its resemblance to a chocolate chip cookie. Effective in desert and mountain environments.
	Fly	Graniny Gorki Lab 2F (bathroom stall)	A foul-smelling camo uniform. It smells so bad that it attracts flies, but it also makes enemies think twice before coming in for a proximity encounter.
	GA-KO	Chyornyj Prud	GA-KO pattern camo uniform. Wearing it enables you to hear Kerotan's calling.
	Leaf	Obtain Backpack	Camo pattern developed to provide cover in forested areas. Effective in underbrush.
	Maintenance	Groznyj Grad Weapons Lab: East Wing (locker room, 2nd trip)	Maintenance crew uniform.
	Naked	Obtain Backpack	Nothing worn on the upper body. Does not provide much camouflage.
	Officer	Groznyj Grad Weapons Lab: East Wing (Raikov event)	The officer's uniform that Raikov was wearing.
	Olive Drab	Default	Commonly known as OD. A single-color battle uniform for general infantry use. Does not provide much camouflage.
	Raindrop	Dolinovodno (Op. Snake Eater)	Camo pattern used extensively in Eastern Europe. Effective in the rain.
	Scientist	Rassvet (EVA meeting event)	Scientist's uniform.
	Sneaking	Groznyj Grad Weapons Lab: East Wing (locker room, 2nd trip)	The latest battle uniform developed by the Soviet Union. Cuts all damage in half and reduces stamina consumption.
	Snow	Chyornaya Peschera Cave	Camo pattern designed to provide cover in snowy environments. Effective against white backgrounds.
	Spirit	Defeat The Sorrow	The Sorrow's camo uniform. Eliminates footstep noise. Also allows wearer to drain stamina by choking enemies in CQC.
	Splitter	Bolshaya Past South	Camo pattern often used on German airplanes during World War II. Effective in urban environments.
	Squares	Obtain Backpack	Camo pattern consisting of an array of squares. Makes it difficult to distinguish the silhouette of the wearer. Effective against brown backgrounds.
	Tiger Stripe	Obtain Backpack	Striped camo pattern resembling a tiger's coat. Effective in wooded and grassy areas as well as against soil and mud.
	Tree Bark	Obtain Backpack	Camo pattern designed with hunters in mind. Pasted with photos of tree trunks and leafy branches. Effective when pressed against trees.
	Water	Bolshaya Past Base	Camo pattern used extensively by the old German Defense Force. Effective when underwater.

FACE PAINT

	NAME	LOCATION
	Black	Obtain Backpack
	Desert	Ponizovje Warehouse
	Mask	Obtain Backpack
	No Paint	Obtain Backpack
	Oyama	Graniny Gorki Lab 1F (west vent shaft)
	Snow	Bolshaya Past Base
	Splitter	Default
	Woodland	Obtain Backpack
	Zombie	Rassvet (Snake Eater mission)

ADDITIONAL CAMOUFLAGE (BONUS OR DOWNLOAD)

	NAME
	Auscam
	Banana
	Brown
	Desert Tiger
	DPM
	Flecktarn
	Green
無	Infinity
	Kabuki
	Tuxedo
	Water

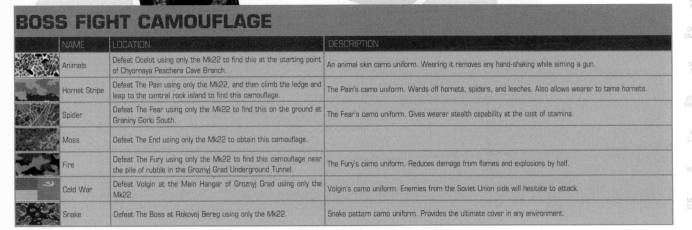

BOSS FIGHT CAMOUFLAGE

	NAME	LOCATION	DESCRIPTION
	Animals	Defeat Ocelot using only the Mk22 to find this at the starting point of Chyornaya Peschera Cave Branch.	An animal skin camo uniform. Wearing it removes any hand-shaking while aiming a gun.
	Hornet Stripe	Defeat The Pain using only the Mk22, and then climb the ledge and leap to the central rock island to find this camouflage.	The Pain's camo uniform. Wards off hornets, spiders, and leeches. Also allows wearer to tame hornets.
	Spider	Defeat The Fear using only the Mk22 to find this on the ground at Graniny Gorki South.	The Fear's camo uniform. Gives wearer stealth capability at the cost of stamina.
	Moss	Defeat The End using only the Mk22 to obtain this camouflage.	
	Fire	Defeat The Fury using only the Mk22 to find this camouflage near the pile of rubble in the Groznyj Grad Underground Tunnel.	The Fury's camo uniform. Reduces damage from flames and explosions by half.
	Cold War	Defeat Volgin at the Main Hangar of Groznyj Grad using only the Mk22.	Volgin's camo uniform. Enemies from the Soviet Union side will hesitate to attack.
	Snake	Defeat The Boss at Rokovoj Bereg using only the Mk22.	Snake pattern camo uniform. Provides the ultimate cover in any environment.

INTRODUCTION

CHARACTERS

SYSTEM

WEAPONS

ITEMS

FOOD

CURE

PROLOGUE VIRTUOUS MISSION

OPERATION SNAKE EATER

SNAKE VS MONKEY

BONUSES & EASTER EGGS

KEROTAN LOCATIONS

INTERVIEWS

METAL GEAR SOLID COMIC

BACKPACK

Whenever Snake procures a new item or weapon, it is stored in his Backpack. To equip an item, it must first be withdrawn from the Backpack. Snake can carry up to eight items and eight weapons at a time.

To withdraw equipment from the Backpack, open the Backpack screen and choose Weapon or Item. Select a piece of equipment from the list and press ● to withdraw the item from the Backpack. To store an item in the Backpack, highlight it and press the ● button.

While viewing the Weapon or Item window of the Backpack screen, hold R2 or L2, respectively, to open the appropriate window in the lower corner of the screen. Move the Left Analog Stick left or right to scroll through available items and view their description. For a quick method of dumping all items into the Backpack, hold L2 or R2 and press ● to dump items quickly.

Pay attention to the weight of items when withdrawing equipment from the Backpack. The more weight Snake carries, the faster he consumes Stamina. Make him more efficient by carrying only what is needed, and leave the rest in storage.

FOOD

When Snake's Stamina runs low due to strenuous activity, open the Survival Viewer and the Food screen to consume food. To maintain his Stamina level and operate at maximum efficiency, Snake must hunt and gather food in the wilderness. Collect fruit, mushrooms and animals by attacking them with a gun or knife. Punches and kicks directed at flora and fauna can also make them ready for consumption. Equip the Thermal Goggles to reveal the heat signatures of hard-to-see foods and animals.

Live animals can be killed and turned into rations, or captured in a cage by shooting them with a tranquilizer dart. Once Food is acquired, it can be viewed and eaten in the Food screen.

Live animals can be kept and eaten at any time, or set loose to terrify unsuspecting guards. Dead animals, vegetables and fruit gradually decay over time, and eventually become rotten. Before eating food, check the screen closely to see if flies are perched on the packaging. One fly on a food package means a 50% chance that the food will give the eater a stomachache. Two flies on a food icon means a 100% chance that the food will make a person sick.

If rotten food is eaten, Snake gains a Stamina increase but also suffers from a stomachache that gradually decreases health. Administer a Digestive Medicine in the Cure screen to return Snake to normal health. Rotten food can be thrown in front of guards to distract them. When a guard eats rotten food, he gets sick and must leave his post.

CURE SCREEN

Open the Cure screen in the second portion of the game to administer medical treatment to wounds and to take medicine for illnesses. Refer to the Cure chapter in this guide for a complete medical education.

MAP

Open the Map screen to view Snake's surroundings. As Snake proceeds through areas, black sections of the map become filled in with white. Scroll the map upward, downward, left or right until the white bar outside the map is highlighted to view previous areas. Press ● to switch to the previous map in the chosen direction. While viewing maps, hold ▲ or ● to zoom the map in or out, respectively.

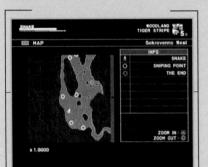

Icons appearing on the in-game map are designed to help you navigate certain areas. Items such as planted TNT or C3, active Claymores, empty or full Mousetraps, and destination points are marked on the maps. During the battle against the Cobra Unit sniper The End, white circles on the map mark his possible sniping locations. A red circle marks The End's current sniping location, once he reveals himself or fires his weapon. When certain guards are interrogated, they might say "Up ahead...there are more of us..." Open the menu after this statement to see the locations of enemy guards marked on the maps. Check the map often to determine entrances and exits from areas, as well as other useful information.

CONTROLLING THE CAMERA

The standard view in the game is from a top-down or slightly angled from top-down vantage point. If you race ahead in this view, you might stumble upon enemies before even seeing them. To gain a better view of your surroundings, you must manipulate the camera angle using the unique features of the game.

Press ▲ to enter First Person View, and rotate the Left Analog Stick to view your surroundings. Unfortunately Snake cannot move or hide in First Person View, and he risks detection to see the path ahead.

INTRODUCTION

CHARACTERS

SYSTEM

WEAPONS

ITEMS

FOOD

CURE

PROLOGUE, VIRTUOUS MISSION

OPERATION SNAKE EATER

SNAKE VS MONKEY

BONUSES & EASTER EGGS

KEROTAN LOCATIONS

INTERVIEWS

METAL GEAR SOLID COMIC

Whenever possible, control the camera angle by pressing Snake's back against a wall or tree. Move to the surface's edge to view what is around the corner. Hold L2 or R2 to peek around the corner to the left or right, respectively. Corner peeking enables an even wider view of the area beyond. While corner peeking, move the Right Analog Stick to angle the camera even wider.

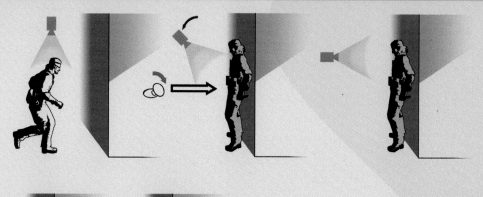

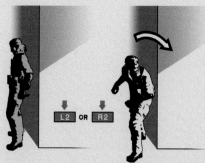

While moving in top-down perspective, move the Right Analog Stick to adjust and widen the camera angle in the direction Snake is heading. If you plan to proceed in this direction for a while, or if you want to keep tabs on an enemy to your side while moving north, move the camera to a wider angle in the desired direction and depress the Right Analog Stick (R3) to lock the camera. Controlling the camera is a bit unconventional compared to typical third-person, follow-behind cameras in other games, but with some experimentation it can benefit to your game play.

MOVEMENT TYPES

Running through areas is not the only option available, and is usually not the best choice. Snake is capable of moving through areas in a variety of modes. Study the environment before proceeding and determine the best movement mode to get through the area undetected.

RUNNING

Move the Left Analog Stick as far as possible to run full-throttle in any direction. This movement mode is good for crossing large areas without enemies. Be aware that Snake makes the most noise while running. Continuous running consumes Stamina at a gradual rate

WALKING

Move the Left Analog Stick slightly to walk through areas. Snake still makes a small amount of noise while walking, and enemies may hear him. Walking consumes Stamina more quickly than running.

STALKING

Press the directional buttons to move Snake silently in Stalking mode. Stalking consumes Stamina more rapidly than running or walking, due to the intense effort of moving without making noise. Use Stalking mode to sneak past enemies in very close proximity, or when you want to sneak up behind a foe to grab him.

CRAWLING

Press  firmly to go from a standing position directly to a prone position on the ground. Move the Left Analog Stick to crawl across the ground. While crawling, Snake makes no noise and maintains the highest possible Camo Index according to the Camouflage and Face Paint he's wearing. Crawling consumes Stamina more rapidly than running or walking.

WADING

Move into shallow waters to begin wading. Snake moves slowly and quietly through the water, making only a slight amount of noise. However, his upper torso is visible and he may be spotted by enemy patrols.

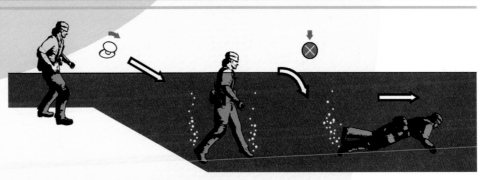

SHALLOW DIVING

While standing in shallow water, press to crouch and then move the Left Analog Stick in the direction Snake is facing to lie down. Snake enters underwater mode. Press ⊗ or ⬤ to swim through the shallows. This method of movement allows Snake to cross shallow water areas more quickly than wading, but he makes a lot of noise.

TREADING WATER

Move into water until Snake reaches a deep area where his feet do not touch the ground to automatically begin treading water. Move the Left Analog Stick to swim forward across the water's surface. Snake treads water faster if all his weapons are holstered.

SWIMMING

While treading water in deep areas, press ⊗ to dive under the surface. The view automatically switches to first person perspective. Move the Left Analog Stick to look around and control Snake's direction of swimming. Press ⊗ or ⬤ to swim forward, and tap either button rapidly to accelerate. Press △ repeatedly to rise toward the surface, depending on Snake's swimming depth.

SHIMMYING

While hanging from a ledge, rope or branch, move the Left Analog Stick to make Snake shimmy from hand to hand along the ledge in either direction. Press L2 and R2 simultaneously to perform a chin-up while hanging. If Snake's Grip Gauge begins to run low, press Action to climb up, in order to avoid falling damage or death.

DIVE ROLLING

While running at full speed in any direction, press ⊗ to perform a dive roll. Dive rolls can be used to trip guards and knock them to the ground momentarily. When executed with precise timing, dive rolls also allow Snake to leap over low rails and crash through glass windows.

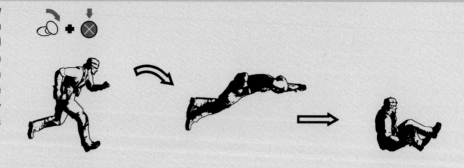

ACTIONS

As mentioned in the controller configuration listing at the start of this chapter, the Action button △ is context-sensitive. It enables Snake to perform various actions that depend on where he's standing and what he's facing. Action button functions include the following:

CLIMBING OBSTACLES

Snake can climb onto crates and platforms waist-high or lower. Press his back up against the box or ledge, and then press △ to climb onto the elevated surface.

CLIMBING TREES

A tree with at least one side covered in thick ivy can be climbed. Face the tree or press Snake's back against it, and then press ⓐ to climb to the first branch. Snake can walk a little way further out on the branch, or he can drop and hang from the branch by pressing ⓐ again. Snake can hang under the branch as long as the Grip Gauge holds out.

CLIMBING LADDERS

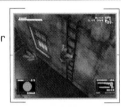

Standing at the base of a ladder, press ⓐ to grab the rungs. Move the Left Analog Stick up or down to ascend or descend a ladder. To descend a ladder from above, stand at the top of the ladder and press the Action button.

HANGING

When facing a rail or when Snake's back is pressed against a rail, press the Action button to jump over the rail and hang from the ledge. From this position, Snake can shimmy left or right along the ledge as long as his Grip Gauge holds out. Snake can also hang from branches and ropes in the same manner. Press ⓧ to drop from a rail or branch. If an enemy soldier is positioned under Snake when he drops, the enemy could be knocked unconscious.

DROP-CATCH

While hanging from a ledge or a rope, Snake can drop and catch onto the next ledge down or a rope directly below. Press ⓧ to drop from Snake's current hanging spot. Then tap ⓐ with just the right timing as Snake passes the ledge or rope that you want him to catch. If you don't press ⓐ just right, Snake could fall to his death. While falling to the ledge or rope below, rapidly tap the ⓐ button to help catch on instead of falling.

OPENING DOORS

If Snake runs into doors, he slams them open with considerable noise. To open a door quietly, stop momentarily in front it and move the Left Analog Stick gently in the door's direction to open it at a more deliberate speed. Also, press Action ⓐ to open a door Snake is facing. The pressure applied to the button controls the force with which Snake opens the door.

OPENING LOCKERS AND TOILET STALLS

Stand facing a locker or toilet stall door and press ⓐ to open the door. Step inside the locker to collect an item or to hide. Face an open locker and press ⓐ to close it, or press Snake's back against the locker door. Locked lockers can be forced open by setting TNT charges on them, or by punching the locker door or toilet stall door until it falls off its hinges. If the locker door falls inward, no item is inside the locker.

DISGUISE GESTURES

While wearing the Scientist disguise inside enemy facilities, press ⓐ to adjust Snake's glasses in a stereotypically geeky fashion. Perform this gesture when guards are suspicious of Snake's disguise to help convince them of his authenticity. When wearing the Officer uniform, press and hold ⓐ to salute soldiers. To avoid raising suspicion, don't salute for too long or salute scientists.

INTRODUCTION

CHARACTERS

SYSTEM

WEAPONS

ITEMS

FOOD

CURE

PROLOGUE VIRTUOUS MISSION

OPERATION SNAKE EATER

SNAKE VS. MONKEY

BONUSES & EASTER EGGS

KEROTAN LOCATIONS

INTERVIEWS

METAL GEAR SOLID COMIC

WEAPON ATTACKS

Press and hold ● to aim a pistol at enemies. When aiming in the overhead view, move the Left Analog Stick to point Snake's gun at enemies. In overhead view, Snake fires with general aiming. To aim at enemy vital spots, hold **R1** while aiming or firing and move the Left Analog Stick to adjust your aim. While trying to shoot someone with stealth, it is better to use a pistol fitted with a suppressor and aim for vital spots in First Person View. During all-out firefights, aiming in overhead view and firing an assault rifle set to full-auto is more advantageous. During boss fights, there is usually little time to line up an accurate shot in First Person View unless otherwise specified in this guide's walkthrough.

While shooting in First Person View, press **L2** or **R2** to strafe a step to the left or right. Strafing helps you to dodge enemy shots, but it makes aiming more difficult. Press **L2** and **R2** simultaneously to stand on Snake's tiptoes, which is good for peeking and aiming over tall obstacles.

DRAGGING BODIES

When soldiers are tranquilized or dead, there is a chance other sentries might notice their bodies and radio headquarters for reinforcements. Be sure to hide the bodies of guards you kill or tranquilize to avoid raising an alert. To drag a guard's body, holster all weapons and stand at the body's head or feet. Press and hold ● to pick up the body, and move the Left Analog Stick to drag it around a corner or into a good hiding spot where no one else patrols.

Bodies can be stashed in lockers inside enemy facilities. Open the locker, and then drag the dead or unconscious person into the locker. After a brief animation, Snake closes the door and seals the person inside the compartment. Unconscious or sleeping guards stored in a locker or toilet stall remain knocked out indefinitely until Snake moves to another area.

ACQUIRING ITEMS

Items are located in various spots in the environment. Pick up items by touching them. If Snake's inventory is full of the item he is trying to collect, the item remains uncollected.

Check your weapons before approaching additional ammunition. If Snake is only a bullet or two short of his maximum carrying capacity, it might be wasteful to collect an additional ammo box just to receive one or two rounds. Collect ammunition boxes when Snake has roughly 10-20% of the maximum ammo-carrying capacity for that weapon, in order to maximize your resources.

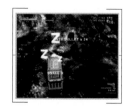

To determine what an item is before collecting it, stand beside the item and look at it in First Person View. To try to determine the identity from a distance, equip the Binoculars and zoom in on the item. Try to read the label on the side of the package.

SHAKING GUARDS

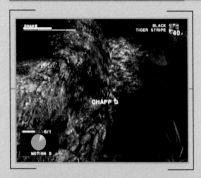

Additional items can be obtained by shaking the bodies of dead or tranquilized guards. To shake a body for items, pick it up and drop it. In Normal difficulty, dead guards drop only one item and tranquilized guards drop two. If additional ammo or medical supplies are needed, start tranquilizing and shaking guards in the hope of acquiring additional goods.

USING ITEMS

To use an item in the Item Window, first remove it from the Backpack and have it ready for Snake to use. Press L2 to open the Item Window, and use the directional buttons or the Left Analog Stick to cycle through the available items. When tools and gadgets are equipped in the Item Window, they become active. Equipment such as the Motion Detector, Mine Detector or Anti-Personnel Sensor work constantly to monitor enemy positions or to detect explosive traps set nearby. When Life Medicines are equipped in the Item Window, Snake uses one automatically to recover health if the Life Gauge is reduced completely.

Some items must be used manually. This includes Pentazemin, Fake Death Pills and Revival Pills. Life Medicines can also be used manually at any time to increase the Life Gauge. To use an item manually, hold L2 to keep the Item Window open, cycle to the desired item, and press ● to use or consume it.

BATTERY POWER

Electronic devices consume battery power. When Snake's battery is completely drained, all electronic devices become useless. Batteries recharge automatically by drawing upon Snake's energy. Unequip electronic devices and allow time for the battery to recover power. Acquiring additional batteries enables longer use of electronic devices. Eat Russian Glowcaps to recover battery power immediately. Battery power recovers more rapidly if Snake lies prone on the ground for a while, and when his Stamina is high.

KNOCKING

When Snake's back is pressed up against a wall or surface, press ● to knock. Use knocking noises to attract the attention of guards when you want to draw them off their usual patrol paths. Take the opportunity to run along a different path and slip past the guard unnoticed. The best environmental situation in which to practice this is an area where crates are stacked in the center of a room

INTRODUCTION

CHARACTERS

SYSTEM

WEAPONS

ITEMS

FOOD

CURE

PROLOGUE: VIRTUOUS MISSION

OPERATION SNAKE EATER

SNAKE VS MONKEY

BONUSES & EASTER EGGS

KEROTAN LOCATIONS

INTERVIEWS

METAL GEAR SOLID COMIC

PUNCH/KICK COMBOS

Press ● even while a weapon is equipped to punch an enemy. If Snake is equipped with nothing or a pistol, press ● repeatedly to perform a punch-punch-kick combo. Use this attack to knock enemies off their feet, to kill wild animals for food, or to knock fruit and vegetables loose from the ground or from tree trunks.

When used against an enemy, the three-hit combo must be used to knock a guard down several times before he falls unconscious. You can extend the full combo by performing two punches, pausing for a brief instant, then performing two more punches, pausing, and so on until the kick is finally delivered. By extending the combo longer, the likelihood of knocking a guard unconscious sooner becomes more likely.

CQC (CLOSE QUARTERS COMBAT)

CQC stands for Close Quarters Combat. The idea is to grab an enemy unarmed or with a knife and/or CQC-capable handgun equipped. The first step is to master sneaking up to enemies and quietly grabbing them without causing an alert. Use the directional buttons to Stalk up to a foe quietly until you're just a step away, and then press and hold ● to grab him. Once Snake has the enemy, release the CQC button and press a different button to perform the desired action with the hostage. A large part of CQC is timing and reflex. Otherwise, Snake merely grabs an enemy and slits his throat rather than allowing you to do anything else.

When equipping weapons, check the weapon icon for the "CQC" mark. This indicates whether CQC is available while the weapon is equipped. Make sure that you are ready to perform CQC before moving in to take an enemy. Otherwise you'll end up punching and kicking the person rather than controlling the situation.

DIRECT THROW

Unlike all other CQC moves, this one does not require that you first grab the enemy. When standing a step behind the enemy, press ● and move the Left Analog Stick simultaneously. Snake grabs the enemy and throws him to the ground as hard as he can. The guard is instantly knocked unconscious. This is a ruthlessly efficient move that can greatly increase your game ranking if you implement it properly.

GRAB

Hold ● when just you're a step or two away from an enemy to grab him. Enemies can be grabbed no matter which direction they face, even if they have just noticed Snake. The grab is the first step in performing the following CQC moves. Once the enemy is under your control, quickly press another button to perform another action, or release ● slightly just to hold the enemy for the moment. If the CQC button is pressed too hard, Snake immediately slits the enemy's throat.

INTERROGATE

First grab an enemy as described above, then release ● and swiftly depress the Left Analog Stick. Snake points a knife at the prisoner's throat and demands information. Release and quickly re-press the Left Analog Stick to extract more information. Guards under duress sometimes provide valuable information, and sometimes they outright lie just to get away.

SHIELD

When equipped with a handgun, grab the enemy and then quickly press to use him as a human shield against other foes. Guards in the surrounding area will not fire weapons as long as Snake holds a guard hostage, but they may try to run in and cut him with a knife. Use First Person View while holding a human shield to aim at and shoot other guards.

THROW AFTER CAPTURE

Having grabbed a guard in a chokehold, move the Left Analog Stick and tap to throw the enemy to the ground. Once an enemy is face down, point a gun at his head to make him surrender.

SLIT THROAT

Grab an enemy and then continue to hold . Snake slits the enemy's throat with his knife.

CHOKE/SNAP NECK

Grab a guard by the neck, and then begin tapping  rapidly to choke him unconscious. Continue tapping  to break his neck.

DRAG

Moving a live prisoner is extremely difficult, and we recommend it only for advanced CQC users. First grab the enemy, but immediately relax the pressure you apply to the  button without releasing it. Then move the Left Analog Stick to drag the struggling captive to a secluded location. This move is extremely valuable for grabbing a guard in the open and then dragging him to an isolated spot for a little interrogation or whatnot.

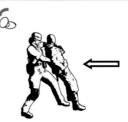

SPECIAL EVENT ACTIONS

During certain circumstances or when specific equipment is available in the area, press the Action button ⚠ to perform special actions.

MOUNTED GUNS

Mounted machine guns and anti-aircraft guns can be grabbed and fired. Position Snake directly behind the artillery and press ⚠ to take hold of the weapon. The view automatically shifts to First Person View. Move the Left Analog Stick to aim and press ⦿ to fire. Press ⚠ again to release the weapon.

CALLING PARTNER

During circumstances in which Snake must lead a partner character through hostile territory, press ⚠ to wave the partner forward. The partner must be no more than about ten feet away from Snake, and his or her line of sight to Snake must be free of obstructions. Move ahead of the partner, then stop and signal for the person to come forward. The signal can be issued whether Snake faces the partner or has his back to the person. The partner character mimics Snake's posture, stopping when he stops and crouching when he does.

ENEMY STATUS

Icons appearing above guards' heads indicate their status and whether or not they are aware of Snake's presence.

ENEMY STATUS INDICATORS

ICON	ENEMY STATUS	ACTION
?	Suspicious of something he saw from the corner of his eye.	Continues staring for a moment, and if he sees nothing further, returns to his patrol route.
!	Noticed a strange sound or saw a strange object, such as a cardboard box out of place or a dead body.	Moves in to investigate.
!	Spotted Snake.	Enters Alert stage, tries to notify other guards in the vicinity or calls for backup on the radio.
✿ ✿ ✿	Unconscious.	Will soon recover consciousness. Leave the area quickly or kill the guard.
ZZZ	Asleep.	Recovers consciousness when the effect of a tranquilizer or sleep-inducing mushroom eventually wears off. Leave the area in the near future.

ALERT STAGES

When an alert stage is triggered because an enemy spots Snake, try to escape and hide. If the guards cannot find Snake, then the alert passes through several phases before everything returns to normal. If Snake proceeds to the next area, the alert level is the same in the next location, unless the area is part of a new stage or a cut scene occurs upon entering. Each alert phase lasts for 99.99 seconds, so long as nothing happens to arouse the guards' suspicions again. Further signs of movement or the discovery of dead or sleeping soldiers might reset the alert phase to 99.99 seconds.

ALERT PHASE

Alert phase is triggered when a guard spots Snake or sees an explosion triggered by Snake. Other guards in the area respond to the initial guard's signal. Guards equipped with radios attempt to call HQ to send in an attack team. Alert phase can be canceled immediately if Snake is able to kill or neutralize the guard who spotted him. Otherwise, knock down enemies or kill them and escape to a good hiding spot when no one is looking. The timer then begins counting down to the end of Alert phase.

EVASION PHASE

Evasion phase occurs when the Alert Phase timer expires. Enemies have lost sight of Snake, but they continue to actively search the area for him. Guards may patrol areas off their normal routes. Guards actively search up high in trees, in lockers, in crawlspaces, and under furniture or vehicles. They become suspicious of cardboard boxes that seem out of place, and they will open locker doors. The timer runs continuously throughout Evasion phase.

CAUTION PHASE

Caution phase is triggered either when the Evasion phase timer runs out, or if guards hear an explosion or gunfire somewhere in the area but do not see it. Replacements are brought in to patrol the routes of dead or unconscious guards. Enemies patrol their routes more quickly, and they are more alert. The timer runs continuously during Caution phase, but resets to 99.99 if the guards spot dead soldiers, footprints or other signs of infiltration.

INFILTRATION EXPLAINED

To figure out how to play a *Metal Gear Solid* game, think of all the good spy movies that you've seen. Movie spies creep slowly and quietly through enemy territory, they wear disguises, and they use weapons fitted with suppressors to take down guards without being seen or heard. Whenever a spy and his beautiful love interest are discovered, they are instantly surrounded by guards and taken to a jail cell to face torture, death, or worse. Either that, or a firefight breaks out and the spy must utilize amazing combat skills to survive. Play the game with classic spy movies in mind, and you have a better shot at understanding how the game is designed.

Upon entering each new area, observe the enemy soldiers from a distance using binoculars or a sniper rifle scope. Monitor their positions and patrol routes. Search the environment for possible ways to sneak around the soldiers, such as vent ducts, stacks of crates, low walls, or other obstructions around which the enemies cannot see. Move slowly or crawl from one section to the next, being careful not to make noise. Change your camouflage as necessary and stay low to the ground to maintain the highest possible Camo Index.

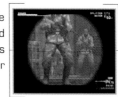

Shoot guards in the head with bullets or tranquilizers to neutralize them and reduce the risk of detection. Drag bodies out of sight, and hide them where other guards do not patrol. Even if a major objective, a useful item, or the target of your mission is nearby, avoid rushing ahead until all guards in the area are eliminated with stealth and silence. It's like a game of hide-and-seek, only you are always "it" and everyone else is looking for you.

INTRODUCTION

CHARACTERS

SYSTEM

WEAPONS

ITEMS

FOOD

CURE

PROLOGUE VIRTUOUS MISSION

OPERATION SNAKE EATER

SNAKE VS. MONKEY

BONUSES & EASTER EGGS

KEROTAN LOCATIONS

INTERVIEWS

METAL GEAR SOLID COMIC

ADVANCED TACTICS

This section's tips and tricks should make the game much easier to complete. Plus, you can really impress onlookers by doing many of these things during the game!

TACTICAL RELOAD

One of the most important strategies to employ is the "tactical reload." If a weapon magazine hits empty while you're firing, Snake performs a manual reload that can use up valuable time and expose him to danger. After firing a few shots with a weapon, double-tap R2 to reload the gun in hand almost instantly. This strategy is even more important when using the RPG-7 or the M37 shotgun against boss enemies. Never allow a weapon to run out of bullets in the clip. In fact, perform a tactical reload after every few shots so that Snake never has to waste time reloading in battle.

SEEING WHERE YOU CANNOT SEE

Sometimes corner-peaking or viewing an area does not reveal the locations of all the patrolling guards. Make use of the Motion Detector, the Active Sonar, or the Anti-Personnel Sensor to detect the approximate positions of nearby enemies before infiltrating further inward. View an area with Thermal Goggles to spot heat signatures emanating from well-camouflaged guards, pitfall traps and tripwires. Never rush into an area without first using gadgets to check the area for possible dangers. Sight alone often is not enough.

Just be aware of the caveats of using these items. For instance, a sonar signal emitted to detect life forms in the area might be overheard by guards or dogs patrolling close by. The Motion Detector weakly marks locations of all life forms, including wildlife, and consumes battery power with frightening speed. Do not use or equip these items more than necessary.

TRANQUILIZERS OR BULLETS: A TOUGH CHOICE

The enemies patrolling the paths between you and your objective must be taken down somehow. Otherwise, you may slip past only to be discovered when the guard turns around. Snake has weapons at his disposal to neutralize guards and prevent them from spotting him and giving away his position. But whether or not the guard should be merely put to sleep with a tranquilizer dart or permanently retired is a tough choice.

Lifting and dropping tranquilized guards might shake out useful items and ammunition in their pockets. In Normal difficulty mode, sleeping guards can be shaken to acquire at least two items. Dead guards can also be shaken, but only one item can be obtained. Additionally, kicking sleeping guards repeatedly awakens them. Then you can aim your gun at their back and hold them up for two more items.

However, tranquilizers eventually wear off. Guards awaken and return to their patrol routes. If you have not yet left the area, the chance of being discovered is greater. Unless you're certain that you're leaving the area shortly, it may be better to kill guards altogether. Killing guards enables more time to spy on other guards and study their patrol patterns, without worrying that the sleeping guy behind you might suddenly awaken.

WAKING SLEEPING GUARDS

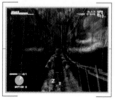

Until you get used to grabbing guards from behind or inflicting fatal head shots at medium to long range, use the tranquilizer gun to knock out guards so that you can move in and take advantage of them. In order to hold up or interrogate a guard, he must be awake at the time. Awaken sleeping guards by standing over their bodies and performing a punch-punch-kick combo. The kick of this move stirs the guard, reducing the time he remains tranquilized.

Continue kicking the person in the torso or head, and keep an eye on the "Z" icons appearing over his head. As the "Z" icons become infrequent, the guard starts to wake up. Move above the guard's head so that as he rises, Snake is poised to strike from behind. Guards that come out of sleep are a bit suspicious; so don't wait too long to take action.

HOLD UPS

Get the drop on guards by sneaking up behind them and pointing a pistol at their back. When Snake gets the drop on a guard, he commands the enemy to "freeze!" The guard puts his hands up and surrenders. Keep your weapon aimed at the guard, and use the Left Analog Stick to circle around to his front side. Enter First Person View and threaten the guard by pointing the gun at his head. Threatened guards beg for their lives and offer bribes, such as rare items. Move the gun away from his head and back again to make him drop two items. Then tranquilize or kill the guard and collect your stolen goods. If you have already knocked out a guard and shaken two items loose from his body, he can still be held at gunpoint to obtain two more items.

HEAD SHOTS

Whether you're attempting to tranquilize a guard or smoke him for good, always aim for the head to ensure one-shot takedowns. A head shot proves instantly fatal, or in the case of a tranquilizer, the drug's effects set in so fast that the guard falls unconscious instantly. Shooting a guard anywhere else could expose your hiding spot and cause him to sound an alert.

DISARMING SHOTS

When fighting a soldier, you can disarm him by aiming for his right shoulder and upper arm. Shoot him in the arm until he drops his weapon. From this point onward, he is incapable of attacking except to run up and slash with his knife. Guards forced to charge are easy to mow down with additional gunfire.

JUMP OUT SHOTS

When fighting soldiers in a narrow area, press Snake's back against a corridor wall at the corner, or against the trunk of a tree. Sidestep until Snake is close enough to the corner that he can corner-peak. Equip a weapon and press ● to step out from the corner and attack. After firing a few shots, release ● to duck back behind cover. A jump out shot executed with the right timing allows Snake to kill one or more guards with a volley of bullets, then leap back to safety quickly before enemies can retaliate. Utilize cover this way during battle to increase combat effectiveness and reduce the damage you receive.

CORNER GRENADE TOSS

The same way Snake can perform a jump out shot described above, he can also toss grenades at enemy patrols from the safety of cover. While pressing Snake's back against a wall near the corner, equip a grenade and hold R2 or L2 to lean around the corner. Press and release ● quickly to toss a grenade. As usual, the distance Snake throws the grenade depends on the pressure applied to the ● button. Try to throw a grenade when enemies are reloading or during a brief pause in their fire, so that Snake does not accidentally drop the live grenade at his feet.

HANGING SHOTS

While hanging under a tree branch or a below a thin platform, press ● to draw an equipped weapon and aim at targets below. Snake's weapon must be equipped before he drops under the branch, rope or platform, because weapons and items cannot be changed or equipped while hanging.

INTRODUCTION

CHARACTERS

SYSTEM

WEAPONS

ITEMS

FOOD

CURE

PROLOGUE VIRTUOUS MISSION

OPERATION SNAKE EATER

SNAKE VS MONKEY

BONUSES & EASTER EGGS

KEROTAN LOCATIONS

INTERVIEWS

METAL GEAR SOLID COMIC

EXPLODING BARRELS

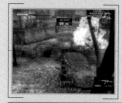

When attack teams stand near barrel drums, shoot the barrels to create an explosion. Enemies caught in explosions suffer burns, shrapnel, and falling damage from being flung. There is little likelihood of them surviving such attacks.

ROLLING BARRELS

Barrels lying on their sides can be rolled toward enemy groups to create chaos. Move behind a barrel and press ▲ to roll it in the direction that Snake is facing. As long as the enemies are downhill or on the same level as the barrel, it knocks them over on contact like bowling pins. Aim at the barrel and shoot with just the right timing to explode it in their midst!

DISABLING RADIOS

When a guard equipped with a radio spots Snake, he usually attacks and then runs for cover. From his hiding position, he calls HQ for help. Prevent him from calling in by shooting the radio in his hand. Another way to disable communications is to toss a Chaff Grenade. Either way, use the Binoculars or First Person View to identify guards with radios before you take action in any area. If the radioman is down, other guards become isolated and easy to kill even if they're alerted.

PROVISIONS STOREHOUSES AND MUNITIONS DEPOTS

Small buildings containing food items, ammunition, weapons, and other provisions stacked against the wall and on shelves are enemy supply points. These outposts can be destroyed to weaken the enemy presence in the area. To destroy a storehouse or depot, toss a Grenade through the open door or set TNT charges and detonate them from outside the building.

Demolishing a food storehouse causes the soldiers in the area to go hungry. Every few seconds, they complain of hunger, giving their positions away. Infiltrating areas becomes much easier when nearby enemies can be heard complaining.

Totaling a munitions depot causes soldiers in the area to run short on ammo. Each soldier is typically equipped with an AK-47, an M1911A1 and a knife. Without a munitions depot in the area, soldiers are restricted to one magazine full of ammo for each weapon. Therefore, when a soldier runs out of AK-47 ammo, he discards the weapon and pulls out the M1911A1 pistol. When the clip in his pistol empties, the soldier either runs in terror or charges at Snake with nothing but a knife. Attack teams entering the area are also restricted in terms of ammunition, so they provide little reinforcement for the already weakened patrols.

THROWING FOOD TO ENEMIES

Food items can be extracted from the Backpack and equipped in the hand via the Weapons Window. From a safe hiding place, throw food into soldiers' patrol paths to distract them. If the provisions storehouse in the area has been demolished and soldiers are complaining of hunger, they tend to ignore Snake even if they see him and go right for the food.

Soldiers can be inflicted with status ailments if they eat rotten or poisonous food. Don't be too hasty to discard decaying food items if they can be used to make guards sick, knock them out, or put them to sleep.

SCARING GUARDS WITH ANIMALS

Throw scary or poisonous live animals, such as spiders and snakes, at patrolling guards to freak them out and send them screaming out of the area. Shoot down hornets' nests near guards. The swarm emerges from the hive and attacks the closest human being. By knocking hornets' nests out of trees, it may be possible to chase an entire enemy squad out of an area.

PATROL DOGS

Bloodhounds sometimes patrol fences and perimeters alongside their human counterparts. Patrol dogs are extremely sensitive to noise, even to the sound of a gun fired with a suppressor. Sniping patrol dogs is unwise, because they emit a piercing yelp on death. Guards in the vicinity are alerted by this sound, and they move in quickly to investigate. Patrol dogs can be distracted by throwing them meaty foods to snack on, and they can be temporarily disabled by throwing Smoke Grenades at them.

DISGUISES

Wide-open forest and jungle areas have relatively few patrols compared to enclosed facilities, such as the Graniny Gorki research lab and Groznyj Grad fortress. Find an applicable type of uniform camouflage (disguise) and wear it in the facility to move past guards without drawing attention.

Avoid bumping into guards, or they become suspicious. If a guard orders Snake to stand still or pay attention, do not turn away or try to run. Allow the guard to examine you and decide that you are just another harmless civilian employee. Some of the more brutal guards may knock Snake to the ground. Avoid retaliation and wait until the guard walks away or tells you to get back to work.

While wearing a scientist or maintenance worker disguise, the guards pay no attention to Snake. But other scientists or maintenance workers who see Snake's face may become curious or suspicious because they do not recognize him. If scientists or maintenance workers identify Snake as an imposter, they cry out and dash for the nearest alarm. Whenever a scientist or maintenance worker approaches, turn your back to him or her. The staff member eventually gives up trying to figure out Snake's identity and moves on.

When disguised as a certain GRU Major, scientists seem to disregard your presence unless you bump into them. Guards inside Groznyj Grad stop and salute as you approach. Press the Action button ▲ to return the salute. Hold the pose for a moment, then drop your salute and walk away. Failure to salute or holding your salute longer than the guard does arouses suspicion, and it could cause an instant mission failure.

SILENT SNIPING

The Dragunov Sniper Rifle (SVD) allows for extremely accurate killing at long range. However, no suppressor is available for the weapon. Its report may attract the wrong kind of attention. In situations where silence is golden, equip the XM16E1 with a suppressor and set the rate of fire to single shot. Hold the First Person View button while simultaneously holding L1 to steady the rifle on your shoulder, and aim down the barrel sights. This method of aiming creates a medium-range zoom. The ring sighting on the nozzle of the gun enables extremely accurate head shots. All in all, the XM16E1 is a versatile weapon capable of going from pseudo sniper rifle to fully-automatic machinegun in a heartbeat.

FUNNY RADIO TALK

The support team in contact with Snake via radio can be a funny, quirky, and entertaining bunch of people. For example, equip the Naked Camouflage and speak to Sigint to witness a hilarious conversation. Para-medic is a virtually nonstop source of amusement, and even Major Zero has odd moments when he turns into a complete dork. Be sure to contact the support team members via radio even if you don't need assistance, just to witness some truly humorous moments in the game.

EASTER EGGS

Metal Gear Solid 3: Snake Eater's creators obviously endeavored to create a suspenseful, action-filled story of espionage and political intrigue set in Cold War Russia. However, they also share their unique sense of humor by including many humorous tidbits and references to other popular Konami games that could be overlooked if you don't know in advance where to look or when. Consult the Easter Eggs chapter in this guide to find numerous instances where the creators' humor or love of videogames comes to the fore!

INTRODUCTION
CHARACTERS
SYSTEM
WEAPONS
ITEMS
FOOD
CURE
PROLOGUE
VIRTUOUS
MISSION
OPERATION
SNAKE EATER
SNAKE VS
MONKEY
BONUSES &
EASTER EGGS
KEROTAN
LOCATIONS
INTERVIEWS
METAL GEAR
SOLID COMIC

WEAPONS

A stealth operative left to his own resources must have a comprehensive knowledge of the weapons available in the field. With the descriptions and tips provided in this chapter, any infiltrator should be shooting with grace and precision in no time!

Basic Weapon Actions

Press R2 to open the Weapon Window, and move the Left Analog Stick to cycle through the weapons available. Release R2 to equip the desired gun or device. Press R2 to holster a weapon, and then press R2 to quick-draw the last held weapon. Fire most weapons by pressing and releasing ●. Some weapons operate by touch-sensitive control, meaning that the operation depends on how firmly the ● button is pressed. Press ● lightly to raise and aim a weapon. When ready to fire, press harder and release to shoot. Some assault rifles actually begin firing when ● is pressed hard, so operate weapons carefully. To obtain in-game information and usage tips for weapons, equip them in the hand and call either The Boss or Sigint, depending on who your current tactical advisor is during the mission.

Tactical Reload

When the magazine of a weapon runs out, Snake begins to reload the weapon manually. While doing this, he becomes exposed to enemy attacks. For greater efficiency in battle, perform a "tactical reload." While holding an empty or almost empty weapon, press R2 to unequip it, then equip it again. When the weapon reappears in Snake's hand, it is fully reloaded and ready to fire. A tactical reload can be achieved by double-tapping the R2 button really fast. Tactical reloads are essential, especially when using slow-loading weapons such as the M37 and the RPG-7.

Suppressors

If you find a suppressor item for a weapon, press and hold R2 to open the Weapon Window. Cycle the menu to the weapon that can be silenced, and press ● to attach a suppressor. Repeat the same operation to remove the suppressor.

Suppressors deteriorate with each use, to the point where they break and fall off the weapon. The gauge displayed at the top of a weapon's icon indicates the suppressor's remaining durability. As the gauge reaches zero, fire each shot carefully to ensure that all shots remain silenced. Otherwise, your next shot sounds a report that alerts nearby enemies. When your first suppressor breaks, attach a new one if it's available.

Silencers should be attached to weapons only during stealthy infiltration, when no alert condition is effective and the enemies have no knowledge of Snake's presence. If enemies become alerted, or if the situation is a boss fight against an extremely powerful foe, conserve suppressors by removing them until the heavy fighting ends.

Rate of Fire

Certain assault rifles are fitted with a switch that enables the user to change the weapon's rate of fire from single-shot to 3-burst shot, or even to fully automatic, depending on the weapon's capabilities. When dealing with lower numbers of enemies, it's advisable to switch to single-shot or burst-shot to conserve ammunition. Additionally, a suppressed XM16E1 can be used as a medium-range sniper rifle when set to single-shot firing.

Weapon Storage and Retrieval

Newly acquired weapons are not immediately available. Instead, they are stored in Snake's Backpack. To prepare a weapon for use, press START to open the Survival Viewer and select the Backpack option. The window on the right displays the weapons currently available. Highlight this window and press the Select button ● to open the weapon equip screen. Highlight each weapon in the list of available equipment, and press the Select button ● to store or remove it from the Backpack.

Snake can carry up to eight weapons at a time. The combined weight of all weapons carried determines the rate at which Snake consumes Stamina. Remove needed weapons from the Backpack so that Snake can use them at a moment's notice, but be sure to store heavier weapons as much as possible to reduce Stamina consumption.

CLOSE-RANGE WEAPONS

SURVIVAL KNIFE (KNIFE)

Weight:	0.5kg
Magazine:	NA
Capacity:	NA
CQC:	Yes
Suppressor:	No
Rate of Fire:	NA

A serrated hunter's knife used in Close Quarters Combat (CQC). Tap ⬤ repeatedly to perform a rapid series of slashing and stabbing motions designed to quickly sever a target's vital arteries. Press and hold ⬤ to stab an enemy with a hard thrust. The Survival Knife is essential in performing all CQC actions as described in the Systems chapter.

FORK (FORK)

Weight:	0.1kg
Magazine:	NA
Capacity:	NA
CQC:	Yes
Suppressor:	No
Rate of Fire:	NA

This mission requires on-site weapons procurement. That means Snake must use whatever items he can find to attack enemies. When stripped of his gear, Snake must make do with this discarded kitchen utensil located in his prison cell. As with the Survival Knife, pressing ⬤ causes Snake to perform a series of rapid slashing and stabbing actions in a pattern designed to sever a target's vital arteries. Press ⬤ hard to perform a powerful forward thrust. The main difference between the Fork and the Survival Knife is that all food sources stabbed with the Fork are instantly consumed.

CIGAR GAS-SPRAY (CIG SPRAY)

Weight:	0.3kg
Magazine:	NA
Capacity:	NA
CQC:	Yes
Suppressor:	No
Rate of Fire:	NA

A narcosis gun that emits sleeping gas from a small tube shaped like a cigar. This espionage weapon is thought to be a test model currently in development for use by KGB spies. When at extremely close range, press and release ⬤ to blow a cloud of sleeping gas at a person's head. No matter which direction the person is facing, he or she falls asleep if the gas cloud surrounds his or her head. Found in the Graniny Gorki Lab facility.

KNOCK-OUT HANDKERCHIEF (HANDKER)

Weight:	0.1kg
Magazine:	NA
Capacity:	60
CQC:	No
Suppressor:	No
Rate of Fire:	NA

A handkerchief soaked with a knockout drug. Allows Snake to put an enemy to sleep just by grabbing him in CQC. Press ⬤ to wave the hanky around, spreading the knockout drug. The handkerchief can absorb only enough drug for one use, and then must be dipped in anesthetic. If Snake waves it in the air too much, he knocks himself unconscious.

TORCH

Weight:	0.5kg
Magazine:	NA
Capacity:	NA
CQC:	No
Suppressor:	No
Rate of Fire:	NA

A piece of white birch dipped in turpentine. Illuminates dark areas and never burns out. Wave it back and forth to attack enemies or shoo away bats with the ⬤ button, and press ⬤ to ignite or douse the torch. When lit, the torch is practically a beacon for enemies. When not lit, it's effective as a club.

SIDEARMS

MK22 (MK22)

Weight:	0.8kg
Magazine:	9
Capacity:	41
CQC:	Yes
Suppressor:	Yes
Rate of Fire:	Single

The Mk22 provided for this mission is a test model of a suppressor-equipped pistol currently in development by the Navy. The CIA has modified it into a tranquilizer gun. The suppressor-equipped pistol from which it is derived, the M39, is being developed for Special Forces use; "Mk22" will be the weapon's name if it is officially adopted. It bears a slide-lock mechanism that keeps the firing sound to a minimum. However, it must be reloaded by hand after every shot, so make each shot count by aiming at an enemy's vital spots. The rounds it fires resemble miniature tranquilizer darts. When one strikes a target, the impact causes a needle contained within the cartridge to shoot out. At the same time, propellant inside the round pushes the plunger, thus injecting the tranquilizer into the target. An enemy can be knocked out immediately by shooting him in the head. But if you hit the arm or leg, the tranquilizer takes some time to set in. Press ● lightly to aim, press hard and release to fire. Hold ▣ R1 to aim down the sights in First Person View.

M1911A1 (M1911A1)

Weight:	1.0kg
Magazine:	7
Capacity:	36
CQC:	Yes
Suppressor:	Yes
Rate of Fire:	Single

Fires .45 ACP rounds. The gun uses a simple single-action system, reducing the frequency of jams. The weapon can be fired while standing in waist-deep mud or sand. The .45 can be equipped with a suppressor to reduce the noise of its gunshot. To attach a suppressor, open the Weapon Window ▣ R2 and press the Enter button ● to attach or detach the suppressor. However, the suppressor deteriorates each time the weapon is fired.

SINGLE ACTION ARMY (SAA)

Weight:	1.0kg
Magazine:	6
Capacity:	30
CQC:	No
Suppressor:	No
Rate of Fire:	Single

The single action army revolver was first manufactured in 1873 and has been in production ever since then, except for a short hiatus. The name "single action army" came about after the U.S. Army adopted it as their official sidearm in 1875. Sometimes also called the "Peacemaker," owing to the fact that a lot of sheriffs used it to keep law and order in the old west. This model is specifically the "Black Powder" model, which uses .45 Long Colt rounds. The SAA is powerful enough to fire a 255-grain bullet at an initial velocity of 800 feet per second. The muzzle energy is almost 10% higher than the .45ACP bullets the M1911A1 uses. Great stopping power, but at the cost of greater reload time. Press and release ● to aim from the hip, or hold ▣ R1 to enter First Person View and steady your firing arm. Hold ▣ L1 to aim down the barrel sights for greater accuracy. While equipping the gun, enter First Person View and move the Right Analog Stick in any direction to perform a gun trick. Rotate the Right Analog Stick continuously to keep spinning the gun. While Snake spins the gun, release ▣ R1 to watch Snake perform tricks. Bullets fired from the gun ricochet off walls and surfaces even after passing through guards' bodies. This is a fun weapon with which you can develop astonishing gun skills.

ASSAULT WEAPONS

SCORPION (SCORPION)

Weight:	1.3kg
Magazine:	30
Capacity:	101
CQC:	No
Suppressor:	No
Rate of Fire:	Single/Continuous

A compact sub machinegun manufactured in Czechoslovakia. Production of this model began only three years prior to the time of this mission. The Vz-61 model featured in the game fires .32ACP rounds with a closed bolt system. This allows for a high degree of precision even when firing in semi-auto mode. Another special feature of this model is the rate reducer, a mechanism that functions as a shock absorber, locking the bolt in place for a split second when it withdraws to its rear position. This reduces the firing rate to a reasonable level and makes the gun easier to control in full-auto mode. The Scorpion fires 750 rounds per minute. This model is fitted with a laser sight. Hold ▣ L1 to shoulder aim down the barrel sights, although aiming should not be a problem with the laser sighting.

XM16E1

Weight:	2.9kg
Magazine:	21
Capacity:	101
CQC:	No
Suppressor:	Yes
Rate of Fire:	Single/Burst/Continuous

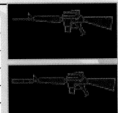

A new type of rifle currently being developed by the U.S. Army as a .22-caliber, high muzzle velocity rifle with full-automatic capability. This particular prototype is a modified AR-15 fitted with a bolt forward assist, quite possibly acquired in South Vietnam. Hold R2 to open the Weapon Window and press ● to attach a suppressor. Press ● lightly to aim, and press harder to fire. The weapon can be shoulder mounted in order to sight down the barrel by holding L1. When fitted with a suppressor, barrel sighting can be used to snipe enemies at medium range. While the Weapon Window is open, press ▲ to switch between single-shot, 3-shot burst, and full-auto fire.

AK-47

Weight:	3.5kg
Magazine:	30
Capacity:	151
CQC:	No
Suppressor:	No
Rate of Fire:	Single/Continuous

The AK-47 is the official assault rifle of the Soviet army. The first model was completed in 1946, and by 1949 it had become the standard assault rifle of the Soviet military. It fires 7.62 mm x 39 rounds, which were developed in 1943, and its clip is a 30-round box magazine originally designed for a different assault rifle. Press ● lightly to aim, press hard to fire. Can be aimed from the shoulder for barrel sighting by holding L1. While the Weapon Window is open, press ▲ to switch between single-shot firing and fully-automatic mode.

M63

Weight:	4.5kg
Magazine:	501
Capacity:	501
CQC:	No
Suppressor:	No
Rate of Fire:	Continuous

An American-made system weapon with mostly interchangeable parts, developed in the year prior to Operation Snake Eater. This model is based on similar Southeast Asian weapons. With interchangeable features, the parts can be mixed and matched to create any number of various weapons. Switching barrels and magazines around allows for the creation of everything from an assault rifle or a carbine to a light machinegun or even a belt-feeding machinegun. Not only does this save the trouble of organizing a bunch of different weapons on different lines, but it also cuts down on the amount of training soldiers need to operate it. The model featured in the game is a lightweight belt-feeding variety. Press ● to aim, press harder to fire. Continuously fires up to 501 bullets.

M37

Weight:	2.9kg
Magazine:	4
Capacity:	21
CQC:	No
Suppressor:	No
Rate of Fire:	Single

The M37 is a 12-gauge pump-action sawed off shotgun. Press and release ● to fire. Although hardly an accurate weapon, one blast sends a nearby enemy flying. The cone-shaped spray of pellets strikes one or more enemies in a cluster. The force blows enemies some distance backward even if they are not killed. A weapon best used against guard clusters and boss enemies.

SVD (DRAGUNOV SNIPER RIFLE)

Weight:	4.6kg
Magazine:	9
Capacity:	51
CQC:	Yes
Suppressor:	Yes
Rate of Fire:	Single

The Soviet Union's top-of-the-line, semi-automatic sniper rifle, adopted by the military in the year prior to Operation Snake Eater. SVD stands for the Russian words that mean "Dragunov semi-automatic sniper rifle." The SVD uses a new ammunition specifically designed for the weapon. The new rounds have a steel core and are 2.5 times more precise than regular rifle bullets. When the SVD is equipped, Snake enters First Person View automatically. Hold L1 to sight through the scope. Press ▲ to change the scope's zoom from x3 to x10 as needed. Press and release ● to fire. Aiming improves and steadies when Snake lies flat on his stomach.

RPG-7

Weight:	6.3kg
Magazine:	1
Capacity:	20
CQC:	No
Suppressor:	No
Rate of Fire:	Single

The RPG-7 is a state-of-the-art portable anti-tank weapon developed as the successor to the RPG-2. This weapon first saw active deployment in 1962. The launcher and the grenade together weigh more than 20 pounds. The RPG-7 triggers First Person View automatically when equipped. Hold L1 to sight through the scope for more accurate firing. It can be fired from a standing or crouched position, but not when prone.

INTRODUCTION

CHARACTERS

SYSTEM

WEAPONS

ITEMS

FOOD

CURE

PROLOGUE: VIRTUOUS MISSION

OPERATION SNAKE EATER

SNAKE VS. MONKEY

BONUSES & EASTER EGGS

KEROTAN LOCATIONS

INTERVIEWS

METAL GEAR SOLID COMIC

CONCUSSIVE WEAPONS

GRENADE (GRENADE)

Weight:	0.3kg
Magazine:	NA
Capacity:	20
CQC:	No
Suppressor:	No
Rate of Fire:	NA

An RGD-5 standard blast-fragmentation grenade used by the Soviet army composed of two steel-plated casings. Each casing has an inner fragment liner that causes it to burst into over 300 shards when the grenade explodes. The grenade delivers heavy damage to any enemies within its blast area. The safety pin is on the opposite side compared to American models. The safety releases when the grenade is thrown, and the bomb explodes about three seconds later. To throw a grenade, press and release ●. Snake throws the grenade farther depending on how hard the button is pressed. Pressing ● lightly enough drops the grenade at Snake's feet, and pressing it harder causes him to lob it long distances. Aiming grenade throws is easier when performed in First Person View.

WHITE PHOSPHOROUS GRENADE (WP G)

Weight:	0.8kg
Magazine:	NA
Capacity:	20
CQC:	No
Suppressor:	No
Rate of Fire:	NA

A grenade that uses white phosphorous chemicals to create an incendiary effect upon detonation. The U.S. military used these during World War II, when they were known as "Willy Petes," named after the first two initials of White Phosphorus. White phosphorous is a waxy substance that spontaneously combusts in reaction to oxygen. The temperature of combustion reaches 5,000 degrees Fahrenheit. Any human targets within the area of effect are set ablaze and seriously burned. If Snake happens to be caught in the blast radius, he should either dive into water or remove burning camouflage briefly to extinguish the flames. Press ✕ to perform dive rolls repeatedly to extinguish the flames.

STUN GRENADE (STUN G)

Weight:	0.5kg
Magazine:	NA
Capacity:	20
CQC:	No
Suppressor:	No
Rate of Fire:	NA

A grenade that knocks the enemies within its blast radius unconscious without hurting them. The flash of light produced by the grenade is produced by magnesium, which is also used in camera flashes. Throw Stun Grenades in the same manner as normal Grenades.

CHAFF GRENADE (CHAFF G)

Weight:	0.8kg
Magazine:	NA
Capacity:	20
CQC:	No
Suppressor:	No
Rate of Fire:	NA

An anti-electronics weapon that scatters a cloud of metal foil in the air to interfere with radio signals. With a Chaff Grenade, the functions of enemy radios and electronic devices can be disrupted for a short period of time. However, as long as the chaff dances in the air, electronic devices such as the Motion Detector and Active Sonar become inoperative. These are thrown in the same manner as normal Grenades.

SMOKE GRENADE (SMOKE G)

Weight:	0.5kg
Magazine:	NA
Capacity:	20
CQC:	No
Suppressor:	No
Rate of Fire:	NA

A grenade that creates a smokescreen around the detonation area. The combustion agent is a mixture of zinc oxide, ammonium chloride, aluminum, and other products. The grenade releases a thick cloud of grayish-white smoke that resists dispersion. The smoke confuses enemies by blocking their field of vision, enabling Snake to make a quick getaway. If thrown at the enemy position, the smoke enables Snake to sneak up on enemies. Smoke Grenades can be used to throw off trained patrol dogs that may be pursuing Snake.

TNT (TNT)

Weight:	1.6kg
Magazine:	NA
Capacity:	16
CQC:	No
Suppressor:	No
Rate of Fire:	NA

"TNT" is short for trinitrotoluene, a pale yellow crystalline compound made from a tri-nitrified mix of nitric acid and sulfuric acid. With low sensitivity and chemical stability, it is portable and easy to handle. TNT has a low melting point, and can easily be shaped by boiling or steaming it. Each TNT pack comes with its own remote detonator. Press ● to set the TNT, then move a safe distance away and press ● to detonate it. Locations where you have planted TNT are displayed on the in-game map. After planting TNT, Snake can equip and use other weapons. This is effective in creating traps for pursuing enemies. Multiple TNT charges can be set, and then detonated one by one by pressing ● repeatedly. However, TNT can be detonated only when Snake activates the triggering device while in the same area.

C3 (C3)

Weight:	1.6kg
Magazine:	NA
Capacity:	4
CQC:	No
Suppressor:	No
Rate of Fire:	NA

A type of plastic explosive developed in the West for special operations following World War II. Composed of 77% RDX and 23% moldable plastic. C3 can be molded into different shapes like clay. It's less volatile than TNT, so a little heat or shock isn't enough to set it off. It is extremely easy to handle and highly effective. These portions are set up with a synchronized timer device that sets off all four bombs simultaneously. Press ● to set the C3 near the fuel tanks in the Groznyj Grad Weapons Lab's Main Wing. To attach the C3 directly to the tank, press Snake's back up against the tank and press ● to attach the C3 to the tank.

CLAYMORE (CLAYMORE)

Weight:	1.6kg
Magazine:	NA
Capacity:	16
CQC:	No
Suppressor:	No
Rate of Fire:	NA

The Claymore is an M18A1 anti-personnel directional mine developed by the U.S. after the Korean War. The curved casing is packed with a pound and a half of high-grade explosives. The side facing the enemy is lined with 700 steel ball bearings that spread upon detonation. An electric motion-detector detonator triggers the Claymore to explode whenever something comes in close range. The presence of Claymores can be determined by equipping the Mine Detector, or by spotting them with the Thermal Goggles. Planted Claymores can be safely dismantled and picked up by crawling over them. To plant a Claymore, face the direction from which the enemy might approach and press ● to set the device.

MISCELLANEOUS WEAPON ITEMS

BOOK (BOOK)

Weight:	0.1kg
Magazine:	NA
Capacity:	10
CQC:	No
Suppressor:	No
Rate of Fire:	NA

A publication that contains adult oriented material. When placed in guard patrol paths, they become helplessly overwhelmed and forced to stare at the lurid pictures contained within. Use the opportunity to take the guard by surprise or escape.

MAGAZINE (MAGAZINE)

Weight:	0.1kg
Magazine:	NA
Capacity:	100
CQC:	No
Suppressor:	No
Rate of Fire:	NA

An empty gun clip obtained by reloading a weapon. Snake can throw Magazines to create noise. The sound a Magazine makes when it hits the ground can divert the enemy's attention, creating a distraction.

MOUSETRAP (MOUSETRAP)

Weight:	0.4kg
Magazine:	NA
Capacity:	16
CQC:	No
Suppressor:	No
Rate of Fire:	NA

A portable tool for capturing small animals alive. Press ● to place the trap on the ground in an area with live animals. After a few moments, it might catch a Rat, Frog or Snake. A Mousetrap requires bait to catch an animal. If an animal has taken the bait out of a trap without setting it off, crawl over the trap to pick it up. Then lay out another trap. Locations where Snake has set Mousetraps can be viewed on the in-game map.

DIRECTIONAL MICROPHONE (MIC)

Weight:	1.5kg
Magazine:	NA
Capacity:	NA
CQC:	No
Suppressor:	No
Rate of Fire:	NA

A highly sensitive electronic microphone that picks up sounds from long distances and even behind walls. Equip the Directional Microphone to listen for footsteps or animal sounds in the environment. The directional microphone can help pinpoint enemy locations at long ranges when all other methods fail.

ITEMS

Snake wouldn't be the one-man army that he is without his Backpack of high-tech gadgetry. Although he begins Operation Snake Eater with just a small collection of essential items and tools, as the mission grows and evolves so does his assortment of survival implements. Snake's items range from sophisticated Thermal Goggles and Motion Detectors to something as simple as a cardboard box.

Each of the items that will eventually constitute Snake's complete inventory has a specific purpose. Some items are designed to be used on a regular basis, such as the Active Sonar, while others, like Cardboard Box A and Cardboard Box B, will be used only once. It's important to take note of this because it underscores the emphasis that Snake must place on searching high and low to find each of the items. There are points in Operation Snake Eater where Snake must have a particular item to proceed. Failure to find this item earlier in the mission may result in failure.

TOOLS OF THE TRADE

Snake can fit all of the items he acquires in his Backpack, but only eight items can be equipped at any given time. Enter the Backpack Menu to adjust items that will be equipped in the Items Menu. Consider keeping the Thermal Goggles, Active Sonar, and the Binoculars equipped at all times, as they are especially useful. Snake can never unequip the Revival Pill, as it is implanted in his teeth.

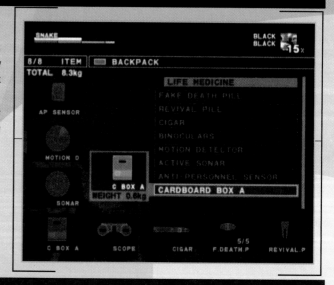

ACTIVE SONAR

WEIGHT	CAPACITY	PURPOSE
3.2kg	1	Sensor that detects animals with sound waves. Consumes battery power when used.

The Active Sonar is similar to the Motion Detector, but it can detect stationary beings, whether they are animals or humans. The downside to using the Active Sonar is that it does not run constantly and it makes a loud ping each time its sound waves are emitted. This noise can betray Snake's position if a guard is nearby and hears it. Push L3 to use the Active Sonar, and inspect the icon in the upper right corner of the screen to see where nearby animals and humans are. Can also be used to repel Vampire Bats.

ANTI-PERSONNEL SENSOR

WEIGHT	CAPACITY	PURPOSE
1.5kg	1	Vibrates when detecting lifeforms. Consumes battery power while used. All other vibrations will be OFF when activated.

The Anti-Personnel Sensor is for those who prefer to *feel* the presence of another being, as opposed to seeing it represented on the Motion Detector or Active Sonar screens. Once equipped, the Anti-Personnel Sensor consumes battery power slowly but steadily, and the controller vibrates whenever another lifeform, be it man or beast, is near. It's very easy to forget that the Anti-Personnel Sensor is equipped and inadvertently drain your batteries. The unit works well, but the Motion Sensor and Active Sonar are less likely to be left on by accident.

BINOCULARS

WEIGHT	CAPACITY	PURPOSE
1.0kg	1	Military binoculars allowing long-distance reconnaissance.

Equip the item to automatically begin peering through its high-powered lenses. Snake cannot move while he is using the Binoculars (a.k.a. Scope). Press ▲ to zoom in and ● to zoom out. The Binoculars provides a brighter image of the environment and can be useful in scouting out enemy locations in the distance. Use them often to study enemy movements and to look for far-off sources of food or other items.

BUG JUICE

WEIGHT	CAPACITY	PURPOSE
0.7kg	25	Bug repellent. Keeps away hornets and leeches while in effect.

Equip Bug Juice and press ● to apply it to Snake's skin and camouflage. The Bug Juice works well against hornets but it does wear off quickly while in the water, so its usefulness against leeches is marginal at best.

CARDBOARD BOX A

WEIGHT	CAPACITY	PURPOSE
0.6kg	1	Says "To the Weapons Lab: East Wing" on the side.

Snake can hide in a cardboard box at any time, but Cardboard Box A is conspicuously labeled specifically for the Groznyj Grad area. Resist the temptation to use this box unless in an area where similar boxes are located. Not only will it then make a great hiding place, but Snake can also use the box to ship himself inside a guarded area.

CARDBOARD BOX B

WEIGHT	CAPACITY	PURPOSE
0.6kg	1	Says "To the Weapons Lab: Hangar" on the side.

Snake can use this box to gain access to the most tightly guarded area in Groznyj Grad—but only when the time is right! Resist the temptation to hide in this box until you're near other, identical boxes. By equipping this box, Snake can hide inside it and safely ship himself deep within enemy territory.

CARDBOARD BOX C

WEIGHT	CAPACITY	PURPOSE
0.6kg	1	Letters on the side cannot be read.

This plain cardboard box doesn't display any labeling that could possibly alert guards to it being out of place. Equip the box when nearby enemy buildings to hide inside it until the coast is clear. The box has a small handle hole through which Snake can see. Hiding under the cardboard box is an effective way to evade guards, but be extra careful to remain motionless. The slightest nudge while under the box is all it takes to raise the guards' suspicion.

INTRODUCTION

CHARACTERS

SYSTEM

WEAPONS

ITEMS

FOOD

CURE

PROLOGUE VIRTUOUS MISSION

OPERATION SNAKE EATER

SNAKE VS. MONKEY

BONUSES & EASTER EGGS

KEROTAN LOCATIONS

INTERVIEWS

METAL GEAR SOLID COMIC

CAMERA

WEIGHT	CAPACITY	PURPOSE
0.7kg	1	A simple photographic device for taking pictures.

The camera makes it possible for Snake to take photographs of locations, enemies, animals, and whatever he else he fancies. Equip the Camera and use ▲ to zoom in, ● to zoom out, and ● to take the picture. Each photograph must be saved to its own unique slot on the Memory Card. Access the Special menu from the Main menu to view the photos in the viewer.

CIGAR

WEIGHT	CAPACITY	PURPOSE
0.1kg	1	Highly addictive and hazardous to your health.

Equip the Cigar to immediately start smoking it. Snake can use the Cigar as part of his survival kit to burn off leeches. He can also use it to help illuminate narrow passages and tunnels. Snake's health does slowly diminish while the Cigar is equipped, so use it sparingly.

CROCODILE CAP

WEIGHT	CAPACITY	PURPOSE
1.6kg	1	A hat that resembles the head of a crocodile.

The Crocodile Cap is one of Snake's best disguises ever. Equip this accessory and then slowly wade or swim through the water. Guards in the area will assume Snake is just another wild animal and will continue with their patrols without hesitation. Although the Crocodile Cap is very effective on the water, it is of little use to Snake when he's on solid ground. Similarly, Snake must remember to move through the water slowly when wearing the Crocodile Cap. The disguise won't fool anyone if Snake jumps and splashes about.

FAKE DEATH PILL

WEIGHT	CAPACITY	PURPOSE
0.1kg	5	Espionage pill developed by the CIA. Can fake death temporarily.

Hold R2 and press ● to use. This item allows Snake to fake his own death to confuse enemies. Although it can be used at any time, enemies will not fall for it while under "Alert" status. The "Snake is Dead" screen appears after the pill is taken. Don't panic—just wait until the coast is clear and then use the Revival Pill.

KEY A

WEIGHT	CAPACITY	PURPOSE
0.1kg	1	Card key obtained from Granin. Opens red door in the southeast of Ponizovje warehouse.

Snake gets Key A when he meets with Granin in the basement laboratory at Graniny Gorki. Key A does not have to be equipped in order for it to be used. The door at Ponizovje Warehouse opens automatically as Snake approaches it.

KEY B

WEIGHT	CAPACITY	PURPOSE
0.1kg	1	Key obtained from EVA. Opens door in the east of Krasnogorje Mountaintop.

Snake must meet with Eva at the ruins atop the Krasnogorje Mountains in order to get this key. Key B opens the door on the east side of the last mountain section. The door at Krasnogorje Mountaintop will open automatically as Snake approaches it; he does not need to have it equipped.

KEY C

WEIGHT	CAPACITY	PURPOSE
0.1kg	1	Key obtained from EVA. Opens door to hangar at weapons lab main wing.

Snake acquires this key only after learning what he has to do to bring down the Shagohod. Eva gives it to him when he awakens in the cave behind the waterfall. Snake does not need to equip this key in order to unlock the door to the hangar.

LIFE MEDICINE

WEIGHT	CAPACITY	PURPOSE
0.2kg	10	Developed by USSR. Restores life.

Hold **R2** and press ● to use. Life Medicine restores one bar of Snake's Life Gauge. If equipped, Snake uses it automatically upon running out of Life. Save as many of these rare items as possible for the challenging battles that come late in the game.

MINE DETECTOR

WEIGHT	CAPACITY	PURPOSE
3.0kg	1	Makes sound upon detection of Claymores on the ground. Consumes battery power while used.

Equip the Mine Detector when in an area with Claymores. The unit beeps as Snake draws closer to the Claymore, thereby warning him to drop into a prone position. The Mine Detector is of only moderate usefulness because Snake will likely stumble onto a Claymore before knowing to be on the lookout for them. Snake can pick up Claymores by crawling across them, and using the Thermal Goggles instead of the Mine Detector makes doing so much easier.

MOTION DETECTOR

WEIGHT	CAPACITY	PURPOSE
1.8kg	1	Sensor that detects an object's motion. Does not detect stationary objects. Consumes battery power while used.

Equipping the Motion Detector adds a circular icon to the HUD. The unit sends out a signal in a sweeping 360-degree path that detects any moving item and displays it as a white blip on the upper right corner of the screen. Snake's field of vision is shown as a brighter cone on the icon, making it possible to tell from which direction the movement is coming. The benefit to using the Motion Detector is that it runs constantly and silently, so long as there are batteries to power it. The downside to using the Motion Detector is that it does not reveal stationary guards, and numerous wildlife moving around can complicate the reading.

NIGHT VISION GOGGLES

WEIGHT	CAPACITY	PURPOSE
1.0kg	1	Electronically amplifies dim light signal for visualization. Allows one to see in the dark. Consumes battery power while used.

The Night Vision Goggles are extremely useful in pitch-black conditions, such as inside a cave. Equipping them allows Snake to automatically begin viewing his surroundings in a bright, greenish hue. The Night Vision Goggles can be used in both third person and First Person View and it's possible to equip a weapon and use it while wearing them. Be warned, however, that these goggles are meant for extremely dark situations exclusively. Using them in bright conditions is akin to having a Stun Grenade explode at Snake's feet.

REVIVAL PILL

WEIGHT	CAPACITY	PURPOSE
0.0kg	N/A	Espionage pill developed by the CIA. Can wake up from fake death.

Hold **R2** and press ● to use. This item allows Snake to resuscitate himself after using the Fake Death Pill. Wait for the enemies to disperse while watching the "Snake is Dead" screen, and then use the item via the Item Window. Do *not* select the Exit or Continue options on the screen. This item is implanted in Snake's tooth and cannot be unequipped.

THERMAL GOGGLES

WEIGHT	CAPACITY	PURPOSE
1.0kg	1	Visualizes heat source distribution. Allows one to see in the dark. Consumes battery power while used.

Equip the item to automatically begin viewing the environment through these high-tech goggles. It's possible to explore in third person or peer through the goggles in First Person View while wearing them. Snake can also equip and fire weaponry while wearing the Thermal Goggles, making them especially useful for hunting prey. Thermal Goggles display a range of colors that correspond to the temperature signature of the item being viewed. Colors range from blacks and dark blues for cold objects (the ground, water, trees, etc.) to bright oranges and yellows (humans, animals, the sky, etc.).

INTRODUCTION

CHARACTERS

SYSTEM

WEAPONS

ITEMS

FOOD

CURE

PROLOGUE: VIRTUOUS MISSION

OPERATION SNAKE EATER

SNAKE VS. MONKEY

BONUSES & EASTER EGGS

KEROTAN LOCATIONS

INTERVIEWS

METAL GEAR SOLID COMIC

FOOD

In true survival fashion, Snake must rely on nature's gifts to provide him with the strength and stamina needed to continue with his mission. Fortunately, the terrain that he crosses in Operation Snake Eater is loaded with edible plants and animals. He'll never be far from a meal, and it's always fast food!

Hunting and foraging can be done at almost any time, in any environment. The region of Tselinoyarsk is loaded with wild animals and native plants that thrive in habitats ranging from watery mangrove forests to rocky mountaintop bluffs. Those looking to conserve ammunition can take comfort knowing that every animal can be killed with a Survival Knife, and many with just a series of CQC attacks. However, it is often safer and more expedient to use the Mk22. To that end, some may decide to utilize Snake's entire arsenal to assist in the hunt—those looking to capture the rarer animals will certainly benefit from using the Thermal Goggles and Dragunov sniper rifle.

VOMITOUS SNAKE

>> Did Snake eat some spoiled food? Is he out of Digestive Medicine? No problem. Enter the Survival Viewer and press R1 to view Snake in full size. Hold the Right Analog Stick to the left or right to spin Snake around in circles. Make Snake spin for roughly 30 seconds and then press START in mid-spin. The Survival Viewer gives way to the game screen and Snake vomits. Although this can be performed at any time, forcing Snake to regurgitate rids his system of the spoiled food. Unfortunately, it also lowers his Stamina, so using the Digestive Medicine is still the way to go.

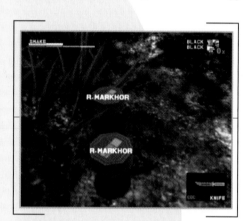

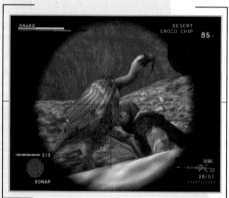

When it comes to making sure Snake has enough food to eat, there are several options at the player's disposal. Animals and plants can be destroyed and prepared as canned meals in a ration-like form. Food put into Snake's Backpack in the form of canned rations (not to be confused with the Russian Ration food item) will start to spoil over time. Eating spoiled food can make Snake sick and require the use of Digestive Medicine. Pay close attention to the icons that appear beside the food's name in the Food Menu, as flies will appear on the icon as time passes.

One fly means there is a 50% chance that Snake will get sick from eating the food.

Two flies means there is a 100% chance that Snake will get sick from eating the food.

Of course, Snake doesn't have to kill his prey. In addition to the dozen slots in his Backpack for prepared food, there are also three cages for live animals. Naturally, Snake can't cage large animals such as the Indian Gavial crocodile or the Markhor goat, but he can use his Mk22 to tranquilize and cage the majority of smaller animals he encounters. Similarly, the Mousetrap can also be used to catch a live animal. Capturing live animals has two key benefits: 1) There is no risk of the food spoiling, and 2) Snake can toss live, poisonous animals at enemies to scare them. Few sights compare to that witnessed from tossing a King Cobra or Coral Snake at an unsuspecting guard!

As hinted on the previous page, not all of the creatures that Snake encounters should be eaten. A great way to find out, besides reading the rest of this chapter, is to give Para-Medic a call on the Codec. Not only does she provide encyclopedic knowledge on each species that Snake has captured, but she'll even alert him to what might be encountered in areas he visits for the first time.

There are strange beings afoot in the jungle after dark, and many of them are quite rare. Snake encounters several nocturnal creatures throughout his trek across the jungle. Keep those Thermal Goggles at the ready when roaming the woods at night, as you might miss some tasty—and rare—vittles!

Lastly, there is the issue of taste. Snake may be an expertly trained field operative with an amazing set of survival instincts, but he still has personal taste. The amount of Stamina obtained from eating food is proportional to Snake's fondness for the item. As one might expect, not all of nature's bounty is exceedingly tasty—especially when it's uncooked and dripping with blood! Even worse, some of the items have unexpected side effects, such as poisoning and drowsiness.

The Effect tables paired with each food item provide the initial amount of Stamina that Snake regains from eating it. As Snake eats the same food repeatedly, he gradually grows accustomed to the taste and acquires a liking for it. This results in larger Stamina boosts later in his mission. A good example of this is the Russian Ration. This 1960s USSR version of field rations provides minimal Stamina gains when Snake first consumes it. Later, as the Russian Rations become more plentiful and Snake develops a taste for them, he gains more Stamina from each can he eats.

FLORA

MUSHROOMS

RUSSIAN OYSTER MUSHROOM

Map Entity: Mushroom A

The Russian Oyster Mushroom is an edible variety that belongs to the Shimeji family. It's known to be particularly rich in vitamin B1 and Niacin. It's typically found growing on tree stumps and hollow logs.

HABITAT	EFFECT
Very common mushroom found in most forested areas.	Barely noticeable stamina recovery.

URAL LUMINESCENT MUSHROOM

Map Entity: Mushroom B

The Ural luminescent mushroom is found only in Tselinoyarsk. It looks like a shiitake mushroom, and it's often found growing on the trunks of trees. If it looks like a shiitake mushroom, then it must be edible, right? Yep. There is no guarantee that it'll taste like a shiitake mushroom, though.

HABITAT	EFFECT
A very rare mushroom only found in certain wooded areas.	Came down with food poisoning.

SIBERIAN INK CAP

Map Entity: Mushroom C

The Siberian Ink Cap is a mushroom from the ink cap family. Its life cycle is transitory. As soon as the spores mature, the cap starts to turn black, liquefy, and melt away. In its immature state, before it melts away, it's valued as a source of food. Just be sure not to eat them while you're drinking alcohol. Ink Caps contain coprin, which inhibits the function of aldehyde dehydrogenase. This prevents the body from breaking down alcohol, causing a buildup of acetaldehyde. It will give you a major hangover.

HABITAT	EFFECT
Very common mushroom found throughout the region.	Barely noticeable stamina recovery.

FLY AGARIC

Map Entity: Mushroom D

The fly agaric is a relative of the deathcap mushroom that grows only in that region. You'll find it growing on the ground, but it's poisonous, so if you pick one up, don't eat it. If you do eat one, go into the Survival Viewer immediately and use Cure to take some antidote. The poisons found in the fly agaric include fallotoxins and amatoxins. When you eat it, the initial symptoms include nausea, stomach pain, and diarrhea. Finally, your liver and kidneys will break down into a sponge-like substance and you die.

HABITAT	EFFECT
Relatively rare mushroom that grows in select forests.	Came down with food poisoning.

RUSSIAN GLOWCAP

Map Entity: Mushroom E

The Russian glowcap is a kind of luminescent fungus—a mushroom that glows in the dark. It's bioluminescent, just like a firefly. It uses the so-called luciferin-luciferase reaction. To put it simply, luciferin reacts with luciferase in the presence of magnesium two plus ions, breaking it down into oxyluciferin and carbon dioxide. The carbonyl groups in the oxyluciferin are initially in an electrically excited state. When they return to their base state, they give off light.

HABITAT	EFFECT
Lives in caves and dark, damp tunnels underground.	Battery recharged after eating.

SPATSA

Map Entity: Mushroom F

The Spatsa is a gray mushroom that grows on the ground. "Spatsa" in Russian means "bringer of sleep." The Spatsa puts you to sleep when you eat it because it contains a type of anesthetic substance similar to alkaloid. Eating a Spatsa and falling asleep might cause your Life and Stamina to recover as well.

HABITAT	EFFECT
Grows in select forests, on the ground near trees.	Become sleepy.

BAIKAL SCALY TOOTH

Map Entity: Mushroom G

The Baikal Scaly Tooth mushroom is used as an antidote to poison. It usually grows on the trunks of trees, so look for it there.

HABITAT	EFFECT
A rare mushroom found in select forested areas.	Barely noticeable stamina recovery.

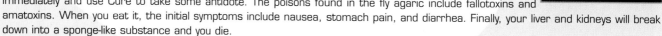

FRUIT

YABLOKO MOLOKO

Map Entity: Fruit A

Its Russian name roughly translates as "milk apple." It's a type of star apple. The juice is thick and sweet, like milk—hence the name. And if you cut one in half lengthwise, you'll see a star-shaped ring radiating out from the center. The star-shaped part has a gelatinous texture and is said to be especially tasty.

HABITAT	EFFECT
A red fruit that grows on trees in forests and swamps.	Slight stamina recovery.

RUSSIAN FALSE MANGO

Map Entity: Fruit B

The Russian False Mango is a mango-like fruit found only in Tselinoyarsk. The egg-shaped fruit is sweet and tangy with a pleasing aroma; just like a mango. Also, the seeds can be used to make a medicine that aids in digestion. It might come in handy if you ever have an upset stomach.

HABITAT	EFFECT
Can be found growing on trees in most jungle areas.	Good stamina recovery.

GOLOVA

Map Entity: Fruit C

Golova is a fruit that's found only in that region. It's related to the jackfruit, which is commonly found in Southeast Asia. Golova means "head" in Russian. It's probably called that because the fruit grows to about the size of a human head. It's supposedly pretty good to eat, with a uniquely sweet flavor. The fruit itself is fairly large, so you could make a meal out of it. Golovas grow directly off the trunk of the tree.

HABITAT	EFFECT
Found throughout most forested areas.	Excellent stamina recovery.

MISCELLANEOUS FLORA

VINE MELON

Map Entity: Vegetable

The Vine Melon is a kind of melon commonly found in Tselinoyarsk. Like the name says, it's a melon that grows on a vine. The flesh is crisp and delicious. The Vine Melon is full of potassium and carotene, so it's good for you as well. Next time you see a vine, why not check to see if there's a melon growing on it?

HABITAT	EFFECT
Moderately rare vegetable found in some forests.	Decent stamina recovery.

FAUNA

SNAKES

KING COBRA

Map Entity: Snake A

The king cobra is the world's largest venomous snake. Its large size means that it has a lot of venom to inject. One bite is supposedly enough to kill an elephant. And it's extremely vicious as well, so watch out. If you get bitten by a king cobra and injected with venom, your Life will start to decrease rapidly. As soon as you're bitten, go into the Survival Viewer and use Cure to give yourself a serum injection. The king cobra's diet consists mainly of other snakes. Be careful or you might end up as its next meal.

HABITAT	EFFECT
A moderately rare nocturnal snake found in forested areas.	Good stamina recovery.

INTRODUCTION

CHARACTERS

SYSTEM

WEAPONS

ITEMS

FOOD

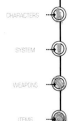

CURE

PROLOGUE VIRTUOUS MISSION

OPERATION SNAKE EATER

SNAKE VS MONKEY

BONUSES & EASTER EGGS

KEROTAN LOCATIONS

INTERVIEWS

METAL GEAR SOLID COMIC

TAIWANESE COBRA

Map Entity: Snake B

The Taiwanese cobra is native to Taiwan and southern China. It's quite vicious, and carries a potent neurotoxin in its fangs. Be careful. If it bites you, go into the Survival Viewer immediately and use the Cure option to inject yourself with serum.

HABITAT	EFFECT
Found in caves, mountainous areas, and some forests.	Very good stamina recovery.

THAI COBRA

Map Entity: Snake C

The Thai cobra is a large venomous snake that carries an extremely potent neurotoxin. Be careful not to get bitten. If you do get bitten, go into the Survival Viewer and use Cure to give yourself a serum injection. The Thai cobra originally comes from Indochina, Thailand, and southern China. The ones in that area were probably imported as pets and research subjects before they escaped and turned feral.

HABITAT	EFFECT
Found in caves and some mountainous areas.	Moderate stamina recovery.

CORAL SNAKE

Map Entity: Snake D

The coral snake is venomous and originally hails from the Americas. Its venom is a very potent neurotoxin, so don't let it bite you. If you do get bitten, go into the Survival Viewer right away and use Cure to neutralize the poison with a serum injection. The colorful red and black patterns on the coral snake are a warning sign. Apparently, the bright, flashy colors and pattern let other animals know that it carries a deadly poison.

HABITAT	EFFECT
Found near swampy areas with plenty of trees and water.	Good stamina recovery.

MILK SNAKE

Map Entity: Snake E

The milk snake closely resembles the coral snake, but it's actually not venomous. Even so, you'll still take damage if it bites you so don't get too close. The milk snake is much less aggressive than the coral snake, although the two look almost identical.

HABITAT	EFFECT
Likes forested areas with access to water.	Barely noticeable stamina recovery.

GREEN TREE PYTHON

Map Entity: Snake F

The green tree python isn't venomous, so no need to worry. It's fairly docile, too, so it's not likely to attack you. The green tree python originally comes from Australia and New Zealand. It's a really pretty green color, and it lives in trees.

HABITAT	EFFECT
Nocturnal snake that lives in branches of trees.	Moderate stamina recovery.

GIANT ANACONDA

Map Entity: Snake G

The Giant Anaconda is believed to be the largest snake in the world in terms of weight and diameter. It's not poisonous, but its large size makes it extremely powerful. They say it even eats crocodiles. Its only natural predators are man and snake.

HABITAT	EFFECT
Moderately rare snake that lives in swamps and some caves.	Great stamina recovery.

RETICULATED PYTHON

Map Entity: Snake H

The Reticulated Python is said to be the longest snake in the world. The biggest ones can grow up to 10 meters in length. Although they're not poisonous, they're still very dangerous so be careful and around them. They have a highly ferocious temperament and they can swallow whole even large animals like deer and pigs. Their most distinguishing feature is the mesh pattern of their scales. This pattern acts as a highly effective natural camouflage.

HABITAT	EFFECT
Very common snake found in numerous environments.	Great stamina recovery.

SNAKE LIQUID

Map Entity: Snake I

The scientific community is unaware of the existence of this species of snake.

HABITAT	EFFECT
Extremely rare snake found only in a field of daffodils.	Excellent stamina recovery.

SNAKE SOLID

Map Entity: Snake J

The scientific community is unaware of the existence of this species of snake.

HABITAT	EFFECT
Extremely rare snake found only in a field of daffodils.	Excellent stamina recovery.

SNAKE SOLIDUS

Map Entity: Snake K

The scientific community is unaware of the existence of this species of snake.

HABITAT	EFFECT
Extremely rare snake found only in a field of daffodils.	Excellent stamina recovery.

FROGS

OTTON FROG

Map Entity: Frog A

The Otton frog is a large, corpulent species of frog. They're known as a delicacy, so it might be worth catching them for food. The Otton frog was originally found only on Amami Oshima in Japan. Frogs usually have four toes on their front legs, but the Otton frog is unique in that it has five.

HABITAT	EFFECT
Very common frog that inhabits forests and caves.	Good stamina recovery.

TREE FROG

Map Entity: Frog B

The Tree Frog is a green frog that's found throughout Asia. It's arboreal, spending most of its time in shrubs and bushes. The Tree Frogs that live in the jungle are bigger than most normal frogs. There are people who think it's a mutation caused by nuclear testing and waste from the research facility.

HABITAT	EFFECT
Frog common to the floor of most forested areas.	Barely noticeable stamina recovery.

INTRODUCTION

CHARACTERS

SYSTEM

WEAPONS

ITEMS

FOOD

CURE

PROLOGUE VIRTUOUS MISSION

OPERATION SNAKE EATER

SNAKE VS. MONKEY

BONUSES & EASTER EGGS

KEROTAN LOCATIONS

INTERVIEWS

METAL GEAR SOLID COMIC

POISON DART FROG

Map Entity: Frog C

The poison dart frog is native to the tropical rain forests of Central and South America. They normally grow between two and five centimeters in length, but for some reason the ones in that area seem to be much bigger than that. Poison dart frogs are known to carry a potent neurotoxin called pumiliotoxin. Long ago, people used the poison to coat their arrows for hunting. Watch out because if you eat one, you'll get food poisoning.

HABITAT	EFFECT
Small purple frog found in some jungle environs.	Came down with food poisoning.

FISH

BIGEYE TREVALLY

Map Entity: Fish A

The bigeye trevally is a type of mackerel. The adult fish lives around coral reefs, but the young can be found in fresh water areas such as estuaries and rivers. There are stories about people getting ciguatera poisoning after eating the adult fish. Fish that live near coral reefs are sometimes contaminated with a poison known as ciguatera toxin. It apparently gives you food poisoning when you eat it.

HABITAT	EFFECT
Found near mangrove forests and in some caves.	Came down with food poisoning.

MAROON SHARK

Map Entity: Fish B

The maroon shark is found mostly in Southeast Asia. But it's not actually a shark—it's related to the carp. It's also known as the red finned cigar shark, the river barb, and the sultan fish.

HABITAT	EFFECT
Found near mangrove forests and in most clear water.	Decent stamina recovery.

AROWANA

Map Entity: Fish C

The arowana is an ancient fish that lives in tropical freshwater areas. Because of its large size, I don't think you'll be able to capture one alive. Ancient fish like the arowana are living fossils. They've hardly changed their forms since the Devonian and Jurassic periods. Other ancient fish besides the arowana include the coelacanth, the starlet, and the knifefish. Almost all organisms on earth have evolved over time, but these fish have kept the same form for hundreds of millions of years.

HABITAT	EFFECT
Found in lakes and rivers with moderately deep water.	Decent stamina recovery.

BIRDS

PARROT

Map Entity: Bird A

The Alexandrine Parakeet (also known as the Alexandrine Parrot) originally comes from Indochina, and is distinguished by its green body and red beak. It's very talkative and makes a good pet.

HABITAT	EFFECT
Found in Sokovenno South near munitions cache.	Barely noticeable stamina recovery.

WHITE-RUMPED VULTURE

Map Entity: Bird B

The white-rumped vulture is found in India. Its diet consists mostly of dead animals. It's not likely to attack you, but it's a fairly large bird of prey, so you probably won't be able to capture it alive using the tranquilizer gun.

HABITAT	EFFECT
Large bird found only in the mountains.	Very good stamina recovery.

RED AVADAVAT

Map Entity: Bird C

The Red Avadavat is a small bird native to Southern China and Southeast Asia. This is its mating season, so the males ought to be a brilliant red color right now. If you want to catch one alive, use the tranquilizer gun. By catching one and then releasing it, you might be able to distract the enemy's attention.

HABITAT	EFFECT
Very rare bird found in tall grass in select wooded areas.	Slight stamina recovery.

MAGPIE

Map Entity: Bird D

Magpies are members of the crow family. They're distinguishable by their beautiful dark blue and white bodies and their long tails. Their favorite food is insects, but they'll also eat small fish, acorns, and fruit. They're omnivores, which means they'll eat anything.

HABITAT	EFFECT
Found throughout most forested areas, especially in grass.	Slight stamina recovery.

SUNDA WHISTLING-THRUSH

Map Entity: Bird E

The Sunda Whistling-Thrush is a bird native to Java and Sumatra. It's distinguished by its large blue body and long beak. It really stands out in the forest.

HABITAT	EFFECT
Common inhabitant of most forested areas.	Good stamina recovery.

MISCELLANEOUS ANIMALS

COBALT BLUE TARANTULA

Map Entity: Spider

The Cobalt Blue Tarantula injects a highly toxic venom into its prey when threatened. Surprisingly, however, this particular spider can be eaten without any risk of being poisoned. Try to capture the Cobalt Blue Tarantula alive and then toss it at the feet of an enemy. Be sure to watch where you step when you're inside caves and basements.

HABITAT	EFFECT
Lives in basements, caves, and underground tunnels.	Barely noticeable stamina recovery.

EMPEROR SCORPION

Map Entity: Scorpion

The emperor scorpion is said to be the largest scorpion in the world. Its venom is a potent neurotoxin, so take care that you don't get stung. If you do get stung, go into the Survival Viewer and use Cure to inject yourself with serum right away. Try catching one alive with the tranquilizer gun and throwing it at the enemy.

HABITAT	EFFECT
Found in high-altitude mountains.	Came down with food poisoning.

INTRODUCTION

CHARACTERS

SYSTEM

WEAPONS

ITEMS

FOOD

CURE

PROLOGUE: VIRTUOUS MISSION

OPERATION SNAKE EATER

SNAKE VS. MONKEY

BONUSES & EASTER EGGS

KEROTAN LOCATIONS

INTERVIEWS

METAL GEAR SOLID COMIC

EUROPEAN RABBIT

Map Entity: Rabbit

The European rabbit is said to have come from the Mediterranean region originally. But nowadays they're found all over the world. They've been used since ancient times as a source of food, so it might be worth catching them. Rabbits are known to eat their own excrement. It's called caecal feces. When the rabbit eats fiber, the fiber is fermented in the rabbit's appendix, or caecum, and turned into a nutritious substance full of vitamins. The rabbit excretes this substance and then eats it again to absorb the nutrients.

HABITAT	EFFECT
Found in forested areas during both night and day.	Good stamina recovery.

HORNETS' NEST

Map Entity: Nest

The difference between Baltic Hornets and other hornets is that they produce honey in their nests. Inside the nest are larva, pupa, and adults—you can eat them all. In particular, the honey you find inside the nest is delicious and full of nutrients. It's easy to digest and helps pep you up when you're feeling tired. In short, it's the perfect survival food. Honey can also be used on a burn; it creates a protective coating over the skin. When you knock down a hornets' nest, a burn ointment will appear along with it, so don't forget to pick it up.

HABITAT	EFFECT
Found in the branches of trees in most forests.	Excellent stamina recovery.

INDIAN GAVIAL

Map Entity: Gavial

The Indian Gavial is a crocodile that originally lived in freshwater regions in India and Nepal. It's a captive crocodile that was brought here for research purposes, but escaped and became wild again. Indian Gavials are large creatures—adult males grow to over six meters in length. You'll never catch it alive, even if you use the tranquilizer gun. Normally, they're cowardly creatures, but the ones in the forest here are belligerent. Apparently, they attack humans.

HABITAT	EFFECT
Found throughout swamps and mud bogs in the jungle.	Moderate stamina recovery.

JAPANESE FLYING SQUIRREL

Map Entity: Squirrel

Japanese flying squirrels are non-venomous, and they shouldn't attack you. The head, front legs, hind legs, and tail of the Japanese flying squirrel are connected by a membrane of skin, which allows the squirrel to glide from tree to tree. If it catches a good wind, it can glide more than 100 yards.

HABITAT	EFFECT
It's a nocturnal animal that lives in forested areas.	Moderate stamina recovery.

KENYAN MANGROVE CRAB

Map Entity: Crab

The Kenyan mangrove crab is a land-going crab. It lives in burrows dug near seashores and mangrove swamps. It's not poisonous, but it might hurt a little if it attacks you with its pincers. Treat it with caution.

HABITAT	EFFECT
Lives in caves and in and around mangrove forests.	Good stamina recovery.

MARKHOR

Map Entity: Markhor

The markhor is a kind of wild goat that lives in mountainous areas. It's quite large, so you won't be able to capture one alive, even with the tranquilizer gun. The name markhor means "snake eater" in Persian.

HABITAT	EFFECT
Found primarily in hilly, forested areas.	Good stamina recovery.

RAT

Map Entity: Rat

The rats in this region are the descendants of wild Norway rats that were domesticated by humans as pets and lab animals. They're not poisonous, and it's unlikely that they'll attack you. But they're quick little creatures, so you might have a hard time catching one.

HABITAT	EFFECT
Likes dark areas like tunnels and basements.	Decent stamina recovery.

VAMPIRE BAT

Map Entity: Bat

The vampire bat bites its victims and sucks their blood. Bats are known to use supersonic waves to sense their surroundings. So you might be able to keep them away by blasting them with a special kind of sound wave. Alternatively, you could try equipping a torch and waving it around with the CQC button.

HABITAT	EFFECT
Inhabits dimly lit caves and tunnels.	Barely noticeable stamina recovery.

PACKAGED FOOD

INSTANT NOODLES

Map Entity: Noodles

Instant Noodles were invented in Japan just recently. Add some hot water and it's ready to eat. It's cheap and can be stored for a long time. And besides, it's delicious. It's like a miracle food.

HABITAT	EFFECT
Can be found in almost any enemy structure.	Excellent stamina recovery.

RUSSIAN RATION

Map Entity: Ration

Rations are portable meals carried by Soviet soldiers. There are some nasty stories about how they taste, though. Nevertheless, they are designed to last. No matter how long you keep a ration, it'll never go bad. And they're surprisingly good for you, too.

HABITAT	EFFECT
Rations can be found in almost any enemy structure.	Decent stamina recovery.

CALORIE MATE

Map Entity: Calorie

Calorie Mate is an energy supplement that contains all the proteins, lipids, vitamins, carbohydrates, and minerals needed for a balanced diet. It is a well-balanced food. Because of that, it's just perfect for giving your body the nutrition that it needs in combat.

HABITAT	EFFECT
Found in enemy provision supply rooms.	Very good stamina recovery.

CURE

MEDICAL TREATMENT IN THE FIELD

Snake is a lone operative working in a large jungle littered with wild animals, booby traps, and enemies armed to the teeth. It's only natural for him to suffer the occasional war wound. While this is understandable, one must keep in mind that Operation Snake Eater is not your basic counter-intelligence mission. There are no medics walking around and certainly no medicine chests to rely on for instant cure-alls. If this mission is to be successful, Snake will have roll to up his sleeves and perform a host of first aid techniques to stay healthy.

Snake's backpack contains numerous first-aid items that can be used to heal burns, cuts, gunshot wounds, and several other unpleasantries, like stomach poisoning and venomous snake bites. The backpack even contains a cure for the common cold!

A portion of Snake's Health bar turns red when he needs medical attention. Press the **START** button to enter the Survival Viewer and select the option labeled "Cure." An X-ray image reveals Snake's wounds, and a brief description accompanies each injury. Each type of wound requires its own treatment, usually involving several first-aid items. The size of the circle appearing near the wound represents the percentage of the wound that has not yet healed. This circle diminishes in size as each correct medical item is used, but the wound is not entirely cured until all of the necessary items have been applied. Until all of Snake's injuries are completely treated, his Health and Stamina will continue to decrease slowly.

Snake's medical inventory is divided into two separate categories. Use the Left Analog Stick to select an injury, and press and hold the R2 button while using the D-pad to browse his available surgical items. These are the items used to heal burns, cuts, broken bones, gunshot wounds, and to remove arrows and needles. Hold the L2 button and use the D-pad to scroll through the list of available medicine. Select an item to apply to Snake's wound with the ◯ button. An audible confirmation sounds if the chosen item helps heal the currently targeted wound. Consult the following explanations to learn which items are required in each field treatment.

SURGERY

CUTS
Cause

Cuts are often received during CQC combat with an enemy wielding a knife or other item as a melee weapon. Snake can also be cut by grenade blasts, especially if he is in close proximity to exploding barrels and/or shattering windows. Last but not least, Snake will receive many of his cuts from encounters with the region's wildlife. The Indian Gavial crocodiles are especially ferocious!

TREATING CUTS

ITEM NAME	ICON
Disinfectant	
Styptic	
Suture Kit	
Bandage	

BURNS
Cause

As one might expect, Snake's body cannot withstand direct exposure to open flames without being burned. Although Snake can run through small flames, his camouflage can catch fire. If this happens, quickly roll on the ground to put out the flames and administer treatment at once. It's also possible for burns to be incurred from the muzzle flash of an enemy's gun, and from grenade or claymore blasts.

TREATING BURNS

ITEM NAME	ICON
Ointment	
Bandage	

BROKEN BONES
Cause

Broken bones aren't terribly common, but they are serious and must be treated immediately if Snake is to have any hope of maintaining Stamina. Broken bones are typically suffered during CQC combat, especially when fighting a highly skilled enemy. It's also possible to incur a broken bone via the powerful jaws of the Indian Gavial crocodile. Lastly, Snake can suffer this injury during falls from great heights. It's possible for Snake to intentionally drop or jump from substantial heights without injury, but falls of greater than two stories will often result in a broken leg.

TREATING BROKEN BONES

ITEM NAME	ICON
Splint	
Bandage	

GUNSHOT WOUNDS
Cause

Gunshot wounds are an unfortunate side effect of engaging in firefights with multiple enemies simultaneously. Although stealth is almost always the way to go, sometimes Snake can't help being seen—and shot—on occasion. Treat the wound quickly to maintain the Stamina necessary to prevail in the fight.

TREATING GUNSHOT WOUNDS

ITEM NAME	ICON
Survival Knife	
Disinfectant	
Styptic	
Bandage	

ARROWS/CROSSBOW BOLTS
Cause

Although extremely rare, Snake will be shot with a crossbow bolt during the course of his mission. This type of injury can't be helped, but it can be cured.

TREATING ARROW/CROSSBOW WOUNDS

ITEM NAME	ICON
Survival Knife	
Bandage	

HYPODERMIC NEEDLES

Snake encounters an enemy that opts to fire hypodermic needles loaded with anesthesia. A needle wound is not immediately life threatening, but Snake's vision is adversely impacted and his Stamina diminishes while the needle is stuck in him. Remove the needle at once!

REMOVING HYPODERMIC NEEDLE WOUNDS

ITEM NAME	ICON
Survival Knife	

LEECHES
Cause

The swamps of this region are loaded with leeches and although Bug Juice can help repel them, it doesn't work for long. Leeches not only suck the blood from Snake's body, but they also quickly drain his Stamina.

REMOVING LEECHES

ITEM NAME	ICON
Cigar	

INTRODUCTION

CHARACTERS

SYSTEM

WEAPONS

ITEMS

FOOD

CURE

PROLOGUE: VIRTUOUS MISSION

OPERATION SNAKE EATER

SNAKE VS. MONKEY

BONUSES & EASTER EGGS

KEROTAN LOCATIONS

INTERVIEWS

METAL GEAR SOLID COMIC

ILLNESS

STOMACH SICKNESS
Cause

Most of the animals and plants that Snake encounters in the jungle are perfectly fine to eat, so long as they are fresh. Unfortunately, food does spoil over time and the longer it stays in the backpack, the greater the odds that it will go rotten and cause food poisoning when digested. See the "Food" chapter for more information on food spoilage and stomach sickness.

TREATING STOMACH SICKNESS

ITEM NAME	ICON
Digestive Medicine	

FOOD POISONING
Cause

Although there aren't many toxic creatures out in the wild, there are several animal and mushroom species that cause food poisoning when eaten. Food poisoning not only hinders Snake's performance by draining his Stamina, but it also causes a decrease in Health.

TREATING FOOD POISONING

ITEM NAME	ICON
Antidote	

COLDS
Cause

It is entirely possible to complete Operation Snake Eater without ever catching a cold, so long as Snake avoids sneezing guards and stays fully clothed. Wearing a camouflage other than "Naked," especially when swimming, exploring caves, or during rain, goes a long way in keeping Snake healthy.

TREATING COLDS

ITEM NAME	ICON
Cold Medicine	

VENOM POISONING
Cause

Some of the environments that Snake explores are home to venomous snakes, spiders, and scorpions. Although it's understandable to focus on enemy locations, Snake must also be aware of the critters that might nip at his ankles. Being bitten by a venomous creature causes a decrease in Health and Stamina and should be treated as soon as possible.

TREATING VENOM POISONING

ITEM NAME	ICON
Blood Serum	

MEDICAL ITEMS

SURGERY

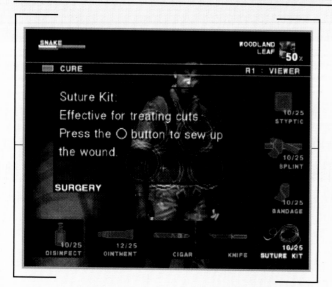

Hold the R2 button to view the available items used in field surgery. These items help heal the inevitable wounds that Snake incurs over the course of his mission. Broken bones can be healed, cuts can be bandaged, and bullets can be extracted. These items can be found by shaking the bodies of fallen enemies (or by holding them up at gunpoint), by plundering enemy storerooms, and by cutting down select plants.

SURVIVAL KNIFE
Capacity: 1

Useful for removing bullets, arrows and needles.

CIGAR
Capacity: 1

Useful for removing leeches attached to the body.

OINTMENT
Capacity: 25

Useful for burn treatment.

DISINFECTANT
Capacity: 25

Useful for treating cuts and gunshot wounds.

STYPTIC
Capacity: 25

Used to stop the bleeding from cuts and gunshot wounds.

SPLINT
Capacity: 25

Helps a broken bone heal by fixing it in place.

BANDAGE
Capacity: 25

Effective for treating burns, cuts, gunshot wounds, and broken bones.

SUTURE KIT
Capacity: 25

Effective for treating cuts by stitching the wound.

MEDICINE

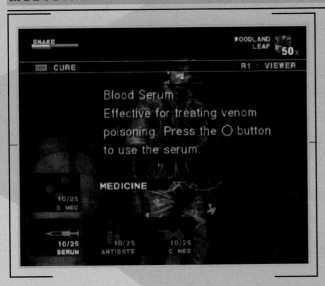

Hold the L2 button to view the available medicinal items. Snake will need these items to cure an internal illness such as food poisoning or if a venomous snake or scorpion bites him. These items can be replenished by finding medical storerooms on enemy bases and by cutting down select plants.

BLOOD SERUM
Capacity: 25

Effective for treating venom poisoning.

ANTIDOTE
Capacity: 25

Effective against food poisoning.

COLD MEDICINE
Capacity: 25

Effective for treating colds.

DIGESTIVE MEDICINE
Capacity: 25

Effective for treating stomach aches.

INTRODUCTION

CHARACTERS

SYSTEM

WEAPONS

ITEMS

FOOD

CURE

PROLOGUE: VIRTUOUS MISSION

OPERATION SNAKE EATER

SNAKE VS. MONKEY

BONUSES & EASTER EGGS

KEROTAN LOCATIONS

INTERVIEWS

METAL GEAR SOLID COMIC

PROLOGUE:
VIRTUOUS MISSION

🌐 NORMAL DIFFICULTY

The following strategy pertains to the Normal difficulty setting. Item placement, enemy quantities and patrol routes may differ from what is described in this chapter when playing other difficulty modes.

Snake (David Hayter)

This brief contains strategy to complete "Virtuous Mission." Each portion of the mission is broken down area by area, including maps with callouts and lists of items located in each zone. While infiltrating, use the Food List to hunt for stamina-replenishing flora and fauna so that Snake stays healthy, active and accurate. These Food Lists do *not* include every single food item, nor do they include items that might be dropped by unconscious, sleeping or held-up guards.

🌐 DIRECTIONS

In all directions provided in this manual, "north" refers to the top of the screen, south refers to the bottom, east is to the right, and west is to the left, much as if you were staring at a geographic map.

MISSION OBJECTIVE:
RESCUE DOCTOR SOKOLOV

CIA operative code-named "Naked Snake" parachutes via high-altitude HALO jump into the jungle region of Tselinoyarsk. Using camouflage, Close Quarters Combat (CQC) and stealth, he must infiltrate an abandoned warehouse several clicks north of his drop zone. His mission is to rescue Soviet defector Dr. Sokolov from the clutches of the KGB, escort him to a safe area, and exit the region via recovery balloon.

FOOD LIST: PROLOGUE STAGE

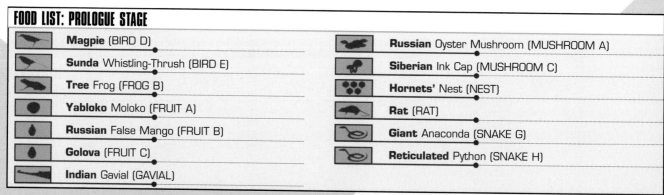

Magpie (BIRD D)	**Russian** Oyster Mushroom (MUSHROOM A)
Sunda Whistling-Thrush (BIRD E)	**Siberian** Ink Cap (MUSHROOM C)
Tree Frog (FROG B)	**Hornets'** Nest (NEST)
Yabloko Moloko (FRUIT A)	**Rat** (RAT)
Russian False Mango (FRUIT B)	**Giant** Anaconda (SNAKE G)
Golova (FRUIT C)	**Reticulated** Python (SNAKE H)
Indian Gavial (GAVIAL)	

DREMUCHIJ SOUTH

ITEMS FOUND

Mk22 BULLET x24

AMMO

Life Medicine (LF MED)

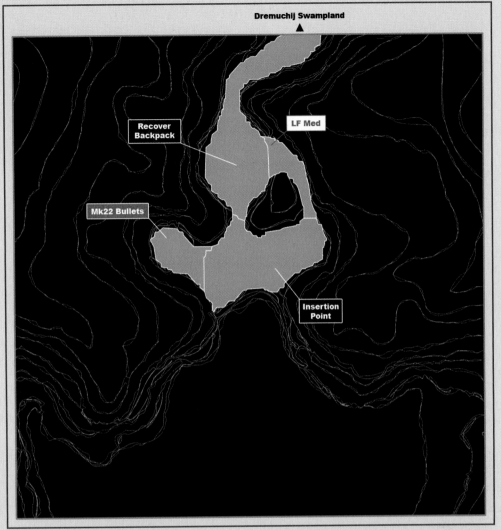

Dremuchij Swampland

Recover Backpack

LF Med

Mk22 Bullets

Insertion Point

Code Name: "Naked Snake"

Jack lands just a few inches short of a high cliff in the Dremuchij area of the Tselinoyarsk forest. After receiving his official codename, "Naked Snake," he must retrieve the backpack that got entangled in the tree a few yards back. There are two routes back to the backpack's location. Either head directly north (toward the top of the screen) from Snake's initial position, drop to the ground, and crawl under the tree trunk, or head east and then north up the slope to a raised ledge where a **Life Medicine** resides. Then slide off the ledge to the base of the tree in the area below.

SNAKE
SPLITTER
OLIVE·DRAB
5 x

LF MED

>> Does your time in the Green Berets have you feeling unfit and flabby? Move south to the cliff's edge and drop over the side. Snake automatically turns and grabs the edge. While hanging from an edge, press the R2 and L2 buttons simultaneously to perform a chin-up. Snake can also perform chin-ups while hanging from a tree branch, such as the one a few feet north of his drop location.

Climbing Trees

Position Snake at the base of the vines growing on the south side of the central tree, and press the Action button ▲ to climb up the vines to the branch. Maneuver carefully out to the end of the branch, toward the backpack, either by lightly moving the Left Analog Stick or by using the Directional Pad. When positioned over the backpack, press the Action button ▲ to drop into a dead hang. When Snake touches the hanging object in this manner, the backpack is obtained along with all of its contents.

FORAGING FOR FOOD

Because this area is clear of enemies, take a moment to gather edible fruits and fungus as well as live snakes and frogs. Directly west of Snake's starting point is a fallen tree. Press the Action button ▲ to climb on top of the lower trunk. Then press the CQC button ⬤ repeatedly until Snake performs a kick. The kicking action should knock loose the mushrooms growing from the log, and you may then obtain them. Drop to the ground behind the fallen trunk and watch the area carefully to find two **Reticulated Pythons**. You may kill them and convert them to rations using the CQC kick, or you can shoot them with the Mk22 to capture them live. Live animals have various uses, and they do not expire like rations do.

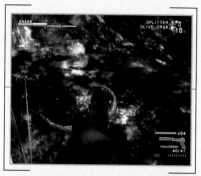

Kick the trees directly north and a little east of Snake's starting position to find several **Siberian Ink Caps**. These are distasteful mushrooms, which can be eaten to restore small amounts of Stamina.

Two **Magpies** like to roost in the tall grass at the top of the slope on the east side of the area. They are extremely difficult to hunt, but they provide good Stamina recovery.

ITEMS FOUND

Bug Juice

Grenades (GRENADE)

Mk22 BULLET x24

Mk22 Suppressor (SP/Mk22)

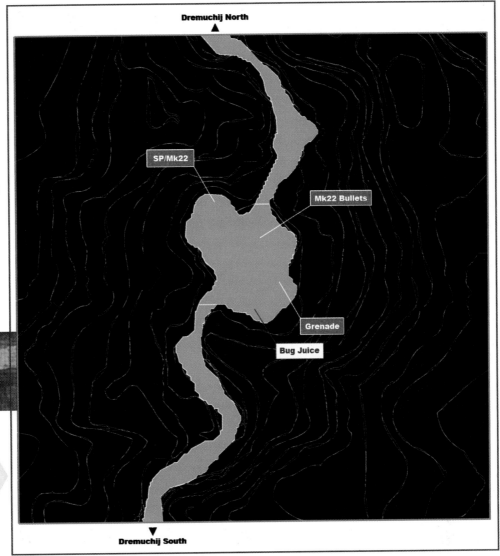

Dremuchij North

SP/Mk22

Mk22 Bullets

Grenade

Bug Juice

Dremuchij South

Snips, Snails and Crocodile Tails

This area is filled with quicksand mud and Indian Gavial crocodiles, which according to Para-Medic are quite belligerent. At the edge of the quicksand, move east and follow the narrow strip of solid ground to the east side of the area. Stay clear of the crocodiles for now, until you procure better weapons. Look around on the ground to locate **Bug Juice** as well as a pack of **Grenades**, then turn and face the central islet. To obtain Indian Gavial meat, blow up the crocodiles with Grenades.

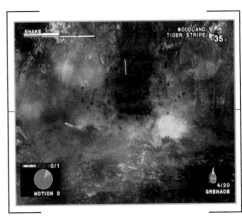

Disturbing the Hive

From the safety of the eastern bank, shoot the **Hornets' Nest** from the tree on the central islet. The hornets emerge from the hive, angered, but Snake should be far enough out of range to avoid their wrath. If your luck isn't so good, Bug Juice can be used to ward off insects such as hornets. Cross through the quicksand toward the central islet before the items disappear, but be sure to keep moving. Otherwise, Snake sinks into the quicksand and dies. Collect the Ointment and the Hornets' Nest ration created from the hive, as well as the **Mk22 Bullets**.

Trudge steadily through the quicksand to the northwest bank. Move around the northern crocodile and collect the **Mk22 Suppressor** behind the reptile. Now move north and collect the **fruit** growing from tree branches, as well as the pieces that have fallen to the ground, and continue into the next area.

VIRTUOUS MISSION

DREMUCHIJ NORTH

ITEMS FOUND

Bug Juice

Grenades (GRENADE)

Mk22 BULLET x24

Thermal Goggles (THERM G)

Stun Grenades (STUN G)

Dragunov Smiper Rifle (SVD)

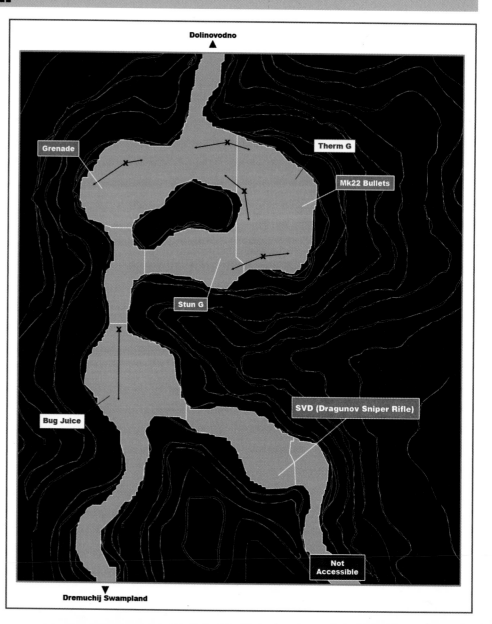

Hiding Inside Trees

Descend to the flat area, move left, and crawl into the south end of the hollow fallen tree trunk. Crawl northward, collecting **Bug Juice**. Continue crawling to the north end of the trunk, look out through the tree trunk's end, and wait for a

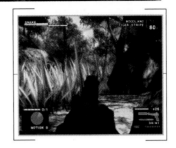

guard to walk slowly into the clearing. Aim the Mk22 at his head and attempt to fire a tranquilizer dart into his face.

THE SNIPER RIFLE

Don't forget to check the path leading southeast from the first area to find the Dragunov Sniper Rifle, good for zooming in on kills but loud in the noise department.

Fun with Guards

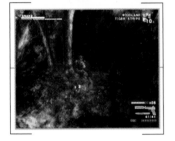

If the guard is successfully knocked out, crawl out of your hiding place and move to the dozing guard. Stand at the guard's head or legs and press ⦿ to begin dragging the body east around the corner, out of the other guards' sight. Here, you can "shake" the guard by picking him up and dropping him repeatedly, causing two or three items to fall out of his pockets. Then you can finish off the guard by crouching near his head and attacking repeatedly with the Survival Knife until the "Z" icons cease.

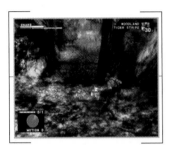

Additionally, you can awaken the guard by standing near his head and performing repeated CQC attacks (press the ⦿ button repeatedly). The final kick of Snake's three-move CQC basic combo should hit the guard's body. Each kick greatly reduces the amount of time the guard remains asleep.

As the guard awakens and slowly rises to his feet, "hold him up" by aiming your gun at his back. After Snake yells "Freeze!" and the guard puts up his hands, continue holding the ⦿ button and move the Left Analog Stick to make Snake circle around the guard. Once in front of the arrested victim, hold 🔲 to enter First Person View and point the gun at his head. Guards can be made to yield several rarely dropped items in this state, even if they have already been "shaken" while unconscious.

If you like, grab the guard by moving in close and holding the CQC button ⦿. Once the guard is entangled in a chokehold, there are numerous ways to interrogate or finish him off as discussed in the System chapter of this guide.

Proceeding from Guard to Guard

Advance north and use tranquilizer darts to prevent the remaining guards in the area from spotting Snake. Shake down bodies for extra items, and be sure to drag sleeping guards around corners to keep them out of sight. Two more guards are positioned along the path heading north from the entrance and then directly east to the exit.

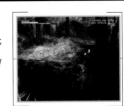
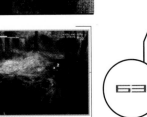

Inside the hollowed-out tree stump to the northwest is a pack of **Grenades.** Inside the tree stump near the east edge of the area is a box of **Mk22 Bullets**. You must overcome a fourth guard patrolling this high grass area in order to acquire these items quietly.

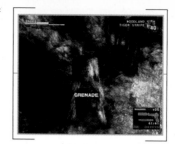
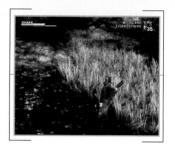

The Thermal Goggles

Crawl through a hollow log in the east sector to obtain the **Thermal Goggles**. The Thermal Goggles display heat signatures in the jungle environment, making it very easy to spot patrolling guards as well as wildlife, fruit, mushrooms and items. Hunting becomes a lot easier now, in case you'd like to return to previous areas to scavenge up more tasty jungle morsels.

DOLINOVODNO

ITEMS FOUND

Pentazemin

Mk22 BULLET x24

XM16E1

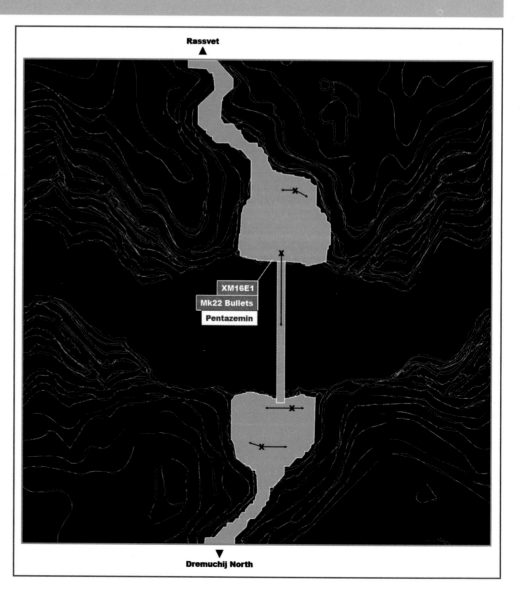

VIRTUOUS
MISSION

This Might Sting a Little...

Entering the area, Snake immediately spots an easy method for dealing with the numerous guards surrounding the bridge. Crouch low in the grass blades near the edge of the drop-off, and check your Camo Index to be sure that Snake is well hidden. Watch the guard patrolling at the bridge's entrance in First Person View. When he moves to the right under the Hornets' Nest, shoot the hive out of the tree. When the angered hornets emerge from the hive, they immediately go after the guard. The guard flees across the bridge, taking the swarm with him. Consequently, the hornets attack the other guards as well, and everyone flees the area!

After crossing the bridge, look up in the tree directly ahead to spot another Hornets' Nest. When the guards return to the area momentarily, drop the second hive on them to chase them out again. If one guard lags behind in this instance, it should be no problem to tranquilize him quickly, shake his body for items, and dispose of him. Quickly move west and follow the narrow path down below the bridge to a ledge where the **XM16E1** is located, as described a few paragraphs ahead.

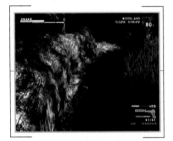

When returning to the upper area, stop a few yards to the west of the exit point and wait for the guards to return yet again. Equip the Motion Detector to approximate the guards' positions, and when they get far enough south, head north to the exit.

SADISTIC DISPOSAL

Guard bodies can be dumped into the gorge simply by dragging them to the edge. Once there, position the body so that Snake is facing the ledge, then pick up and drop the body repeatedly. With each drop, the body slides a little further off the ledge, and eventually drops over the side. This is a great way to hide guard corpses in this area.

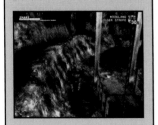

The Shaky Bridge

Slide down the slope and cross the bridge quickly, steering carefully straight down the center. If Snake veers a little too far left or right, the balance of the bridge shifts and Snake falls over the side. Press ⬆ to climb back onto the bridge. If Snake is positioned below one of the vertical planks on the bridge, he cannot climb up. Use the Left Analog Stick to shimmy north or south along the length of the bridge until Snake is at an open spot between support planks, and press ⬆ to climb up.

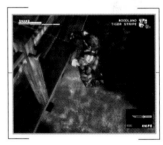

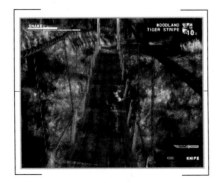

If the side ropes of the bridge are severed by blasts or with the knife, the section's balance becomes highly unstable. Slicing the ropes with the Survival Knife is a good tactic to employ if guards are pursuing Snake across the bridge, as the enemies may lose their balance in the unstable section and fall to their deaths.

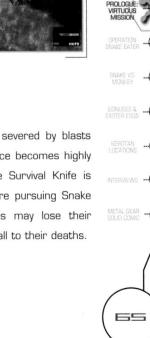

Shimmying under the bridge is also a good way to cross the gorge unseen. With full Stamina, Snake should be able to shimmy from the halfway point of the bridge all the way to the north side. A branch sticks out from a ledge below the north end of the bridge. Snake can drop and catch hold of the branch using a Drop-Catch maneuver. While hanging from the west side of the bridge, press ⊗ to let go and drop. Press the △ button at the instant Snake drops past the branch to grab on. If successful, press △ to swing up onto the branch and walk carefully over to the ledge, where the **XM16E1** and other items are located.

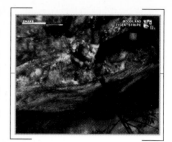

Stashed Under the Bridge

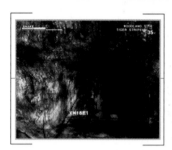

Using either of the methods described previously, navigate to the ledge below the north anchor of the rope bridge. Tucked almost out of sight here are **Pentazemin**, **Mk22 Bullets**, and the **XM16E1** prototype assault rifle. West of the depression is an extremely narrow ledge. If Snake attempts to walk on it normally, he drops and hangs from the side. If this happens, shimmy one direction or the other until the ledge widens out a bit, and then climb back up. Snake has an easier time crossing the narrow ledge if you move just a little ways onto the ledge, press your back against the wall and hold L2 or R2 to sidestep along the surface.

VIRTUOUS
MISSION

RASSVET

ITEMS FOUND

M37

XM16E1 Bullets x80

AMMO

XM16E1 Suppressor (SP/XM16E1)

Life Medicine (LF MED)

Mousetrap

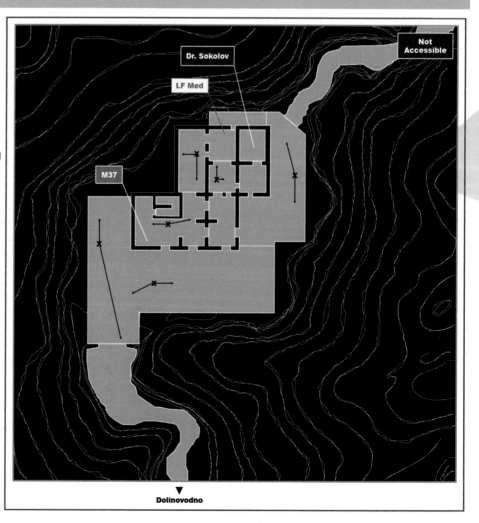

Dolinovodno

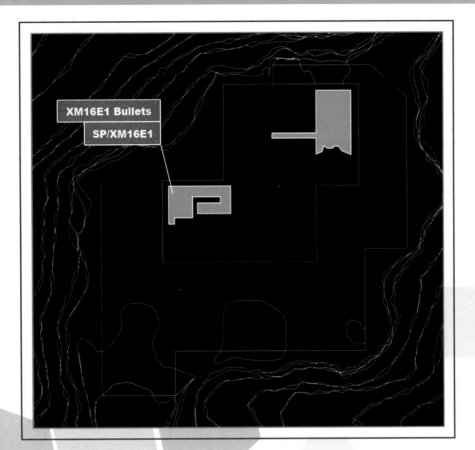

XM16E1 Bullets

SP/XM16E1

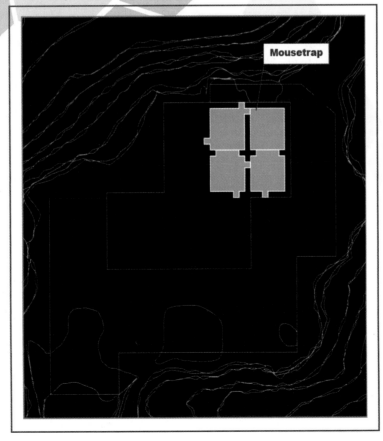

Mousetrap

Approaching the Ruins

The room where Sokolov is held cannot be entered while the guards are in alert mode. Therefore, you must navigate through this area with a minimum of encounters and neutralize the guards along the path quietly to prevent discovery. Rather than discuss all the possible options, this briefing provides a tested attack method for the entire area that should get you to Sokolov without incident. Attempt this strategy to the best of your ability, improvising as needed to compensate for minor guard route variations.

I've reached the abandoned factory where Sokolov is supposedly being held

After the cinema, a guard stands with his back turned a few yards from the brick wall where Snake hides. Move just through the opening of the wall and aim in First Person View. Fire a dart at the ground directly behind the guard to draw his attention. When he turns to

investigate, quickly run behind the wall. If done successfully, the guard hears the noise, turns to look and catches the slightest glimpse of movement near the wall. This should bring the guard all the way down to the wall's opening. Move a few feet down and west of the brick wall opening, wait for the guard to approach, and fire a dart into his face when he stops at the brick wall. Then drag him outside the wall and dispose of him as you please.

The guard that patrols north-to-south in the western yard can be taken down in a similar manner, simply by running back and forth in front of the wall opening until the guard notices the movement. This maneuver brings him down to the wall much more quickly than waiting for him to gradually patrol that far on his own. Tranquilize and neutralize him as well.

Penetrating the Fallen Walls

Move quickly but quietly to the northwest corner of the zone, and press up against the low brick wall at the west edge of the ruins to view the interior. A guard patrols the area, but his route is so wide that the west entry point is unguarded for long periods. Move inside the wall and head south to find the **M37** shotgun located behind some stacked crates. Should an all-out firefight ensue, this is a fun weapon to use when you want to unleash some real stopping power, so be sure to remove it from the Backpack in case of emergency.

Move inward to a wide stack of cardboard boxes, and press your back up against them so that the east portion of the ruins can be viewed. The guard eventually patrols into this area, and he should move directly past Snake without seeing him. Once the guard is a few steps past your position, release the wall press and fire a dart at the back of his head. Drag the guard to the former location of the M37 and do what with him you will.

Direct Route to Sokolov

After downing the guard that checks the west side of the ruins, slowly ascend the metal stairs to the north without making too much racket. Stop on the mid-level platform and look northeast. With correct positioning, you should be able to spot the guard patrolling the enclosed north yard. Fire a tranquilizer dart at his head. Quickly head to the top platform, collect the **XM16E1 Bullets** and **Suppressor**, and then proceed to collect the dozing guard's body in the north yard.

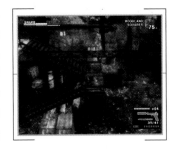 

The next guard in your path is just inside the enclosed area to the east. However, charging through the hole in the wall runs a high risk of exposure. The previously interior room has a noisy wood floor, and the central obstruction makes it difficult to determine the

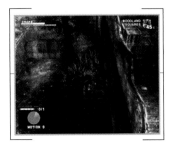 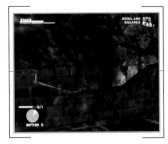

guard's position. Instead, climb onto the stack of crates piled against the wall in the yard. Stand at the northwest corner of the crates, drop to your belly, and look through the hole in the brick. The guard sometimes stops directly across from this hole in the wall. Fire a dart at his head through the hole to take him out easily. Then proceed inside and collect a **Life Medicine** near the upper wall.

Optional Undertaking

The next interior room to the east is just outside the area where Sokolov is kept. If you approach the north door, several very exciting cut scenes ensue. However, with just one guard left, there is ample opportunity for side action. For starters, climb onto either stack of boxes in the room and look through the window to see if you can spot the guard patrolling the east yard. Carefully shoot a tranquilizer dart through the broken window to knock him out, and then go torture him however you like.

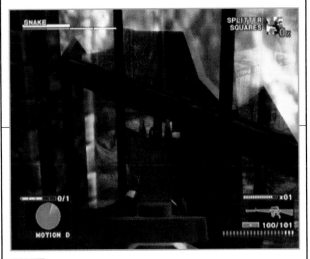

Staring at the outside of the ruins' east wall, you should easily spot a ladder allowing roof access. Simply approach the ladder and press the Action button ○ to climb onto the shingles. The **Sunda Whistling-Thrush** on the roof are easy to shoot or capture at this close range.

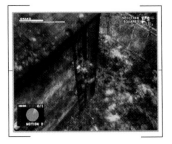 

Ground-level crawl holes around the exterior of the building's east side allow you to intrude into the area under the wooden floor. **Rats** and **Reticulated Pythons** run rampant in the four quadrants of this area. Capture or kill them with the usual methods, or obtain and use the **Mousetrap** located near the north wall. The Mousetrap is used like a weapon. Once the trap is set on the ground, the tasty cheese bait soon attracts a Rat. The Mousetrap captures the Rat live in a cage, so make sure you have one free. Once the Rat is collected, the Mousetrap is retrieved for another use.

LEAVE OCELOT ALONE!

The unconscious Ocelot commander and his soldiers do not reawaken. All of them can be shaken for items as usual, including a **Mousetrap** that Ocelot sometimes drops. However, avoid shooting Ocelot or using the Survival Knife anywhere near his motionless form. If Ocelot is killed, a time paradox is created and the game ends!

Field Surgery

After an amazing series of events and introductions unfolds, head back to the Dolinovodno area to continue. After Snake is betrayed, beaten, and thrown from the bridge, you must learn to use field medical procedures to repair his injuries. While lying helpless on the riverbank, press **START** to enter the Survival Viewer and choose the "CURE" option. The CURE menu displays areas where Snake is seriously injured and requires medical attention.

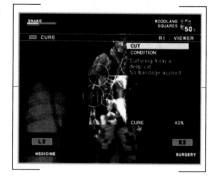

A series of symptoms is listed for each wound. Curing each symptom requires the use of a Surgical Item. For example, cuts require the aid of a Disinfectant, a Styptic, a Suture Kit, and a Bandage. A broken bone requires only a Splint and a Bandage. The order of item use is irrelevant. Once all treatments are applied to the wounded area, the cursor automatically moves on to the next wound. Treat all of Snake's injuries before you proceed.

From this moment on, large amounts of damage that Snake receives during cut scenes and from explosive devices or close-range gunshots must be cured. Additionally, sicknesses such as poisoning or stomach ailments can be remedied using Medicines. Normally, food must be eaten or Life Medicines must be used to recover lost Stamina and Health after Snake cures himself. But for now, Snake is headed back to base to regroup, recoup and later to return...

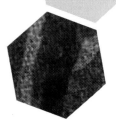

1 | OPERATION SNAKE EATER

Those shotguns are M37s. They're an American model designed for field combat

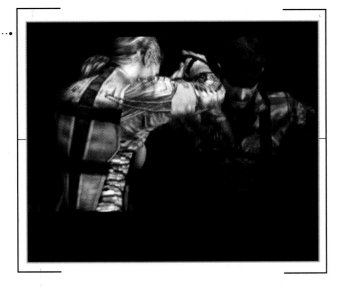

Due to the unfortunate setbacks of Virtuous Mission, a new campaign has been coordinated in the joint interests of the United States and the Soviet Union, two nations forced to collaborate due to the severe threat of the situation. Although badly wounded during the previous mission, operative CIA agent "Naked Snake" has been reassigned to complete this new and more complex mission. The main objectives are to rescue Sokolov, destroy the Shagohod, and to kill the defector and traitor formerly known as "The Boss." Because her COBRA Unit comrades will most likely not stand idly by, Snake is expected to encounter and kill them as well. Hence the reptile-exterminating mission name, "Operation Snake Eater."

MISSION OBJECTIVE ONE: ADAM AND EVA

Snake crash lands in Dremuchij East, an area somewhat near the location of Virtuous Mission. Four days have passed. Snake lands in the middle of the night. His first objective is to meet up with ADAM, a contact within the KGB. ADAM will take you to Sokolov's location to complete the rescue portion of the mission. Unlike before, this is an official mission with full assistance from the U.S. Government.

Snake, you're being given an honor on par with Alan Shepard.

FOOD LIST: ADAM AND EVA STAGE

Magpie (BIRD D)			**Siberian** Ink Cap (MUSHROOM C)	
Sunda Whistling-Thrush (BIRD E)			**Hornets'** Nest (NEST)	
Yabloko Moloko (FRUIT A)			**European** Rabbit (RABBIT)	
Golova (FRUIT C)			**Rat** (RAT)	
Russian False Mango (FRUIT B)			**King** Cobra (SNAKE A)	
Otton Frog (FROG A)			**Green** Tree Python (SNAKE F)	
Tree Frog (FROG B)			**Giant** Anaconda (SNAKE G)	
Indian Gavial (GAVIAL)			**Reticulated** Python (SNAKE H)	
Markhor (MARKHOR)			**Flying** Squirrel (SQUIRREL)	
Russian Oyster Mushroom (MUSHROOM A)				

DREMUCHIJ EAST

ITEMS FOUND

None

Dremuchij North

Insertion Point

OPERATION
SNAKE
EATER

| ADAM AND EVA

| BEYOND THE FOREST BASE

3 | ESCAPE THE CAVE

4 | WAREHOUSE IN THE MANGROVE

5 | GRANINY GORKI LAB

6 | WOODLAND HUNT

7 | ALPINE ASCENT

8 | GROZYNJ GRAD

9 | SHAGOHOD

10 | THE BOSS

Back in Action

Snake is now equipped with the M1911A1, a .45 caliber gun that fires lethal rounds. Any target shot with this weapon may be killed; there is no tranquilizer gun for now. However, you are about to lose this weapon. Use the M1911A1 to your heart's content for hunting until the next cinema.

Snake is completely out of food, so forage in this area to collect new rations. **Reticulated Pythons** still slither through the grass, and nocturnal **Otton Frogs** are quite a delicacy, according to Para-Medic. Check anywhere in the area to spot a rarely seen **Flying Squirrel** crawling on tree trunks or gliding in the air.

Look for small, isolated plants and shrubs near trees and rock walls that are slightly different in color from the surroundings and bear strange flowers, berries or nuts. Use the Survival Knife or the CQC kick action to knock these plants loose. Doing so transforms them into medical supplies for use in surgery and treatment. Now that curing Snake is a big part of the game, be sure to stay fully stocked on medical supplies at all times.

DREMUCHIJ NORTH

ITEMS FOUND

None

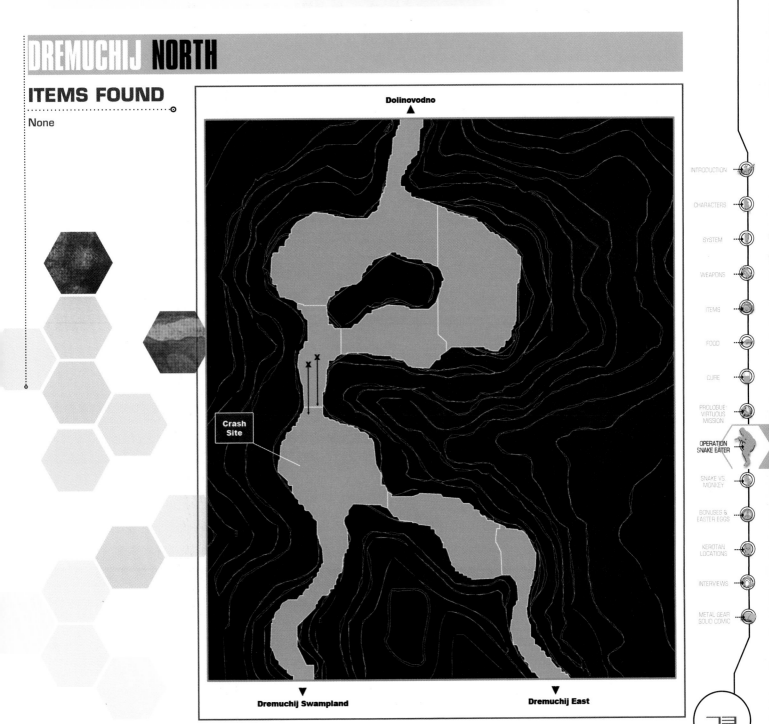

The Crash Site

Snake emerges on a ledge overlooking the area. Once he drops down from this ledge, Dremuchij East cannot be revisited. If you haven't collected food and medicinal supplies, go back and hunt for them before you proceed.

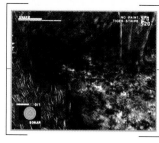

After dropping to the lower section, follow the path and look for a **Green Tree Python** hanging from tree branch directly in front of you. Continue down the path until a scene begins. Two guards enter the area immediately after the scene ends. They immediately spot the destroyed drone and radio back to base. Alert status will be effective in this location for a while, so it is best to just exit the area. Flee from detection by heading southwest to other familiar territories.

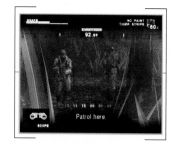

OPERATION
SNAKE
EATER

 1 | ADAM AND EVA

2 | BEYOND THE FOREST BASE

3 | ESCAPE THE CAVE

4 | WAREHOUSE IN THE MANGROVE

 5 | GRANNY GORKI LAB

 6 | WOODLAND HUNT

 7 | ALPINE ASCENT

 8 | GROZNYJ GRAD

9 | SHAGOHOD

10 | THE BOSS

DREMUCHIJ SOUTH

ITEMS FOUND

Grenades

Stun Grenades

Chaff Grenades

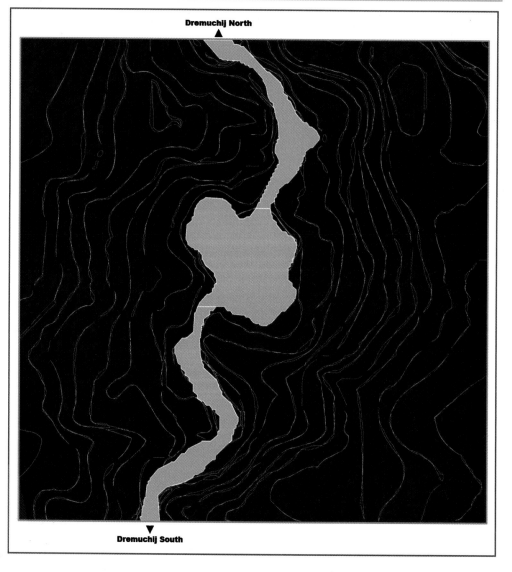

Dremuchij North

Dremuchij South

Dremuchij Swampland ▲

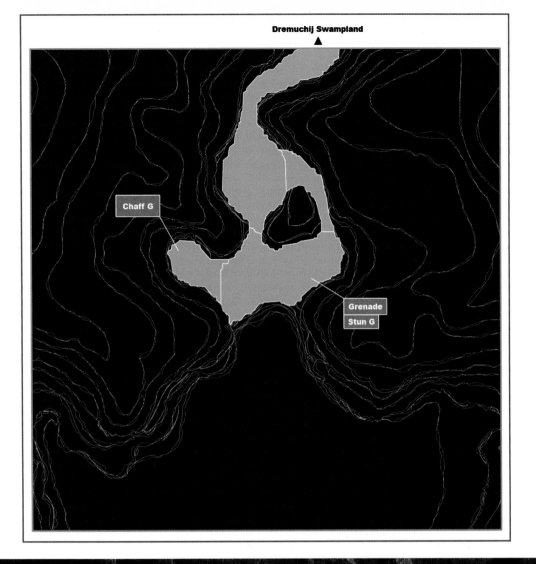

Chaff G

Grenade
Stun G

Stocking Up on Explosives

Head straight through the item-less Swampland area to Snake's drop point during the previous mission. The south section of the area contains several packs of **various grenade types**, as well as rare foods such as a **Markhor** goat and a **European Rabbit** hopping around near the cliff's edge. The goat may butt Snake with its horns if he gets too close, so attack it from the rear with the Survival Knife to obtain its rare restorative meat.

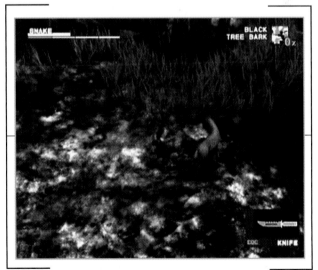

ITEMS FOUND

None

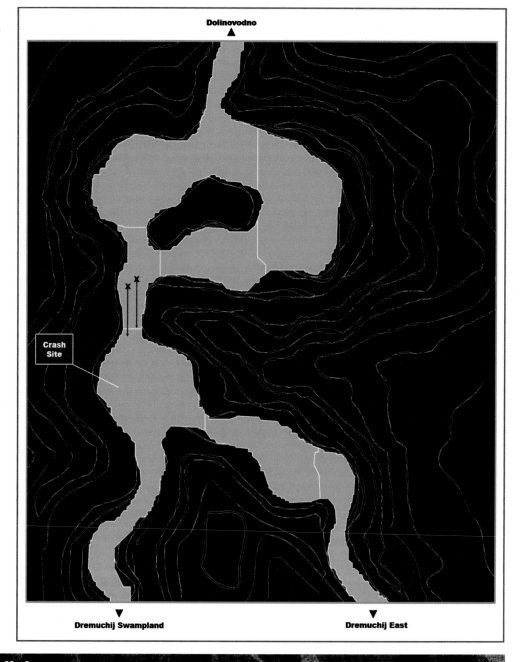

Dolinovodno

Crash Site

Dremuchij Swampland

Dremuchij East

Combat without Bullets

The two guards that entered this area to investigate the drone crash site are now on patrol. When entering from the south for the first time, only one guard remains in the area. The other guard is absent, perhaps reporting to base for help. The lone guard patrols the northwest sector; you can avoid him entirely by moving east to the slope and then north to the exit. The next time you enter the area, the second guard reappears and patrols in a wide circle near the drone wreckage.

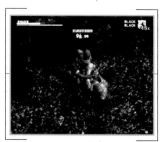

Without a firearm or dart gun to help, CQC tactics and camouflage become more important than ever. Hide behind trees or in plain sight with the Camo Index at the highest possible percentage. Creep up on the guards' locations and find a good place to hide until they pass. Then dash up behind them, press the CQC button extremely hard, and quickly pull down on the Left Analog Stick.

In the CQC maneuver described above, Snake slams the victim to the ground hard enough to render him instantly unconscious. Unconscious guards can be shaken to release several items. Tie up loose ends by slashing at unconscious guards with the Survival Knife in First Person View, aiming at their head and throat.

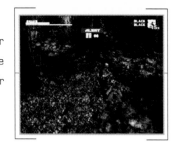

DOLINOVODNO

ITEMS FOUND

Raindrop Camouflage
(UNIFORM/RAINDROP)

Smoke Grenades (SMOKE G)

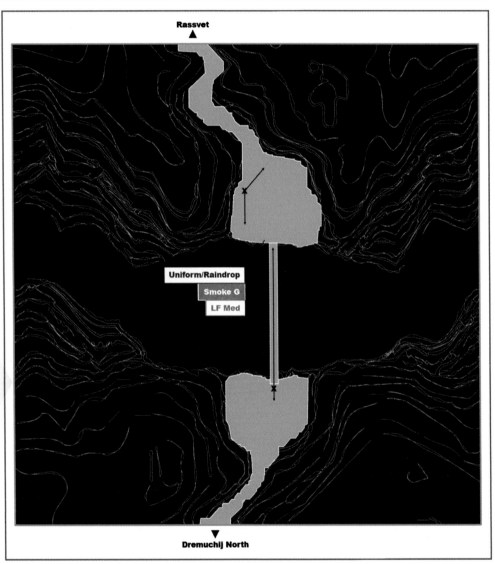

Rassvet ▲

Uniform/Raindrop
Smoke G
LF Med

▼
Dremuchij North

Night Crossing

Guards still patrol this area, but without a gun you cannot shoot down a hive to drive them off. A guard usually stands at the south end of the rope bridge for a moment after Snake enters from the south. He then turns and walks slowly across to the north side. The quickest way to take him down is to follow him very carefully onto the bridge, pressing the Directional Pad button to stalk quietly. Grab him and slit his throat, then drag his body out of sight. Shake his body for an item.

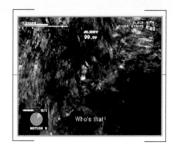

Cross the tilting bridge carefully to avoid falling off the side. Falling off the west side of the bridge and hanging can be detrimental, especially if the guard that patrols the sloping path to the northwest spots you. Sneak up behind the path guard and overtake him with CQC tactics.

Clothes for a Rainy Day

Follow the sloping path down to the alcove hidden in the cliff face beneath the north end of the bridge. Collect the **Raindrop Camouflage** and **Smoke Grenades** stored here, then continue north to Rassvet. The Raindrop Camouflage is most effective in rainy areas or while swimming in discolored water.

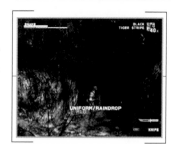

OPERATION
SNAKE
EATER

1 | ADAM AND EVA

2 | BEYOND THE FOREST BASE

3 | ESCAPE THE CAVE

4 | WAREHOUSE IN THE MANGROVE

5 | GRANINY GORKI LAB

6 | WOODLAND HUNT

7 | ALPINE ASCENT

8 | GROZNYJ GRAD

9 | SHAGOBOD

10 | THE BOSS

RASSVET

ITEMS FOUND

AK-47

Smoke Grenades

Thermal Goggles

Cardboard Box A (C BOX A)

Bug Juice

Zombie Face Paint (FACE/ZOMBIE)

Mine Detector (MINE D)

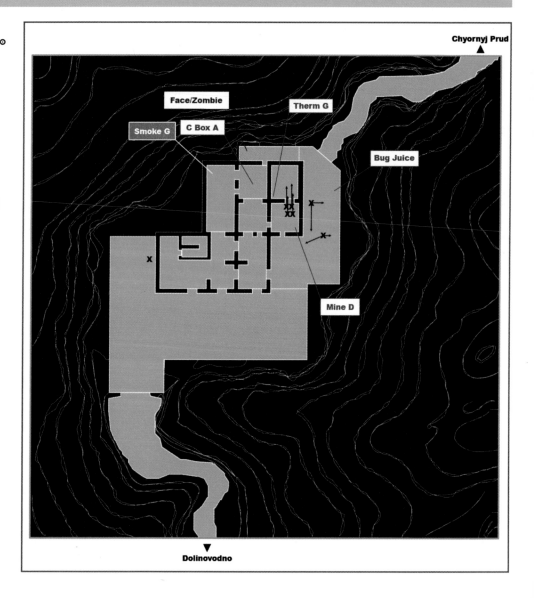

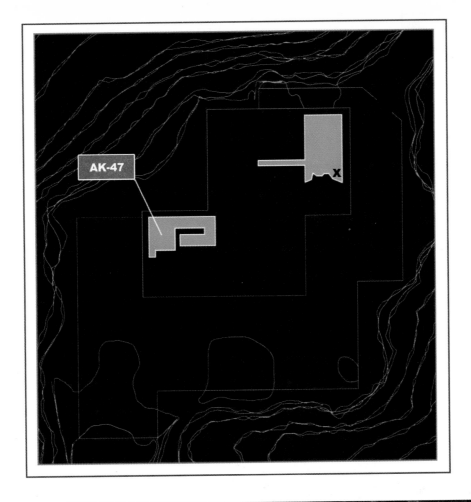

AK-47

X

Home of the Ambushes

The area is strangely devoid of guards. Move into the warehouse ruins, and ascend the stairs to the raised platform to find the **AK-47**. There is a stack of crates in the area beside Sokolov's former holding room. Press the Action button to climb atop the crates and collect the **Cardboard Box A**.

In the yard east of Sokolov's room is some **Bug Juice**. Behind the ruins is the **Zombie Face Paint**. This ghoulish design for Snake's mug will not be very useful until later stages in the game.

Collect the Mine Detector and then enter Sokolov's former holding room. Open the locker in the lower left corner to find another set of **Thermal Goggles**. A cutscene begins upon exiting the room. Snake meets EVA, an accomplice of ADAM. She gives Snake a bevy of gifts, including another **Mk22**, the **M1911A1**, and the **Scientist Camouflage**. During the introductory scenes, you can press R1 when the button icon appears onscreen...

INTRODUCTION

CHARACTERS

SYSTEM

WEAPONS

ITEMS

FOOD

CURE

PROLOGUE VIRTUOUS MISSION

OPERATION SNAKE EATER

SNAKE VS. MONKEY

BONUSES & EASTER EGGS

KEROTAN LOCATIONS

INTERVIEWS

METAL GEAR SOLID COMIC

Ocelot Team Assault

After resting for the night, Snake awakens to a perilous situation. Eight members of the GRU Ocelot unit surround the warehouse and attack. You must kill all eight to escape. Be sure to remove the suppressor from handguns at the start of this all-out engagement.

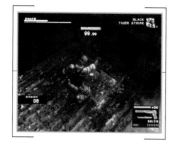

Making a stand inside the room is noble, but extremely dangerous. Follow EVA through the floor hatch by pressing the Action button △ to open it. Crawl southeast under the floorboards and emerge from the hole so that Snake is still inside the ruins.

OPERATION
SNAKE
EATER

1 | ADAM AND EVA

2 | BEYOND THE FOREST BASE

3 | ESCAPE THE CAVE

4 | WAREHOUSE IN THE MANGROVE

5 | GRANINY GORKI LAB

6 | WOODLAND HUNT

7 | ALPINE ASCENT

8 | GROZNYJ GRAD

9 | SHAGOHOD

10 | THE BOSS

The Ocelot team splits in half. Four men are stationed at positions all over Rassvet, while the other four breach the room where they think Snake and EVA are hiding. Stay out of view and watch as the four-man team runs into the building and breaks through the door. Run to a position just outside the doorway and lightly toss a grenade into the room to eliminate all four of them at once!

Two men are positioned in the east yard. Climb onto the crates stacked against the window in the room below Sokolov's former holding cell. Shoot the barrels just outside the window to create an explosion that should kill the two unseen men.

Another man is sniping from the roof. He tends to crouch too close to the south edge of the partially collapsed structure. Position Snake no more than a foot south of the roof's broken edge, and look upward to try to spot the man. Equip the AK-47 and use First Person Aiming R1 as well as barrel sighting L1 to ambush the rooftop soldier.

The final soldier is positioned outside the westernmost wall of the ruins. Approach the wall, lie flat on the ground, and look at the wall in First Person View to locate a hole you

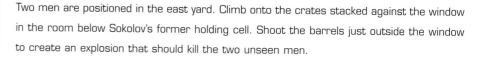

can crawl through. Move toward the hole and get as close as possible without going through. If even a finger on Snake's hand goes through the hole, the watchful soldier spots him. When you're well positioned, look through the hole and aim high at the guard's kneecap with the suppressed M1911A1. Shooting him in the leg causes him to double over in pain, exposing his head. Quickly shoot him in the head to finish him off.

When no more Ocelot soldiers remain, head toward the northeast corner of the area. After a scene, head northeast and exit through the newly opened gate.

2 | MISSION OBJECTIVE TWO:
BEYOND THE FOREST BASE

Though ADAM was unable to show, Snake seems to have found a new ally in the seductive EVA. With ruthless skill she clears the path for Snake to proceed north toward the area known as the "crevice." But to get there, Snake must cross wide-open spaces full of nature's worst predators

as well as dangerous soldiers. Numerous traps and pitfalls start to appear in the jungle. And just before the end, Snake must pass unseen through a heavily fortified enemy base. Snake's journey toward Sokolov and Shagohod is becoming more complicated by the minute.

FOOD LIST: BEYOND THE FOREST BASE

	Arowana (FISH C)
	Golova (FRUIT C)
	Indian Gavial (GAVIAL)
	Siberian Ink Cap (MUSHROOM C)
	Hornets' Nest (NEST)
	European Rabbit (RABBIT)
	King Cobra (SNAKE A)
	Coral Snake (SNAKE D)
	Milk Snake (SNAKE E)

INTRODUCTION

CHARACTERS

SYSTEM

WEAPONS

ITEMS

FOOD

CURE

PROLOGUE VIRTUOUS MISSION

OPERATION SNAKE EATER

SNAKE VS. MONKEY

BONUSES & EASTER EGGS

KEROTAN LOCATIONS

INTERVIEWS

METAL GEAR SOLID COMIC

CHYORNYJ PRUD

ITEMS FOUND

White Phosphorous Grenades (WP G)

AK-47 Bullet x120

AMMO

Smoke Grenades (SMOKE G)

Mk22 Bullets x24

AMMO

Grenades

Crocodile Cap (CROC CAP)

Stun Grenades (STUN G)

M1911A1 Bullets x21

AMMO

GA-KO Camouflage (UNIFORM/GA-KO)

Chaff Grenades (CHAFF G)

OPERATION SNAKE EATER

1 | ADAM AND EVA

2 | BEYOND THE FOREST BASE

3 | ESCAPE THE CAVE

4 | WAREHOUSE IN THE MANGROVE

5 | GRANINY GORKI LAB

6 | WOODLAND HUNT

7 | ALPINE ASCENT

8 | GROZYNJ GRAD

9 | SRAGOHOU

10 | THE BOSS

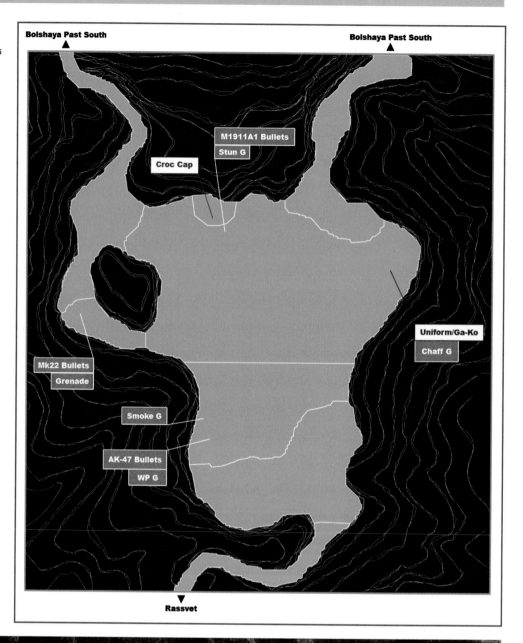

Bolshaya Past South   Bolshaya Past South

M1911A1 Bullets
Stun G
Croc Cap

Uniform/Ga-Ko
Chaff G

Mk22 Bullets
Grenade

Smoke G

AK-47 Bullets
WP G

Rassvet

A Dip in the Water

New types of snakes crawl on the south bank of the lake area, so take a few moments to hunt before proceeding into the waters. **Milk Snakes** and **Coral Snakes** are almost identical, except that Coral Snakes are more likely to bite.

Navigate west along the shoreline and then wade a few feet into the water to obtain **grenades** and **ammo**. In order to reach the next area, Snake must swim across to the north shore, or he can swim to the west shore and head north from there. Both methods of ingress are covered further as you read ahead.

Water Navigation Methods

To cross the pond, simply wade into the water to the deep part, where Snake automatically begins treading water. Use the Left Analog Stick to move Snake in any direction across the water's surface. While treading water, Snake moves faster when he is not holding weapons or items.

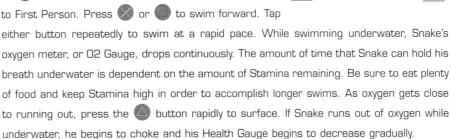

Snake can cross the entire lake treading water, but swimming under the surface is much faster. Press  or ◯ to dive underwater. The view shifts automatically to First Person. Press ✕ or ◯ to swim forward. Tap either button repeatedly to swim at a rapid pace. While swimming underwater, Snake's oxygen meter, or O2 Gauge, drops continuously. The amount of time that Snake can hold his breath underwater is dependent on the amount of Stamina remaining. Be sure to eat plenty of food and keep Stamina high in order to accomplish longer swims. As oxygen gets close to running out, press the △ button rapidly to surface. If Snake runs out of oxygen while underwater, he begins to choke and his Health Gauge begins to decrease gradually.

In shallow areas, Snake wades at an incredibly slow pace. To speed things along, press ✕ to crouch and then move the Left Analog Stick to lie down in the water. Snake enters swim mode. While swimming at such a shallow depth, be careful not to look upward or you may accidentally surface. With this method, you should be able to swim right up to the shoreline before surfacing.

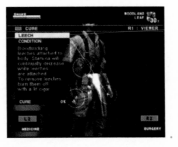

 LEECHES!

If Snake's Stamina Gauge appears to be depleting too rapidly, open the Cure menu and check for the possibility of leech parasites. Leeches are easily removed by burning them off with the Cigar in the Cure menu, but by then the damage is already done. Use Bug Juice frequently to prevent leech parasitism as much as possible while swimming in the water.

Killer Crocs

The water is full of tasty **Arowana** fish, but **Indian Gavial** crocodiles are also present. Equip the Thermal Goggles occasionally to double check their locations and make sure they do not come too close. A crocodile in close range can bite Snake with its powerful jaws and thresh him to death in a heartbeat. Crocodiles in the shallows can be survived, but those floating in the water deal instant death.

Either swim in a wide radius around the crocs, or use underwater-compatible weapons, such as the AK-47 or the M1911A1, to kill them. Dead crocodiles and fish float to the surface, transform into rations, and then drop with weight to the bottom. Equip the Thermal Goggles to spot items in the dark and dirty water.

STOCKPILE RATIONS!

The areas ahead are almost completely devoid of wildlife and useful plants due to the enemies' electrical traps. Before proceeding too far ahead, make sure Snake has a plentiful supply of Indian Gavial and Arowana meat, as well as the mushrooms and fruits available in this area. Progress through the next few areas is slow, and Snake's hunger could become too great if it's neglected!

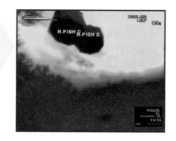

The Western Shore

As mentioned above, there are two exits from this area. But first, swim to the northeast corner of the area to obtain **Chaff Grenades** and the **GA-KO Camouflage**. This bizarrely patterned uniform sometimes makes strange noises that might be heard by enemies. Use caution in wearing it.

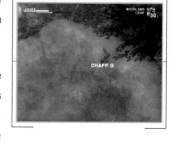

Swim to the west side of the area, where two passages connect to the west bank. Only the south passage allows you to emerge on dry land. Swim under the logs blocking the south passage and collect the **Mk22 Bullets** and **Grenades** on the shore.

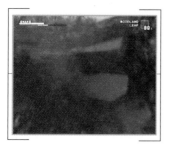

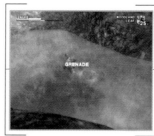

BOOBY TRAP

>> Watch out for the hidden pitfall trap in this area. Equip the Thermal Goggles and look north. The glowing red patch of leaves on the ground is the pit. Stepping on it means instant death.

Climb the tree near the water's edge. Face south on the branch so that Snake hangs from the best side of the rope. Press Action [tri] to drop into a hanging position, and shimmy outward along the rope tied to the branch. Continue outward until Snake is positioned directly over another rope below, then press ✕ to release the rope. Start tapping △ immediately to Drop-Catch onto the lower rope.

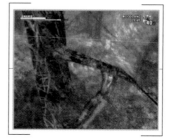

Shimmy along the rope to a small island where the **Crocodile Cap** is located. This cap allows Snake to disguise himself as an Indian Gavial and hide from aerial attacks. Drop off the same ledge into the water to collect **Stun Grenades** and **M1911A1 Bullets x21**. Return via the south passage to the west bank and head north if you wish to exit that way.

Danger Due North

On the north bank, a tripwire is strung between the two trees on either side of the exit. Equipping the Thermal Goggles in this area triggers a call from EVA. If instead you set off the trap accidentally, she calls to make fun of your incompetence. Shoot the tripwire from a safe distance, and you can bypass the spiked log easily.

BOLSHAYA PAST SOUTH

ITEMS FOUND

Claymore (x10 qty.)

 C = Claymore

Splitter Camouflage
(UNIFORM/SPLITTER)

Choco Chip Camouflage
(UNIFORM/CHOCO CHIP)

SO HUNGRY...

There are no food sources whatsoever in this area, so if you run out of supplies and Snake's tummy starts grumbling, you must retreat to the previous area and do some underwater fishing.

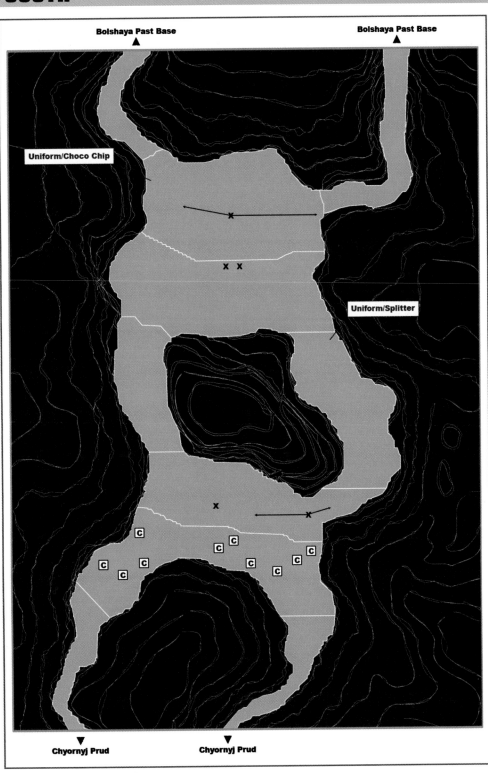

Bolshaya Past Base

Bolshaya Past Base

Uniform/Choco Chip

Uniform/Splitter

Chyornyj Prud

Chyornyj Prud

Electric Barriers

Electrified fences block the passages into the area. Equip the Thermal Goggles to see the electric barrier more clearly. If Snake runs into the fence, the shock damage is somewhat minimal. The true damage is all the noise Snake makes while getting shocked, which usually draws the attention of guards from all over this area. The power supply for the fence is the vertical solid strip at one end or the other. Destroying the power supply with the M1911A1 makes the fence safe, but makes it difficult to clearly see a path under the obstacle. With the Thermal Goggles equipped, examine the fence to find either a broken section of the fence or a dog ditch you can crawl through, depending on which entrance brought you to this area.

OPERATION
SNAKE
EATER

1 | ADAM AND EVA

2 | BEYOND THE FOREST BASE

3 | ESCAPE THE CAVE

4 | WAREHOUSE IN THE MANGROVE

5 | GRANINY GORKI LAB

6 | WOODLAND HUNT

7 | ALPINE ASCENT

8 | GORZNYJ GRAD

9 | SHAGOHOD

10 | THE BOSS

Claymore Array

Continue wearing the Thermal Goggles and crawl across the next sector. **Ten Claymores** set up around the area might go off if you attempt to run through. The Claymores are calibrated to detect a standing target in motion. However, you can pass through in the crawling position without setting off any of them. Crawl over the Claymores to deactivate and collect them for your own use.

Sniping From Above

Climb the tree near the western end of the fence and look down. Shoot the stationary patrol dog with the M1911A1 and don't bother using a suppressor. Even if your shot is silenced, the dog yelps so loudly that a nearby guard becomes curious either way. Soon, he enters the area to investigate. He moves slowly, so wait patiently in the tree for him to come within aiming range, and kill him by the fence to completely clear the swamp area to the east. This is highly advantageous because there is an item to obtain near the quicksand pools.

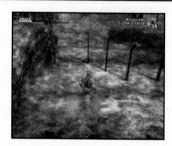 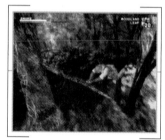

FENCE WITH A CENTER HOLE

A huge hole has been cut out of the electrified fence on the west side of the area. We don't advise proceeding this way due to the two guards posted just a few yards to the north, as well as several tripwires installed in the area beyond. However, if you insist on getting through the raised opening, shoot out the power box at the end of the fence to the right. Then back up and get a running start. Perform a forward roll with just the right timing to dive through the hole in the fence.

New Camouflage

Instead of proceeding northwest, go east to an area full of quicksand. Cross the center strip of land between the two quicksand pools and climb onto the embankment. Press Snake's back against the rock wall and sidestep all the way up to the north end of the thin ledge, where the **Splitter Camouflage** is located. Drop from the ledge to take on the guards in the north portion of the area.

Getting to the Base

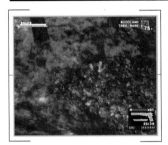

Two guards stand stationary watch on either side of a gap in the electrified fence. Another guard patrols the area beyond the fence, making it difficult to take out both guards at once with an incendiary device. Before proceeding, note that there are several trip wires in this area that rattle cans filled with beans to alert the guards. Use thermal imaging to detect all the tripwires in the area before moving in.

First shoot or tranquilize the lone guard patrolling near the north rock wall. Move to the eastern end of the electric fence and get as close as possible without touching it. Lie flat on the ground to steady your aim and reduce the chance of touching the fence when you extend your arm to aim. Wait until the guard stops at the east point in his patrol route, and hit him in the head with your first shot. It is a tough shot, but it's worth the trouble.

Move to the bottom of the trees to the left of your location, and toss a Stun Grenade between the two guards by the gate. When they are knocked out, slay them. The **Choco Chip Camouflage** is in the hollow tree trunk near the northwest exit. Both exits to the north lead to separate entry points to the Bolshaya Past Base. However, entering via the eastern path is the best strategy for dealing with the next area.

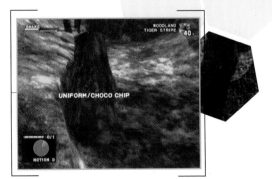

UNIFORM/CHOCO CHIP

BOLSHAYA PAST BASE

ITEMS FOUND

M1911A1 Suppressor
(Sp/M1911A1)

Mk22 Bullets x24 (x2 qty.)

Mousetrap (x2 qty.)

Snow Face Paint
(FACE/SNOW)

Water Camouflage
(UNIFORM/WATER)

Russian Ration

Calorie Mate

Bandages

Digestive Medicine (D MED)

Life Medicine (LF MED)

Antidote

M1911A1 Bullets x21

White Phosphorus Grenades
(WP G)

TNT

AK-47 Bullets x120

Grenades

Stun Grenades (STUN G)

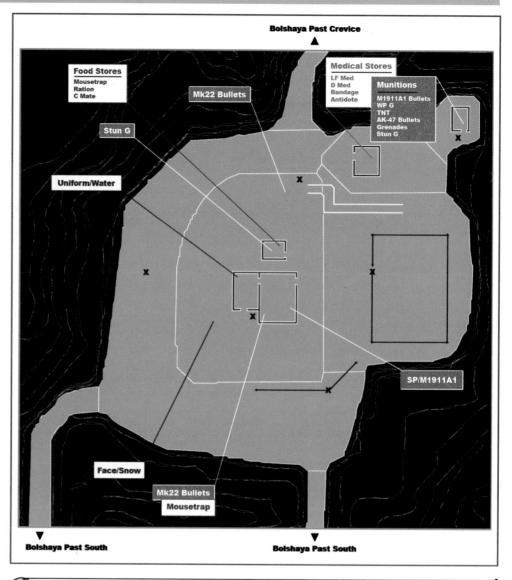

INFILTRATING THE BASE

Entering this area via the eastern path is strategically advantageous. With high visibility and many soldiers, this base is a hotspot where Snake can get trampled repeatedly. This brief provides a tested method for clearing all the soldiers quietly while collecting a truckload of valuable items and equipment. While our method is by no means the only strategy that can be used here, it will aid players in forming their own approach.

Solid Strike

Stand just inside the eastern entrance into the base zone, and watch the guard on patrol by the fence straight ahead. Wait for the guard to pass in front of the mounted .20-caliber machine gun. Then charge the guard and use CQC maneuvers to throw him down hard enough to knock him unconscious. Hide his body behind the trees a few feet to the south, and prepare for the next guard, who patrols around the nearby helicopter.

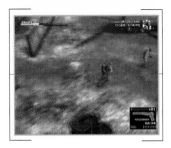

Watch the helicopter guard walk around the south side of the craft. Then charge beyond the fence, run up behind the soldier, and use the hard-toss CQC maneuver to knock him out. Drag him to the ferns directly south of the helicopter to hide his body.

Enter the Barracks

Now head west into the main building.

OPENING DOORS

>> Snake opens doors by collision. If he runs through the door full speed, he barges in, loudly slamming the door open. However, if he stops briefly in front of a door and then moves gently into it, Snake opens the door with precision and stealth. It doesn't matter in this particular case, as no one is inside the barracks. But keep this in mind when you open subsequent doors.

Collect the **M1911A1 Suppressor** by the barracks window. Crawl under the back two bunks to locate a **Mousetrap** and **Mk22 Bullets x24**. A stationary soldier guards the rear door of the room behind the barracks, so do not go through the west door. Instead, exit via the same door you came in.

Trench Trudge

Outside the barracks, head south around the orange wall and drop into the shallow trench. Crawl west on your belly with the Tree Bark Camouflage equipped. When you reach the end, climb out, roll diagonally northwest toward the next trench and drop inside. Follow the second trench north to the **Snow Face Paint**.

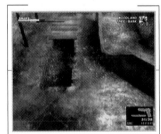

Continue crawling northward in the same trench until you're just past the first diagonal curve in the route. Rise to a knee, look northwest and carefully shoot the guard patrolling rather slowly outside the fence.

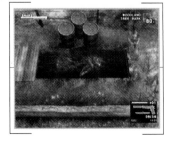

Crawl along the bottom of the trench as the ditch leads north and then east, collecting **Mk22 Bullets x24** from under the platform. Move a little further east in the north trench and stop just past the barrels. Look up and to the left to spot the guard positioned at the .20-caliber machine gun. Stay flat in the trench and shoot him in the back of the head.

INTRODUCTION

CHARACTERS

SYSTEM

WEAPONS

ITEMS

FOOD

CURE

PROLOGUE VIRTUOUS MISSION

OPERATION SNAKE EATER

SNAKE VS MONKEY

BONUSES & EASTER EGGS

KEROTAN LOCATIONS

INTERVIEWS

METAL GEAR SOLID COMIC

89

OPERATION
SNAKE
EATER

1 | ADAM AND EVA

2 | BEYOND THE FOREST BASE

3 | ESCAPE THE CAVE

4 | WAREHOUSE IN THE MANGROVE

5 | GRANINY GORKI LAB

6 | WOODLAND HUNT

7 | ALPINE ASCENT

8 | GROZYNJ GRAD

9 | SRAGOHOD

10 | THE BOSS

GUN 'EM ALL DOWN!

If there is a radio alert, reinforcements come from the north and south exits. If you can grab one of the machineguns facing those positions, mowing down the troops as they enter is quite a bit of fun. Also, a machinegun mounted northwest of the helicopter turns far enough to aim at both the north and south exits, allowing you to combat troops coming from both ends. Take control of a mounted machinegun by positioning Snake directly behind it and pressing the Action button (△). Hold (○) to fire.

The Food Storage Shed

South below the end of the northern trench is a small wooden shed. **Stun Grenades** are located underneath the shed, and this crawlspace is also an excellent hiding spot. Inside the shed are **Russian Rations**, a **Calorie Mate** and a **Mousetrap**. Use the trap to catch the Rat in the shed if you wish.

Getting onto the Main Building's Roof

One more guard has a stationary post at the southwest corner of the main building. Because he blocks access to the roof access ladder, down he must go. Take him out with CQC and then climb the ladder. The **Water Camouflage** is at the northwest corner of the roof.

Taking the Ammo Store

The last remaining guard stands outside the munitions depot in the northeast corner of the area. Head northwest to the small building with an antenna. Inside the communications building are **Bandages**, **Digestive Medicine**, **Life Medicine**, and an **Antidote**.

Go around the north side of the radio building, and crawl along the ground east toward the last building. Crawl up to the east edge of the tall, green grass and shoot the guard standing in front of the door. The munitions depot contains a goldmine of **ammunition** and **various grenades**, as well as **TNT**.

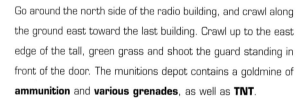

Total the Base!

DY-NA-MITE!

Veterans of previous *Metal Gear* games can think of TNT as the "C4" of the past. Press  to set a block of TNT, move a safe distance away, and press to detonate the explosive. When Snake's back is pressed against a wall, press to affix a TNT block to the spot where Snake's hand rests. Up to five TNT charges can be set simultaneously and then detonated one by one.

Set TNT inside the munitions building, exit, and detonate the explosives to destroy the building. Also, demolish the communications building and food storage shed to weaken the strength of enemy soldiers. Additionally, TNT charges can be used to obliterate the helicopter and the mounted machineguns. When finished playing the Unabomber, continue north toward the crevice.

BOLSHAYA PAST CREVICE

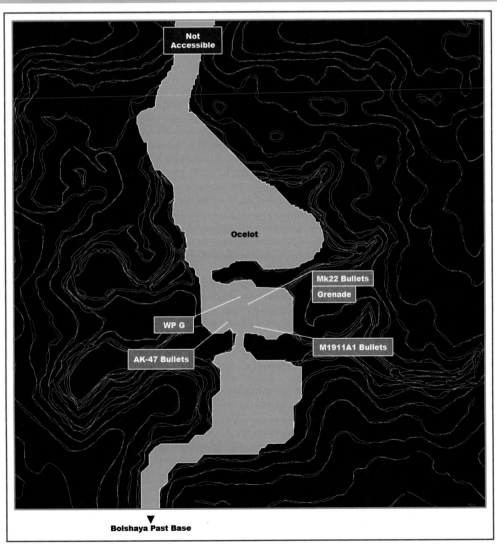

OCELOT

BATTLE-SPECIFIC SUPPLIES

AK-47 Bullets x120

AMMO

Mk22 Bullets x24

AMMO

White Phosphorus Grenades (WP G)

M1911A1 Bullets x21

AMMO

Move left and crouch behind the boulder. Remaining behind cover, quickly shoot the wildlife in the area, including poisonous snakes and rabbits, to prevent them from interfering in this duel. Additional snakes may emerge from the forest later, so check the ground around Snake whenever you hide behind the boulders on either side of the screen, and do a little exterminating if necessary.

You can climb a tree at the east end of the forward ledge to obtain White Phosphorus Grenades. Pick up the handgun ammunition only when you run out of your own. At certain times during the battle, men from Ocelot unit appear in the woods to the south. They cannot be shot, so don't waste the ammo.

NON-LETHAL ALTERNATIVE

Consider defeating Ocelot by draining his Stamina gauge instead of his Life gauge. Follow the strategy outlined on this page, but use the Mk22 exclusively. After the post-battle cinematic, Snake will find the **Animals Camouflage** in the cave next to him as a reward for his efforts.

Watch the north bank and shoot Ocelot when he moves between stones. As the battle progresses, Ocelot gets better at ricocheting bullets off the rocks behind Snake in order to hit him while he is under cover. Run from cover to cover, stopping at the cliff's ledge momentarily to shoot Ocelot as he passes on the other side of the crevice. Staying behind cover for too long serves no purpose, because Ocelot's bullets can find you anywhere.

Three Hornets' Nests hang in the trees above Ocelot. Shoot down a nest, and the hornets drive Ocelot out of hiding. While he stands out in the open waving off the swarm, toss a Grenade his way or fire the AK-47 at him. If Smoke Grenades detonate near his hiding spot, Ocelot steps into the open and starts coughing uncontrollably. Shoot him repeatedly while he's frozen in his tracks.

I've never felt a tension like this before...

Sometimes Ocelot steps out and begins to reload. While this would seem to be nothing more than a cinematic, it is actually your best opportunity to strike. Press **START** to return to playing, aim at Ocelot, and shoot him repeatedly while he reloads.

Above all, Ocelot wants a "fair" fight. If you use Grenades or the AK-47, he considers it "cheating." The Ocelot unit soldiers in the woods to the south shoot Snake from behind if you "cheat." This is supposed to be a duel, pistol against pistol. Whether or not you abide by the unwritten rules is up to you.

3 | MISSION OBJECTIVE THREE:
ESCAPE THE CAVE

Snake's standoff with Ocelot is cut short by interference from The Pain. Forced to jump into the crevice, Snake lands miraculously unharmed in the dank and dark underground cave EVA mentioned. As she described, Snake must navigate through the cave and continue north to complete his mission.

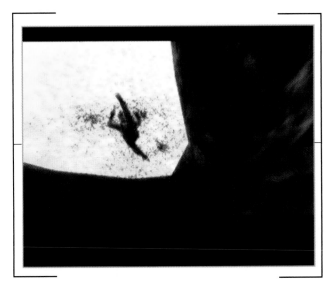

FOOD LIST: ESCAPE THE CAVE STAGE

	Vampire Bat (BAT)
	Kenyan Mangrove Crab (CRAB)
	Maroon Shark (FISH B)
	Arowana (FISH C)
	Otton Frog (FROG A)
	Tree Frog (FROG B)
	Russian Glowcap (MUSHROOM E)
	Rat (RAT)
	Russian Ration (RATION)
	Taiwanese Cobra (SNAKE B)
	Thai Cobra (SNAKE C)
	Reticulated Python (SNAKE H)
	Giant Anaconda (SNAKE G)

INTRODUCTION

CHARACTERS

SYSTEM

WEAPONS

ITEMS

FOOD

CURE

PROLOGUE: VIRTUOUS MISSION

OPERATION SNAKE EATER

SNAKE VS. MONKEY

BONUSES & EASTER EGGS

KEROTAN LOCATIONS

INTERVIEWS

METAL GEAR SOLID COMIC

ITEMS FOUND

White Phosphorous Grenades (WP G)

Torch

Serum (2 qty.)

Cold Medicine (C MED)

AK-47 Bullets x120 (4 qty.)

Night Vision Goggles (N.V.G.)

M1911A1 Bullets x21 (2 qty.)

Russian Ration (RATION)

Battery

Grenades

Mk22 Bullet x24

Bug Juice

OPERATION SNAKE EATER

1 | ADAM AND EVA
2 | BEYOND THE FOREST BASE
3 | ESCAPE THE CAVE
4 | WAREHOUSE IN THE MANGROVE
5 | GRANINY GORKI LAB
6 | WOODLAND HUNT
7 | ALPINE ASCENT
8 | GROZYHJ GRAD
9 | SHAGOHOD
10 | THE BOSS

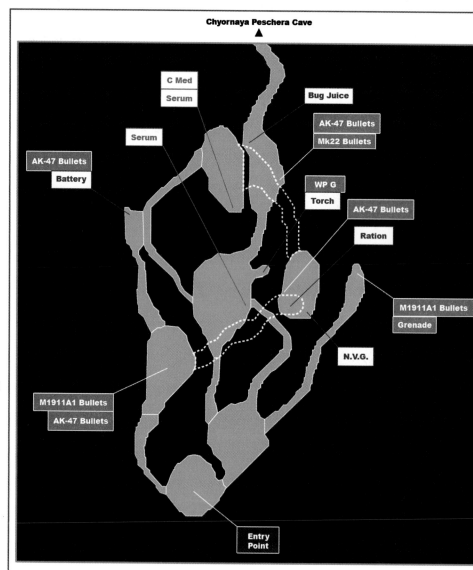

Chyornaya Peschera Cave

C Med / Serum — Bug Juice — AK-47 Bullets / Mk22 Bullets — Serum — AK-47 Bullets / Battery — WP G / Torch — AK-47 Bullets — Ration — M1911A1 Bullets / Grenade — N.V.G. — M1911A1 Bullets / AK-47 Bullets — Entry Point

IT'S DARK IN HERE!

Nearly absolute darkness envelops Snake, making navigation in the caves tricky and confusing. You can deal with the dark in a number of ways. Snake's eyes gradually adjust to the light, making the cave seem brighter and brighter as time passes. This means that if you walk off and leave your console on and the game running, the screen should be brighter when you return. However, Snake's eye adjustment time is incredibly long.

Unable to See

The Thermal Goggles can be equipped to highlight items, animals and mushrooms in the environment. However, the stone walls and corridors remain black and invisible even in this mode. The Binoculars lighten the area being viewed. Use the Binoculars to look around, find an exit, and continue. The Map can be used to determine possible passage locations and inch your way forward. However, this requires that you open the Survival Viewer frequently and it takes time.

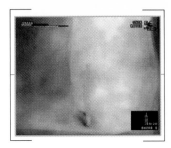

The Cigar casts only a tiny amount of light when Snake smokes it, but in such a dark cave the ember illuminates surprisingly well. Equip it only for short periods to prevent significant health drainage. Smoke Bombs fill caverns and passages with white clouds that reveal the shape and length of corridors and caves. And if all else fails, you might simply adjust the brightness setting of your monitor until the environment is visible. Just be sure to reset your television when you return to daylight.

The Search for Light

Take a moment to peruse your food supplies, since older items may have expired by this point. To determine if food is rotten, view the food icons as displayed in the Weapons menu of the Backpack. Discard any rotten items marked with fly icons. **Kenyan Mangrove Crabs** skitter across the cave floor. These tasty morsels provide good Stamina recovery, and there are plenty of fish and other food sources in the cave to replace your expired goods.

A great light source is just a dozen yards away. Head east from the starting point into a larger cave with three exits. Follow the northwestern passage to a room where water cascades off a higher ledge. In an alcove between the two waterfalls is the skeleton of a lost spelunker, along with **White Phosphorus Grenades** and the **Torch**. Remove the Torch from your backpack immediately and equip it. Now you have a good light source to use until Snake's eyes better adjust to the darkness.

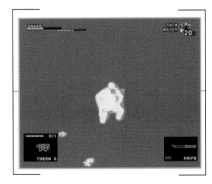

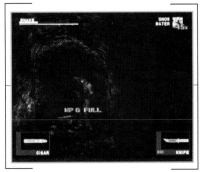

GLOWING FUNGUS

>> A phosphorescent Russian Glowcap mushroom dimly lights the alcove where the Torch is acquired. This mushroom recharges Battery power when eaten, so be sure to stock these for upcoming events. Eat one and then speak to Para-Medic to view an extremely amusing conversation.

Cave-to-Cave Search

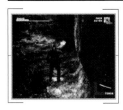

Directly across from the waterfall is a narrow cleft in the wall. Follow this thin passage northwest, and do not fall off the ledge into the area below. Continue north, go prone, and crawl through a floor-level crawlspace.

The cave Snake emerges into is filled with **Vampire Bats**. Collect the medicinal items at the south end of the cave. Carrying the Torch or shooting a weapon in this chamber sends the bats into a flying frenzy. Equip the Active Sonar and press the Left Analog Stick (L3) to emit a signal. Sonar emissions send the bats back to their perches on the ceiling.

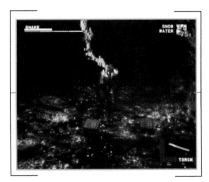

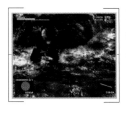

Drop to the ground and crawl through the next passage heading southeast. Emerging, head south and avoid falling into the wide central pit for the moment. Collect the **Night Vision Goggles** located on the south edge of the chasm. The Night Vision Goggles are the best possible way to see in the dark cave at all times, but they consume battery power quickly.

INTRODUCTION

CHARACTERS

SYSTEM

WEAPONS

ITEMS

FOOD

CURE

PROLOGUE: VIRTUOUS MISSION

OPERATION SNAKE EATER

SNAKE VS. MONKEY

BONUSES & EASTER EGGS

KEROTAN LOCATIONS

INTERVIEWS

METAL GEAR SOLID COMIC
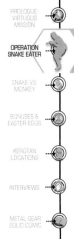

Sunken Treasures

Jump into the central, water-filled pit to find a surprisingly distasteful **Russian Ration**. Swim through the submerged chute to a water-filled tunnel. After catching a breath on the surface, use the Thermal Goggles to easily spot the **M19 Bullets** and **AK-47 Bullets** on the tunnel floor. Be sure to hunt and collect seafood swimming in the water.

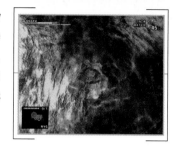
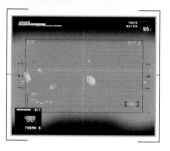

Swim north in the tunnel to a ledge. Press the Action button to climb onto the rock ledge, and then continue forward to a dead end. Pick up the **AK-47 Bullets** and the additional **Battery** stored here. Electronic devices can now run twice as long, enabling longer use of the Night Vision Goggles.

On to the Next Area

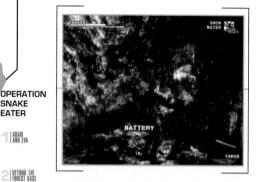

Navigate south to Snake's initial starting point. In the chamber with three paths, follow the short east tunnel. Beside the remains of another unlucky cave explorer are **Grenades** and **M1911A1 ammunition** in addition to more **Russian Glowcaps**.

Return to the main chamber and crawl through the middle passage. Stay alert for a **Taiwanese Cobra** that may attack as you pass through the midpoint of the passage.

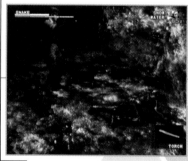

The tunnel emerges atop the waterfall platform. **Serum** lies near the south corner of the falls. *Do not drop off the ledge.* Instead, continue north. Along the way lies another skeleton guarding **ammunition**. Collect the **Bug Juice** on the left as you continue into the next passage.

OPERATION
SNAKE
EATER

1 | ADAM AND EVA

2 | BEYOND THE FOREST BASE

3 | ESCAPE THE CAVE

4 | WAREHOUSE IN THE MANGROVE

5 | GRANINY GORKI LAB

6 | WOODLAND HUNT

7 | ALPINE ASCENT

8 | GROZNYJ GRAD

9 | SHAGOHOD

10 | THE BOSS

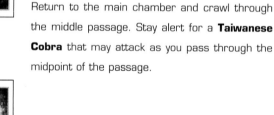

ITEMS FOUND

M37

Mk22 Bullets x24

Snow Camouflage (UNIFORM/SNOW)

M1911A1 Bullets x21

AMMO

AK-47 Bullets x120

AMMO

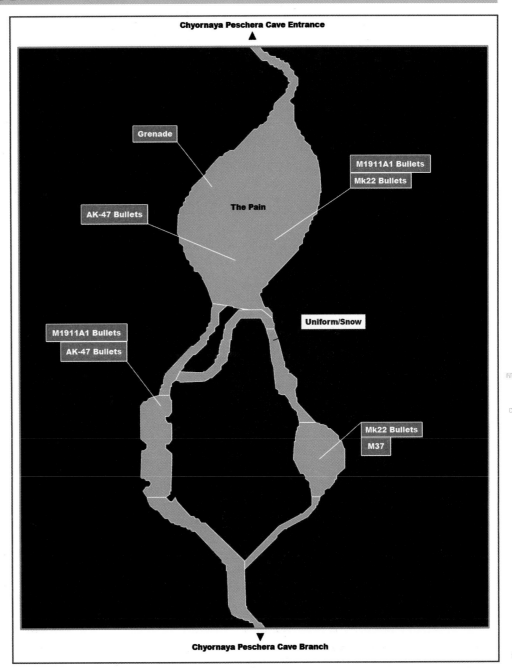

Chyornaya Peschera Cave Entrance

Grenade

M1911A1 Bullets

Mk22 Bullets

AK-47 Bullets

The Pain

M1911A1 Bullets

AK-47 Bullets

Uniform/Snow

Mk22 Bullets

M37

Chyornaya Peschera Cave Branch

A Much Simpler Cave

As soon as Snake enters, divert down the narrow side passage to the right. This path emerges into a bat-filled cave where an **M37** shotgun lies, in addition to **Mk22 Bullets**. Crawl north under a ledge and follow the crawlspace tunnel. The tunnel heightens briefly to allow Snake to stretch his legs and collect the **Snow Camouflage**.

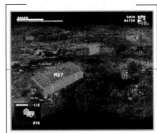

Continue crawling through the next tunnel, which winds all way back to the west side of the map. Emerging, head south to find **Smoke Grenades** and **ammunition.** Head north from there to the sunshine-lit cave.

THE PAIN

OPERATION SNAKE EATER

1 | ADAM AND EVA
2 | BEYOND THE FOREST BASE
3 | ESCAPE THE CAVE
4 | WAREHOUSE IN THE MANGROVE
5 | GRANINY GORKI LAB
6 | WOODLAND HUNT
7 | ALPINE ASCENT
8 | GROZNYJ GRAD
9 | SHAGOHOD
10 | THE BOSS

NON-LETHAL ALTERNATIVE

It's possible to defeat The Pain by depleting his Stamina gauge. Use the Mk22 exclusively during the fight against him to defeat him in a non-lethal manner. Extra bullets can be found on a rock above the water; Snake can acquire them during both portions of the battle. After the fight, follow the narrow ledge on the side of the cave counter-clockwise from the north, and then leap to the platform in the center to find the **Hornet Stripe Camouflage.**

BATTLE-SPECIFIC ITEMS

Grenades

AK-47 Bullets x120
AMMO

M1911A1 Bullets x21
AMMO

Mk22 Bullets x24
AMMO

The Pain controls a swarm of hornets, making direct combat extremely difficult. The Pain's island in the center of the water-filled chamber is inaccessible to Snake, but The Pain can send his hornets over the water's surface to attack with various methods.

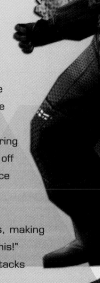

At the start of the battle, quickly shoot The Pain a few times with the M1911A1 or the AK-47. The Pain immediately summons a swarm of hornets to cover his body, rendering him immune to bullets. Perform a dive roll off the islet and swim under the water's surface to avoid The Pain's various attacks.

The Pain announces his impending actions, making it easier to respond. If he screams "Eat This!" or "Tommygun!" he is about to perform attacks that can damage Snake even underwater. Swim laps around the Pain's island to avoid concussions and bullet damage. If The Pain screams out "Grenade!" you can sometimes shoot him if his body is uncovered while he forms a hornet bomb in his hand.

Be sure to have plenty of food on hand, because you'll spend a lot of time underwater. The water is full of Crabs, Maroon Sharks and Arowanas, so do a little fishing if necessary. Just be aware that shooting fish in the water may reveal your position to The Pain. You can return to areas where The Pain's explosives detonated in the water to collect fish killed by the blasts.

Equip the Water Camouflage and the Snow Face Paint for the best invisibility, then dive underwater and remain motionless. When The Pain cannot see you for a while, his hornet armor relaxes and you can ambush him from underwater. Equip the Thermal Goggles and stare at The Pain's platform until he moves to the edge and bends to search the water. If you can see that he is not covered with hornets, shoot him. Make sure you're continually well fed to extend the O2 gauge and hide in the water as long as possible.

Occasionally, The Pain forms a mirror image of himself to draw Snake out of the water. After a short period without comment from The Pain, or if you hear him grunt for no reason, climb out onto one of the small islets to see the identical figures posing on the center island. Equip the Thermal Goggles. The one with the heat signature is The Pain. Unload on him with the AK-47 to inflict major damage. Then dive underwater and resume attacking from below.

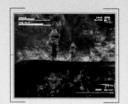

When The Pain's health drops to half, he changes tactics and starts using bullet bee attacks. If hit, you must enter the Cure menu and use the knife to dig out the bullet, then patch the wound with Disinfectant, Styptic, the Suture Kit, and Bandages. Otherwise Snake continuously loses health. Avoid the bullet bees by diving underwater and swimming a lap around The Pain's pedestal.

If you completely run out of ammunition, including the supplies located in the cave during the battle, then climb onto the islets surrounding The Pain's platform and try to throw Grenades next to him.

CHYORNAYA PESCHERA CAVE ENTRANCE

ITEMS FOUND

Claymore (2 qty.) **C** = Claymore

AK-47 Bullets x120

AMMO

M1911A1 Bullets x21

AMMO

Mk22 Bullets x24

AMMO

Slide down the slope and continue forward through the narrow crevice to a semi-clearing. Enter the bat cave on the left by crawling on the ground; **2 Claymores** are set in front of the ammunition packs. Continue along the path to the next cave. Work your way carefully down the ledges, collecting **Glowcaps** along the way.

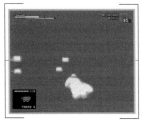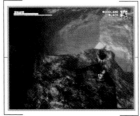

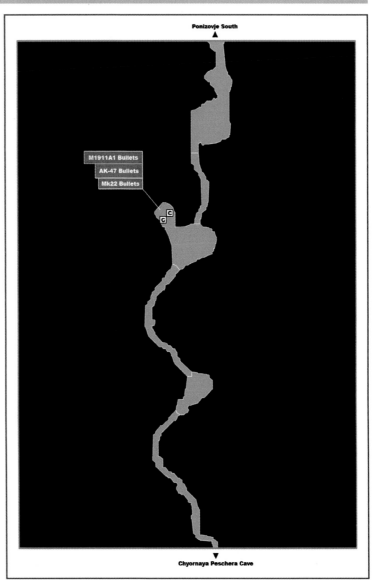

Ponizovje South

M1911A1 Bullets
AK-47 Bullets
Mk22 Bullets

Chyornaya Peschera Cave

4 | MISSION OBJECTIVE FOUR:
WAREHOUSE IN THE MANGROVE

Darkness is falling on the land once again as another day ends in Operation Snake Eater. Undercover of darkness, Snake must penetrate a highly secured area on the path to the research facility to the north. Guards riding hovercraft and patrolling tricky areas make it hard to pass through undetected.

FOOD LIST: WAREHOUSE IN THE MANGROVE STAGE

	Kenyan Mangrove Crabs (CRAB)
	Bigeye Trevally (FISH A)
	Maroon Shark (FISH B)
	Arowana (FISH C)
	Rat (RAT)
	Cobalt Blue Tarantula (SPIDER)

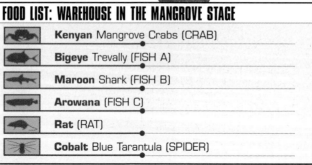

ITEMS FOUND

Chaff Grenades (CHAFF G)

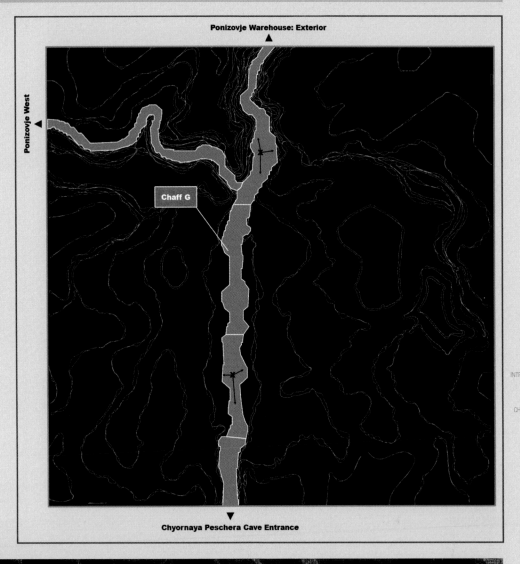

Ponizovje Warehouse: Exterior ▲

◄ Ponizovje West

Chaff G

▽ Chyornaya Peschera Cave Entrance

The Stretch

Wear the Raindrop or Splitter camouflage and equip the Crocodile Cap to help fool the guards floating on their strange hovercraft in this area. When Snake crouches and lies prone in the shallow water, the guards think he is just a crocodile feeding in the stream. Anytime a guard is directly overhead and Snake is out in the open, lie prone with the Crocodile Cap on and stay underwater until the guard moves on. The length of time before the guard goes away can be quite long, so keep Snake's Stamina high at all times to allow for a longer O2 gauge. Swim upstream with the Crocodile Cap on, and the illusion should allow you to pass through. The jets under the guard's vehicles burn Snake and lead to detection if he cries out in pain. While swimming through the shallow stream, watch out for light halos on the water's surface and swim around them if possible.

NO CROCODILE CAP?

>> In case you overlooked the Crocodile Cap, you can avoid detection by stopping under the thick branches overhanging the stream and waiting until guards pass.

Chaff Grenades can be found on the left side of the stream just before you enter a series of raised rock walls. At the split in the path, go left.

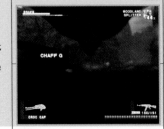

ITEMS FOUND

M1911A1 Suppressor (SP/M1911A1)

Mk22 Bullets x24

M1911A1 Bullets x21

White Phosphorous Grenades (WP G)

Stun Grenades (STUN G)

Mk22 Suppressor (SP/Mk22)

Dragunov Sniper Rifle (SVD)

Mk22 Bullets x24

M37 Bullets x16

AK-47 Bullets x120

TNT

Grenades

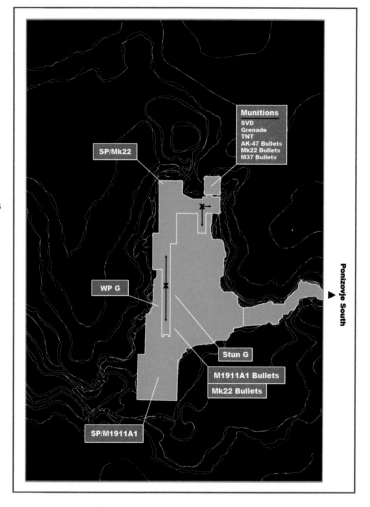

OPERATION SNAKE EATER

1 | ADAM AND EVA
2 | BEYOND THE FOREST BASE
3 | ESCAPE THE CAVE
4 | WAREHOUSE IN THE MANGROVE
5 | GRANINY GORKI LAB
6 | WOODLAND HUNT
7 | ALPINE ASCENT
8 | GROZYNJ GRAD
9 | SHAGOHOD
10 | THE BOSS

The Secret Dock

Two guards patrol the wooden dock platforms in this area. Because there is an armory here and plenty of supplies, this out-of-the-way location is completely worth conquering. Plus, this area can be viewed at two times of day. If you visit this area first, the setting is dusk. But if you go to the upcoming docks area first, this area is enshrouded in night.

The risk of detection here is really high. If you're discovered, the guards radio for backup. The reinforcements for this area are hovercraft guards, so you must avoid being seen at all costs.

Getting onto the Docks

Move slowly across the surface up to the backside of a sunken rowboat, and view the docks area. One guard patrols the long dock to the west, while the other patrols in front of the armory to the north. Watch the guard on the dock furthest out and wait for him to turn and walk north. Submerge and swim southwest to find an **M1911A1 Suppressor** underwater. Then swim north to the bottom edge of the dock and surface.

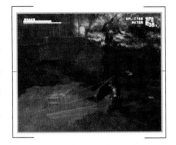 

Empty handed, Snake should be able to remain unseen while treading water at the bottom end of the dock. Wait for the guard to check the south area where Snake is hidden, then press Action [tri] to climb out of the water when he turns. Avoid sneaking directly up on him, because the other guard in the area may see. Crouch and aim at the back of the guard's head, and take him down with a silenced round. Collect the items in the rowboats to either side of the dock.

Close in on the guard patrolling near the armory by lying flat on the dock, and change camouflage to raise the Camo Index. Whenever the guard turns away from the water, crawl north and up the stairs. Crawl onto the concrete area directly west of his route, and shoot him or tranquilize him from this relatively close range. Just watch out for venomous **Cobalt Blue Tarantulas** crawling behind the barrels to the left of the steps.

Blow the Armory

The days of haphazardly sniping with a pistol are over. Inside the armory is the **Dragunov Sniper Rifle**, along with **TNT** and plenty of other ammo. Remember to set a charge and blow the armory to weaken the soldiers in this area.

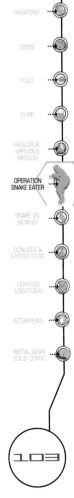

PONIZOVJE WAREHOUSE: EXTERIOR

ITEMS FOUND

SVD Bullet x40

AMMO

M1911A1 Bullets x21

AMMO

M1911A1 Suppressor (SP/M1911A1)

Mk22 Bullets x24

AMMO

Stun Grenades (STUN G)

AK-47 Bullets x120

AMMO

Smoke Grenades (SMOKE G)

OPERATION SNAKE EATER

1 | ADAM AND EVA

2 | BEYOND THE FOREST BASE

3 | ESCAPE THE CAVE

4 | WAREHOUSE IN THE MANGROVE

5 | GRANINY GORKI LAB

6 | WOODLAND HUNT

7 | ALPINE ASCENT

8 | GROZNYJ GRAD

9 | SHAGOHOD

10 | THE BOSS

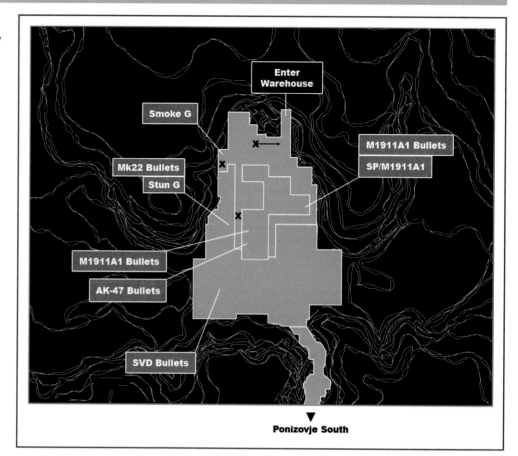

Ponizovje South

Sniper Assault

Snake spots Sokolov, but he is unable to pursue because of Volgin's "Kuwabara Kuwabara." This area is very hard to enter without being spotted. With the SVD in hand, you can snipe all the guards from the entrance. All three of them are radiomen, so you have to pull this off fast. Shoot the guard that patrols near the door in the northeast corner of the dock. Then shoot the one standing at the south end of the dock. By that point, the guard that patrols the northwest corner should come around the crates to see what is happening. Shoot him before he radios in. Even if an attack team enters the area, all they can do is watch the docks. Shoot the barrels on the dock to kill the attack team in massive explosions.

 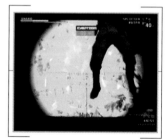

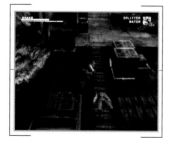

Reload with the **SVD Bullets** submerged in the water in the southwest corner near the canal gate. Check in the rowboats and swim under the docks to find items, and then go inside the warehouse.

THE END'S EARLY DEMISE

Those who found the Dragunov Sniper Rifle and have a quick trigger finger can sidestep a later boss battle. Do so by sniping The End on the dock as he is wheeled back inside the warehouse. Immediately equip the sniper rifle when the cinematic ends and shoot the guard pushing the wheelchair. Continue firing at the wheelchair-bound old man until you kill him. You'll know you succeeded in taking him out if the wheelchair blows up and flies through the air toward Snake's position.

Those playing through the game for the first time are advised to allow The End to be wheeled safely back inside the warehouse. The battle against The End is one of the highpoints in the game; it would be a shame not to witness it firsthand.

PONIZOVJE WAREHOUSE

ITEMS FOUND

Serum

Antidote

Bandage

Desert Face Paint (FACE/DESERT)

Styptic

Disinfectant

Mk22 Suppressor (SP/Mk22)

Instant Noodles (NOODLES)

Calorie Mate

Mousetrap

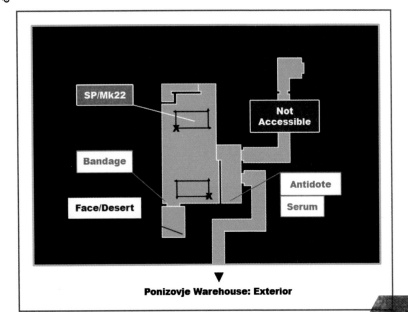

SP/Mk22

Not Accessible

Bandage

Antidote

Face/Desert

Serum

Ponizovje Warehouse: Exterior

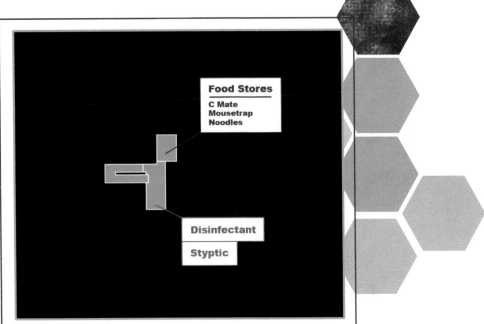

Food Stores
C Mate
Mousetrap
Noodles

Disinfectant

Styptic

Graniny Gorki South

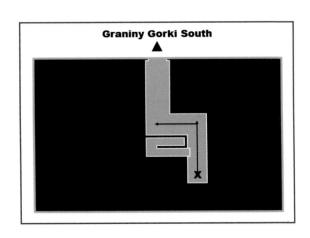

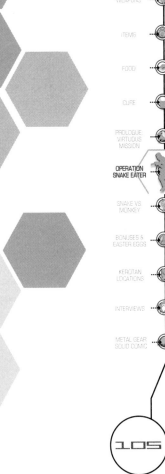

The High Ascent

Ascend the stairs in the corridor and go quietly through the orange doorway. Move quietly south to obtain **Serum** and **Antidote**. The guard that starts in a position near the stairs eventually makes his way to the southwest corner to check the garage door passage. In a crouching or prone position, look west through the rail and watch for the guard to stop in the doorway. Tranquilize or kill the guard, then descend the stairs to the lower floor without being seen by the guard on the top level. Pull the tranquilized guard out of sight and do what you want with him.

Check the position and view of the guard on the top level as you move in to take out the guard patrolling near the stairs. Then move south to a stack of crates. Climb onto the crates, lie flat, and use the SVD to take out the guard on the top level.

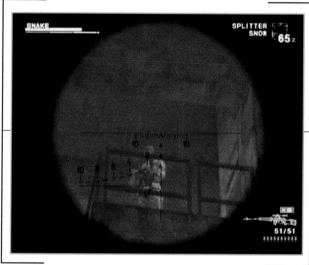

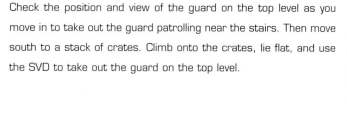

Time now to collect all the items in the area, including the **Desert Face Paint** near the south garage door. Ascend the stairs to the second level, move south, and jump over the rail. Drop onto the central crates and collect the **Mk22 Suppressor**. Then go upstairs again and through the door into the Food Storehouse. Collect the food items and set a TNT bomb to blow up the room, weakening the force in this area.

5 | MISSION OBJECTIVE FIVE:
GRANINY GORKI LAB

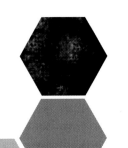

Snake arrives at the woods just outside the area where Major Zero believes Sokolov is being held. The fortifications are severe, not only to keep intruders out but also to imprison the poor scientists forced to work

on Volgin's weapon research. Once inside the building, Snake must don the garb of a scientist just to avoid being detected in the ultra-secure facility. Avoid doing the slightest thing to draw suspicion from guards or the researchers.

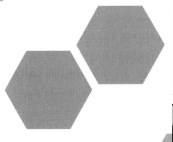

FOOD LIST: GRANINY GORKI LAB STAGE

	Magpie (BIRD D)
	Sunda Whistling-Thrush (BIRD E)
	Calorie Mate (C. MATE)
	Poison Dart Frog (FROG C)
	Yabloko Moloko (FRUIT A)
	Siberian Ink Caps (MUSHROOM C)
	Fly Agaric (MUSHROOM D)
	Instant Noodles (NOODLES)
	European Rabbit (RABBIT)
	Rat (RAT)
	Taiwanese Cobra (SNAKE B)
	Milk Snake (SNAKE E)
	Reticulated Python (SNAKE H)
	Cobalt Blue Tarantula (SPIDER)
	Flying Squirrel (SQUIRREL)

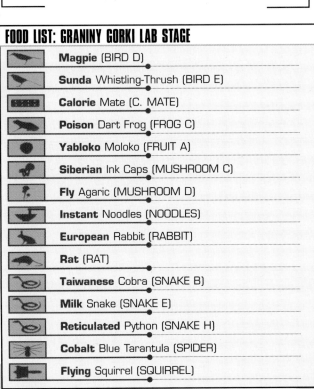

GRANINY GORKI SOUTH

ITEMS FOUND

Life Medicine (LF MED)

Instant Noodles (NOODLES)

Book

OPERATION SNAKE EATER

1 | ADAM AND EVA

2 | BEYOND THE FOREST BASE

3 | ESCAPE THE CAVE

4 | WAREHOUSE IN THE MANGROVE

5 | GRANINY GORKI LAB

6 | WOODLAND HUNT

7 | ALPINE ASCENT

8 | GROZYNJ GRAD

9 | SHAGOROD

10 | THE BOSS

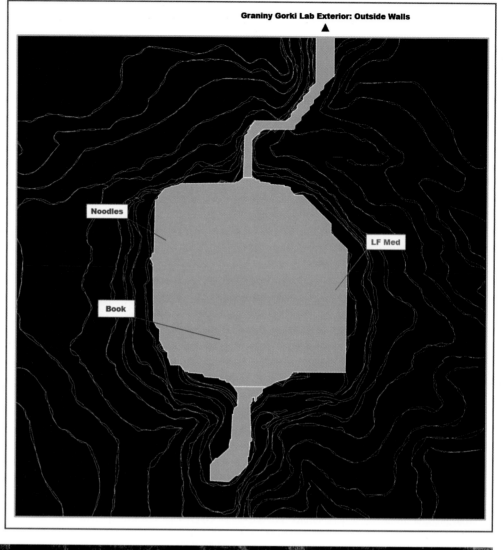

Graniny Gorki Lab Exterior: Outside Walls

Noodles

LF Med

Book

Traps in All the Trees

No guards patrol this area because they have set up traps everywhere to ensnare intruders. Equip the Thermal Goggles to spot the dozen or so traps set in the area. A spike log hung in a tree in the west portion of the area still has a scientist's corpse impaled upon it. Poor guy may have been trying to escape. A **Book** has been left just right of the area's center, and someone dropped **Instant Noodles** in the northwest corner.

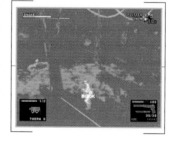 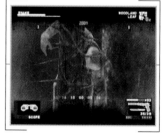

While going for the **Life Medicine** on the east ridge, watch out for a pitfall trap and a trip wire strung between explosives. If you're caught in the snare trap located on the west side of the area, which hangs Snake upside down from a tree, press Action △ to cut loose his foot.

ITEMS FOUND

Mk22 Suppressor (SP/Mk22)

M1911A1 Suppressor
(SP/M1911A1)

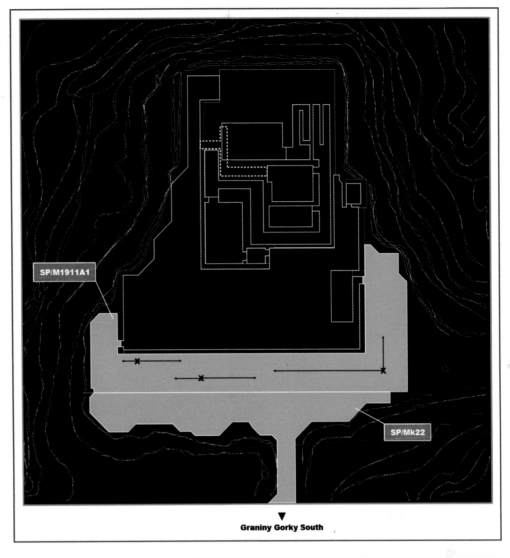

SP/M1911A1

SP/Mk22

▼
Graniny Gorky South

INTRODUCTION

CHARACTERS

SYSTEM

WEAPONS

ITEMS

FOOD

CURE

PROLOGUE
VIRTUOUS
MISSION

OPERATION
SNAKE EATER

SNAKE VS.
MONKEY

BONUSES &
EASTER EGGS

KEROTAN
LOCATIONS

INTERVIEWS

METAL GEAR
SOLID COMIC

KNOCK ON THE DOOR

›› A door that provides another entrance into the facility is at the east end of the exterior wall. However, the door is locked. To enter the interior grounds this way, press Snake's back against the door and press ● to knock. Then run north and hide behind the crates. A guard unlocks the door and emerges. Either sneak in the door behind him or take him down first.

Perimeter Defenses

Crawl into the area, moving east along the wall to the corner, where an **Mk22 Suppressor** lies in the grass. Then crawl west along the wall to the opposite end of the electrified fence. Change camouflage as necessary as you crawl from one type of terrain to another. Kill a **Taiwanese Cobra** crawling in the grass by hitting it with the Survival Knife in a prone position. A **Milk Snake** lurks the west end of the electrified fence, where a hole has been torn in the barbed wire. Crawl through the fence opening when the western sentry moves to the east end of his route.

Move north around the west corner of the wall. Look upward into the tree above to shoot a **Sunda-Whistling Thrush** perched on a branch above. An **M1911A1 Suppressor** lies in the northwest niche. Press your back against the wall near the south corner to spot a ground-level crawl hole leading under the wall into the courtyard.

GRANINY GORKI LAB EXTERIOR: INSIDE WALLS

ITEMS FOUND

Mk22 Bullets x24

M1911A1 Bullets x21

Claymore

Smoke Grenades (SMOKE G)

Oyama Face Paint
(FACE/OYAMA)

XM16E1

SVD Bullets x40

M37 Bullets x16

AMMO

AK-47 Bullets x120

AMMO

TNT

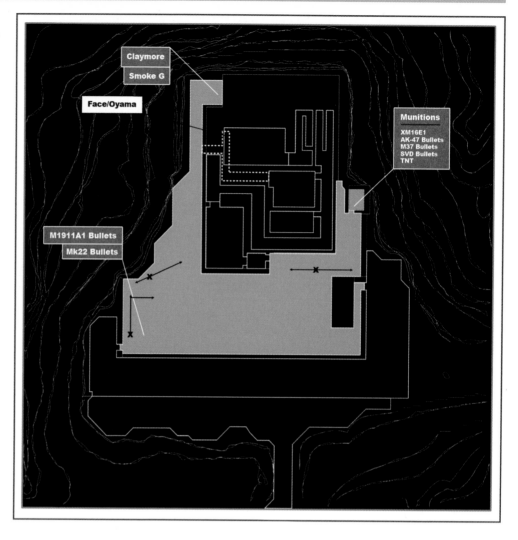

Courtyard CQC

Stay flat on your belly in the grass until the two guards patrol further north. Then crawl east toward the trucks and hide under the south vehicle, where **Mk22** and **M19 bullets** are stashed. Use a suppressed weapon to shoot or tranquilize the guard patrolling the southwest corner of the area. Then watch the guard patrolling the nearby area to the north. When he is moving northeast, leave your hiding spot and grab him. Either knock him out or slit his throat. Snipe the remaining guard patrolling the east side of the courtyard with the SVD, or sneak to his side of the yard and administer an Mk22 dart when he patrols the northeast corner.

A Poor Way to Enter the Facility

In the northwest corner of the area, a packaged **Claymore** and **Smoke Grenades** rest against the building's west wall. A few feet south of the wall is a vent that leads into the central courtyard inside the facility.

The vent breaks into a T-intersection. Go to the left to obtain the strange **Oyama Face Paint**. Do not go south in the vent! The vent leads to a courtyard full of windows, which the soldiers inside the building check all too frequently. If you wear fatigues into the courtyard, any soldier looking out a window from any direction sounds an alert. Even if the Scientist Camouflage is worn in the courtyard, the soldiers arrest Snake and throw him into the jail cell on level B1. This is one way to get inside the facility, but hardly a smooth choice.

Entering the Laboratory

After taking down the guards in the courtyard, explore the northeast corner of the area to find an armory. The familiar **XM16E1** assault rifle is available inside the depot, in addition to several types of **ammo** and **TNT**. Set and detonate charges inside the armory to reduce the enemies' capabilities in this region.

The staff entrance is the door to the right of the double doors. Before going inside, change Snake into the Scientist Camouflage and no face paint.

GRANINY GORKI LAB 1F

ITEMS FOUND
................................o

None (at this point)

 INTRUDER ALERT

Inside the facility, the only way to avoid being detected and immediately surrounded is by wearing the Scientist Camouflage and no face paint. Even then, guards may become suspicious of your movements, especially if you bump into them or try to go through a door at the same time they do. To avoid colliding with guards, watch them through a window to make sure they are standing away from the door before entering.

Blending in with Staff

If a guard becomes suspicious, just stand still, face the guard, and make no sudden movements or attacks. Press △ to adjust your glasses. This convinces a guard to disregard Snake and move on. Some of the guards are brutal sadists, and may punch out Snake just because they feel like it. Do not retaliate. Instead, wait until the guard tells you to get back to work, and beat it out of there!

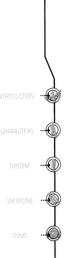

Scientists who see Snake's face peer in closely and soon realize that he's not one of the staff. They become scared and cry out. Guards patrolling nearby immediately set off the alarms when they hear such outcries. Whenever a Scientist is in the room, turn Snake's back to him until the guy gives up trying to recognize you.

Wearing the Scientist Camouflage, Snake cannot use CQC or his normal weapons. He must find special undercover espionage weapons found inside the lab in order to neutralize guards or scientists. To perform normal CQC actions, especially to interrogate guards for directions or tips, position Snake behind a stationary character and switch to another camouflage, such as Naked, and grab the person before he turns and spots Snake.

Move through the lobby to the north end of the corridor beyond. Open the wooden door carefully and proceed east through the foyer to the stairs.

OPERATION SNAKE EATER

1 | ADAM AND EVA

2 | BEYOND THE FOREST BASE

3 | ESCAPE THE CAVE

4 | WAREHOUSE IN THE MANGROVE

5 | GRANINY GORKI LAB

6 | WOODLAND HUNT

7 | ALPINE ASCENT

8 | GORZYNJ GRAD

9 | SHAGOHOD

10 | THE BOSS

GRANINY GORKI LAB B1 WEST

ITEMS FOUND

Cigar Gas-Spray

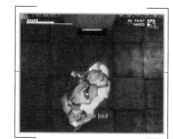

Knockout Handkerchief (HANDKER)

XM16E1 Suppressor (SP/XM16E1)

Battery

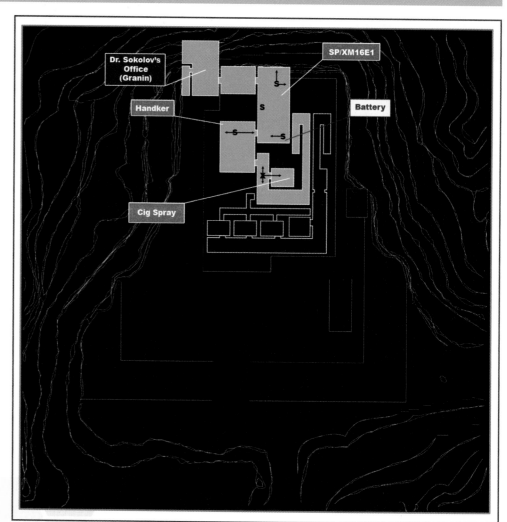

The Scientist's Tranquilizer of Choice

Go into the guard's post and grab the **Cigar Gas-Spray**. When equipped, Snake appears to be smoking a cigar. But in truth the small tube in his mouth emits a highly effective tranquilizer that knocks out one or more personnel standing within one foot directly in front of Snake. Use the Cigar Gas-Spray to knock out scientists and guards before they can identify Snake as an intruder. Enter the wooden door across the hallway from the guard's room.

The scientist in this small break room is quite troublesome to get past. Knock him out swiftly with the Cigar Gas-Spray, and then stuff his body into one of the lockers so that he is not discovered. The left locker contains **Knockout Handkerchiefs**, which work in a fashion similar to the Cigar Gas-Spray. However, due to the fumes emitted by waving the kerchief, Snake runs a risk of knocking himself out!

Playing Goalie

Continue through the northeast door from the break room into a cubicle area where two or three scientists perform research. If any scientist identifies Snake as an impostor, which is a possibility in these tight quarters, he runs to the north end of the room and pulls the alarm switch.

There are two ways to get past the scientists in the middle cubicles and the north portions of the room. Either move to a position parallel to each scientist and turn your back to them until they go back to work, or move to the top of the room and use Cigar Gas-Spray or Knockout Handkerchiefs to tranquilize the scientists as they try to run for the alarm. Check the cubicles in the room to find an **XM16E1 Suppressor** and a **Battery**.

Granin

Go through the northwest door and into next room to meet the drunken Granin. Granin gives Snake **Key A**, which opens the second orange door in the Ponizovje Warehouse a few clicks back. The key works automatically on the door back in the warehouse, even if it's stored in the Backpack. After the scene, return to the lab and run out of the cubicle area as quickly as possible.

Take this

WHERE'S THAT KEROTAN?!

Stand near the froglike character on the shelf against the west wall of the break room and call Para-Medic on the radio. Para-Medic recognizes the doll as Kerotan, a magical character who has been around a long time in Japan. When you're alone in the room, punch the Kerotan doll to make it emit noise. Kerotan can be punched three times before its vocal box breaks. There is one Kerotan in nearly every area of the game, and finding and attacking them all unlocks bonus content. Check the **Kerotan Locations** chapter at the back of this book for more information.

ITEMS FOUND

M1911A1 Bullets x21 or
Cigar Gas-Spray Bullet x5

AMMO

Serum

Ointment

Suture Kit

Bandage

OPERATION
SNAKE
EATER

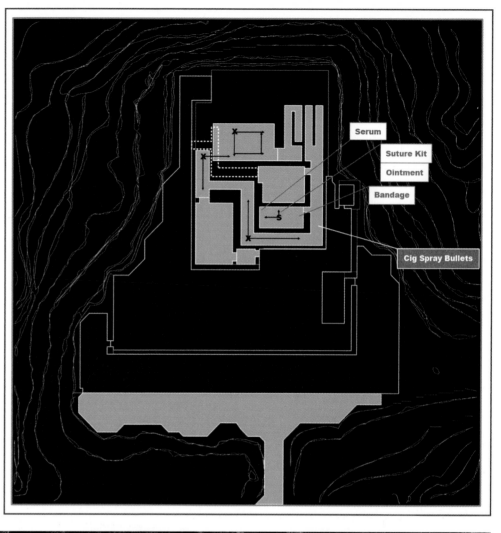

Checking the Rest of the Lab

Return to the first floor and cross the foyer. Head south and to the right down a twisting corridor just above the lobby. Open the second locker on the east wall to find **Cigar Spray Bullets x5**. If you have not obtained the Cigar Gas-Spray weapon, then a pack of **M1911A1 bullets** is in the locker instead.

Go through the wooden door into a small reference room. Turn your back to the scientist or knock him out with Cigar Gas-Spray to prevent him from identifying you. Pick up the medical supplies in the room, then exit and go north past the red door. The red door leads outside to a courtyard surrounded by windows through which Snake can be seen. Even scientists are not allowed to go outside, and Snake will be arrested if he's spotted here. Instead, descend the stairs at the north end of the corridor.

ITEMS FOUND

Antidote

Mk22 Bullets x24

AMMO

SVD Bullets x40

AMMO

M37 Bullets x16

AMMO

Mousetrap

Life Medicine (LF MED)

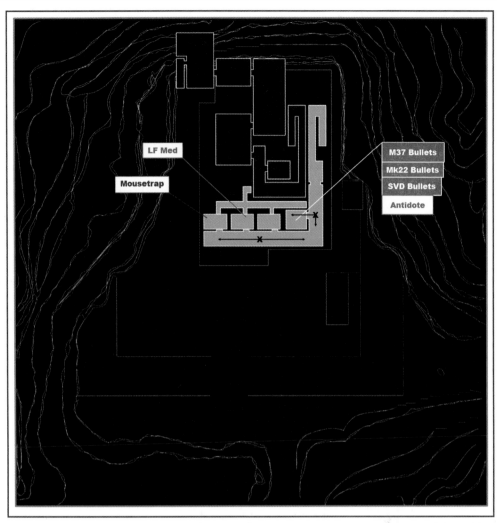

A Guard with Secret Information

Move south in the corridor, and go through the door on the left into a guard's station. Before crawling to reach the **SVD** and **M37 bullets** under the forward desk, make sure that no one is looking, or they'll become instantly alerted. Interrogate the guard who sometimes stands in this room during his patrol to make him divulge a secret radio frequency where music is played. It may be better to follow the guard outside the room, knock him out, drag him north away from the other guard's patrol route, wake him, and interrogate him there before silencing him permanently.

Continue west, avoiding the poison bites of Cobalt Blue Tarantulas in the passage. Proceed to the end prison cell to find another Kerotan doll. Punch the doll to shake him, but avoid performing this action in front of the patrolling guard. Pick up the **Mousetrap** in the last cell, then enter the middle cell and wait for the guard to go away before crawling under the bunk to obtain **Life Medicine**. A series of vent shafts between prison cells allows for hiding and better maneuvering to the Life Medicine during an alert, if necessary.

GRANINY GORKI LAB 2F

ITEMS FOUND

Mk22 Suppressor (SP/Mk22)

Fly Camouflage
(UNIFORM/FLY)

Instant Noodles
(NOODLES)(2 qty.)

Calorie Mate (C. MATE)

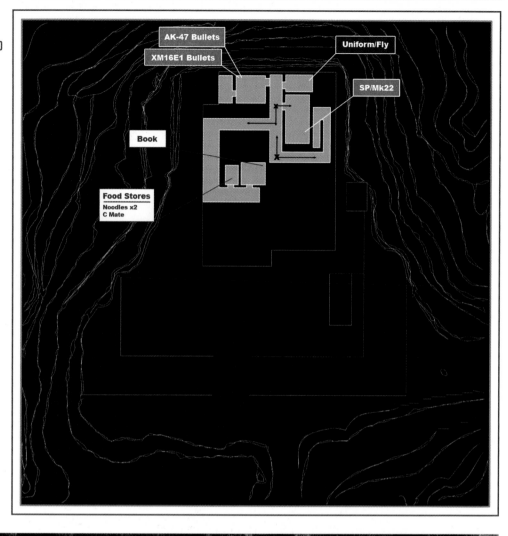

AK-47 Bullets

XM16E1 Bullets

Uniform/Fly

SP/Mk22

Book

Food Stores
Noodles x2
C Mate

The Upper Level

Return to the first floor and take the next set of stairs directly up to 2F. The second floor is part of the same area as the lower level, and guards above and below the balcony can see each other. Proceed cautiously if you're tranquilizing or interrogating guards. Use Cigar Gas-Spray to knock out all the guards patrolling the balcony to prevent trouble during your upcoming actions, and go north into the upstairs library to find an **Mk22 Suppressor**.

The next room to the north in the corridor leads to a restroom. The third stall door is locked. Use punches and kicks when no guards are in the room to break down the door. Be sure to move away as the panel falls, or Snake takes damage. Inside the third stall is the **Fly Camouflage**.

The Food Storeroom

Now go southwest around the balcony. The first door on this side of the upstairs level contains **Instant Noodles** and a **Calorie Mate**. Dispose of other foods clogging the inventory to obtain these superior products.

To destroy this food storehouse and weaken the guards throughout this stage, change out of the Scientists Camouflage and place a TNT charge in the room. Exit the room and go outside through the next door in the corridor to a raised platform above the courtyard. There is a **Book** located there. Press (O) to detonate the charge in the next room, switch back to the Scientist Camouflage, and return inside. Reinforcements arrive to investigate the bomb, but they should move right past Snake in the corridor.

A Good Exit

To get out of the facility with less likelihood of detection, move north past the restroom on the upper level. Check the leftmost locker to find **XM16E1 Bullets**, and open the next locker to find **AK-47 Bullets**. Go through the red door.

Outside, drop over the rail and hang, then drop to the ground below. With the food storeroom inside destroyed, all the guards should now be hungry. All the items previously found in this area should have now reappeared, except the Oyama Face Paint (assuming you previously acquired it). Crawl through the southeast hole in the wall to the exterior fortifications area, and crawl through the hole in the electrified fence. Continue south.

GRANINY GORKI SOUTH

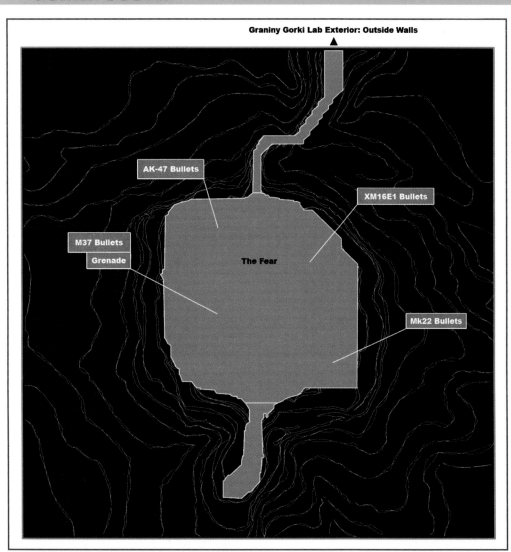

Graniny Gorki Lab Exterior: Outside Walls

AK-47 Bullets

XM16E1 Bullets

M37 Bullets

Grenade

The Fear

Mk22 Bullets

INTRODUCTION

CHARACTERS

SYSTEM

WEAPONS

ITEMS

FOOD

CURE

PROLOGUE: VIRTUOUS MISSION

OPERATION SNAKE EATER

SNAKE VS MONKEY

BONUSES & EASTER EGGS

KEROTAN LOCATIONS

INTERVIEWS

METAL GEAR SOLID COMIC

THE FEAR

BATTLE-SPECIFIC ITEMS

XM16E1 bullets x80

`AMMO`

Grenades

`AMMO`

Mk22 Bullet x24

`AMMO`

AK-47 Bullets x120

`AMMO`

M37 Bullets

`AMMO`

Cure yourself from the wound inflicted by The Fear during the cinema. Use a Serum to negate the poisoning, then use the Knife, Styptic, Suture Kit, and Bandage to repair the crossbow bolt wound. Each subsequent crossbow bolt that pierces Snake should not require poison treatment, but use the other items to extract the bolt and facilitate healing during the battle.

Remove the M37, XM16E1 and AK-47 from the Backpack if necessary. Equip the Thermal Goggles and wear them throughout the fight to avoid the numerous pitfalls, snares, and other traps in the area. Additional ammunition is spread out across the map. Be extremely careful when you go for the **Mk22 Bullets** located in the lower southeast corner of the area, because a trap blocks all access to the item. Shoot the tripwire in First Person View from a safe distance to detonate the hidden explosives, and then collect the ammo.

The Fear bounds from tree to tree in the area around Snake. Therefore, it is a relatively easy matter to track him in First Person View as he leaps, provided you're wearing the Thermal Goggles. When he stops and pulls out is crossbow or begins to speak, unload a machinegun on him. Use the thin red lines in the center of the Thermal Goggles as a crosshair to line up Snake's aim.

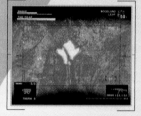

Leaping from tree to tree consumes The Fear's Stamina very quickly. If your constant machinegun attacks keep him on the move, he should be starving and out of energy in no time. After complaining that he's hungry, he uses his crossbow to shoot fungus or wildlife in the area. Sometimes he shoots and eats something poisonous, and damages himself in the process!

When The Fear finishes eating, he rushes up and attacks Snake, removing his Thermal Goggles and weapon. Re-equip your items and go after him. Preempt this assault by chasing him across the ground as he heads for food. Rush him and blast the area with the M37 shotgun. Relatively speaking, The Fear is as easy to defeat as they come in the Cobras.

NON-LETHAL ALTERNATIVE

It's possible to defeat The Fear by depleting his Stamina gauge. Use the Mk22 exclusively during the fight as he jumps from branch to branch. Reloading the Mk22 with a fresh tranquilizer dart takes time, so Snake will be able to get off only one shot before The Fear moves again. The **Spider Camouflage** can be found on the ground nearby after the battle.

6 | MISSION OBJECTIVE SIX: WOODLAND HUNT

With the key offered by Granin, Snake can now proceed northeast beyond the warehouse, through a dense forest, toward the impenetrable fortress

of Grozynj Grad. EVA wants Snake to meet her at the top of Krasnogorje Mountain so she can pass along the key to Volgin's impenetrable fortress. But lying in wait is the most cunning sniper the world has ever known. Could this be...The End?

FOOD LIST: WOODLAND HUNT STAGE

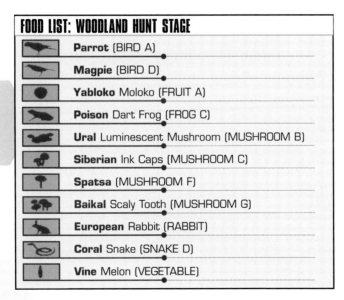

- **Parrot** (BIRD A)
- **Magpie** (BIRD D)
- **Yabloko** Moloko (FRUIT A)
- **Poison** Dart Frog (FROG C)
- **Ural** Luminescent Mushroom (MUSHROOM B)
- **Siberian** Ink Caps (MUSHROOM C)
- **Spatsa** (MUSHROOM F)
- **Baikal** Scaly Tooth (MUSHROOM G)
- **European** Rabbit (RABBIT)
- **Coral** Snake (SNAKE D)
- **Vine** Melon (VEGETABLE)

PONIZOVJE WAREHOUSE

ITEMS FOUND

Serum

Antidote

Bandage

Styptic

Disinfectant

Mk22 Suppressor
(SP/Mk22)

Mousetrap

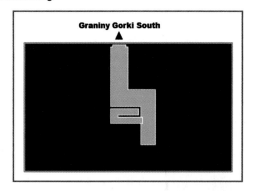

Graniny Gorki South

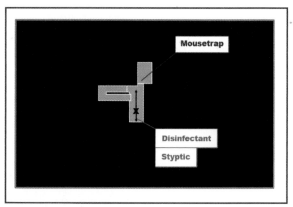

Mousetrap

Disinfectant

Styptic

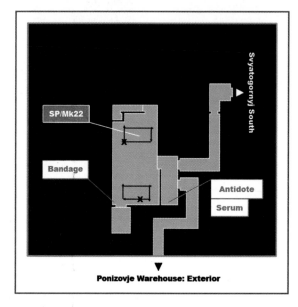

SP/Mk22

Bandage

Antidote

Serum

Svyatogornyj South

Ponizovje Warehouse: Exterior

OPERATION SNAKE EATER

1 ADAM AND EVA

2 BEYOND THE FOREST BASE

3 ESCAPE THE CAVE

4 WAREHOUSE IN THE MANGROVE

5 GRANINY GORKI LAB

6 WOODLAND HUNT

7 ALPINE ASCENT

8 GROZNYJ GRAD

9 SHAGOHOD

10 THE BOSS

Just Passing Through...

When entering the warehouse from the north, the guard that normally patrols the top level takes up a new route on the mid level. Descend the stairs while he is patrolling the south portion of the platform, and then move downstairs and slip behind him for a quick takedown.

All the items in this area have reappeared, except for food items and the Desert Face Paint (unless you didn't acquire it previously). Work your way from guard to guard to the bottom level. The card key Granin provided opens the orange door beside the previous entrance in the southeast corner.

ITEMS FOUND

Book

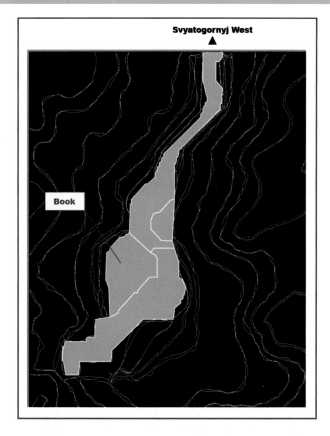

Svyatogornyj West ▲

Book

MELLOW MUSHROOMS

Do not eat the Spatsa Mushrooms unless you're absolutely certain there are no enemies nearby. Eating these mushrooms causes Snake to immediately fall asleep. Although this enables him to replenish his Health and Stamina, it leaves him vulnerable to attack. Consider tossing Spatsa Mushrooms in front of hungry guards to tranquilize them.

The Sloping Garden

No enemies patrol this area. Enter the area a few steps to receive a transmission from EVA. **Styptics** can be harvested from the three green plants by the door. Continue slashing plants as you ascend the slope to obtain a **Splint** and **Cold Medicine**. Cut the mushrooms from the tree near the middle to obtain **Baikal Scaly Tooth**. A **Book** has been discarded on the flat spot to the left.

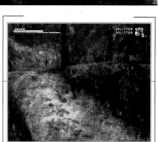

Look for single, long-stemmed mushrooms near trees. When plucked from the environment, both **Spatsa Mushrooms** and **Hanker Bullet x1** pop out!

ITEMS FOUND

XM16E1 Bullets x80

AMMO

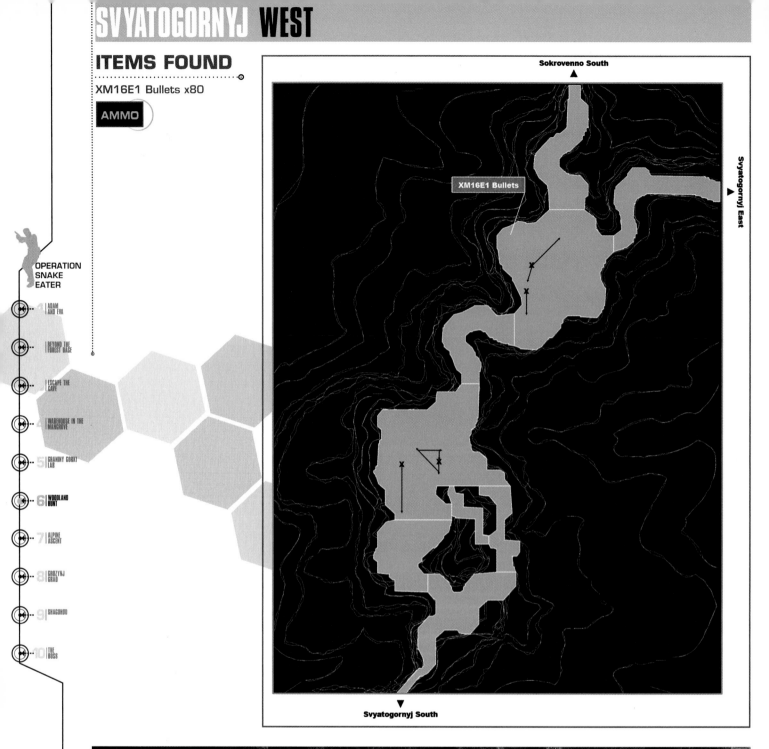

Sokrovenno South

Svyatogornyj East

XM16E1 Bullets

Svyatogornyj South

Well-Camouflaged Guards

Throughout this sometimes-rainy area, the brush is extremely heavy and visibility is poor. Plunge ahead too hurriedly, and you could bump into a guard without seeing him. Use caution and occasionally put on the Thermal Goggles to spot guards and neutralize them.

Moving north, follow the west wall until you reach a climbable tree. Then duck and crawl into the hollow log to left, and crawl to the opposite end. A guard patrols the path below the ridge. Allow him to come near enough to shoot him in the head with a dart or bullet.

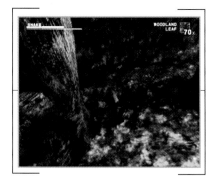

Move to the guard you just took out and shake him for items. Continue north and then head east up a slope. Drop and crawl in the grass with Leaf Camouflage on, and allow a guard patrolling the area atop the ridge to approach you. Neutralize him when he comes into range.

Continue north and follow the path into another wide section of forest. Crawl on the ground as you clear the corner, and shoot the guard that patrols the closest. Go north past him into the grass beyond the logs. Use the sniper rifle on the last guard in the area by facing northeast and firing. Head east to a side area before going north.

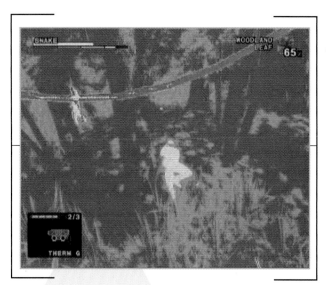

Ammo Bait

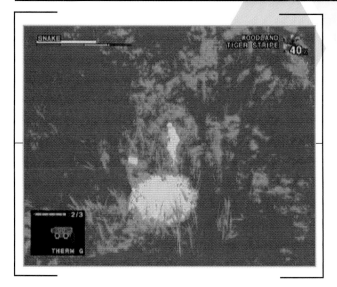

There is a pack of **XM16E1 Bullets** on the west side of the map's upper portion. However, they sit on the opposite side of a pitfall trap. Use the Thermal Goggles to spot the danger, and get the ammo safely.

INTRODUCTION

CHARACTERS

SYSTEM

WEAPONS

ITEMS

FOOD

CURE

PROLOGUE-VIRTUOUS MISSION

OPERATION SNAKE EATER

SNAKE VS. MONKEY

BONUSES & EASTER EGGS

KEROTAN LOCATIONS

INTERVIEWS

METAL GEAR SOLID COMIC

ITEMS FOUND

Calorie Mate x2 (C. MATE)

Russian Ration (Ration)

M37 Bullets x16

SVD Bullets x40

AMMO

XM16E1 Bullets x80

AMMO

Mk22 Bullets x24

AMMO

M63

TNT

XM16E1 Suppressor (SP/XM16E1)

Mk22 Bullets x24

M1911A1 Bullets x21

Book

OPERATION SNAKE EATER

1 | ADAM AND EVA
2 | BEYOND THE FOREST BASE
3 | ESCAPE THE CAVE
4 | WAREHOUSE IN THE MANGROVE
5 | GRANINY GORKI LAB
6 | WOODLAND HUNT
7 | ALPINE ASCENT
8 | GROZNYJ GRAD
9 | SHAGOHOD
10 | THE BOSS

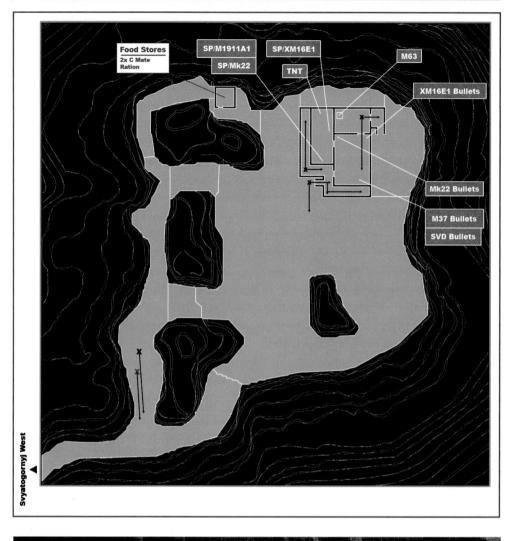

Food Stores
2x C Mate Ration

SP/M1911A1
SP/Mk22
SP/XM16E1
TNT
M63
XM16E1 Bullets
Mk22 Bullets
M37 Bullets
SVD Bullets

Svyatogornyj West

A Two-Man Patrol

Two guards approach together, so take cover. Allow both of them to pass, because the second man is the guy with the radio. Shoot the second guard, enabling you to sneak up behind the other guard.

Cabin in the Woods

Move north, following the narrower western path up the mountain. When the path splits, follow the path to the left. This path takes you above a food storehouse and behind a large cabin in the woods. Taking down the guards around this cabin and getting inside unseen proves very difficult, but it is a good way to hone your skills.

Watch the guard patrolling the cabin's surrounding deck, and drop onto the shed roof when he moves around the corner. Enter the food storehouse to find **two Calorie Mates** and a **Russian Ration**. To avoid an alert, wait to destroy the warehouse until all the guards are neutralized.

Rooftop Ambushes

Exit the shed and equip a suppressed pistol. A guard patrols the deck of the nearby cabin. Wait for him to go to the front. Then run north of cabin while he's not looking, climb up the tree, and drop onto the cabin's roof.

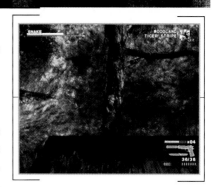

Crawl across the roof heading east. Find a portion where a slat is missing, allowing you to look down into the room below. Aim at the door in the room below. When the guard inside comes into the back room, shoot him in the head.

Crawl to the sides of the rooftop, while avoiding detection by the guard who patrols the yard. Move the Right Analog Stick to look over the sides at the guards patrolling around the cabin. Crawl again to the front of the building and look west. Shoot a guard in the head as he comes south around the west corner of the building. Shoot the other guard walking in the yard, then drop from the roof and go inside.

Cabin Intricacies

The main room contains various types of ammo. Climb over the crates in the back room to obtain the **M63**, an awesome machine gun you will love using near the end of the game. If you need to escape, a trap door in the floor behind the crates lets you slip under the house. Enter the barracks on the west side of the house and crawl under the north bed to find **TNT**. Under the east bed is an **XM16E1 Suppressor**. Collect the other items in the room and return to the previous area in the woods.

DANGEROUS ENEMY AHEAD!

Save before proceeding, or you could be set back several stages by "losing" the upcoming battle.

EMERGENCY DIVE!

>> If something goes wrong and the enemy engages in pursuit, lead them into the cabin. Once all the guards follow Snake inside, head to one of the windows in the bedroom. As you run toward the window, press ⊗ when you're just a foot or so away. With the right timing, Snake dives and crashes through the window into the yard! Now you can get away before the guards can get out of the cabin!

OPERATION
SNAKE
EATER

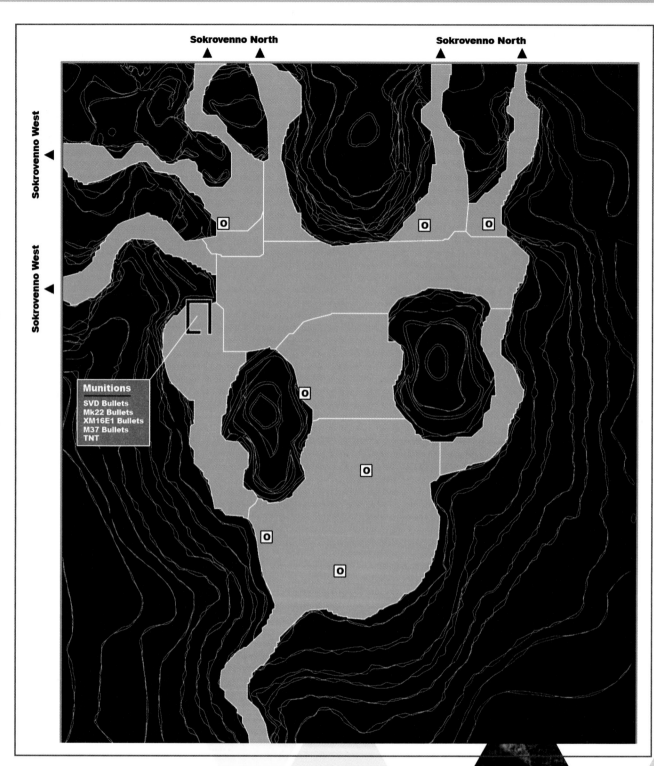

Munitions

SVD Bullets
Mk22 Bullets
XM16E1 Bullets
M37 Bullets
TNT

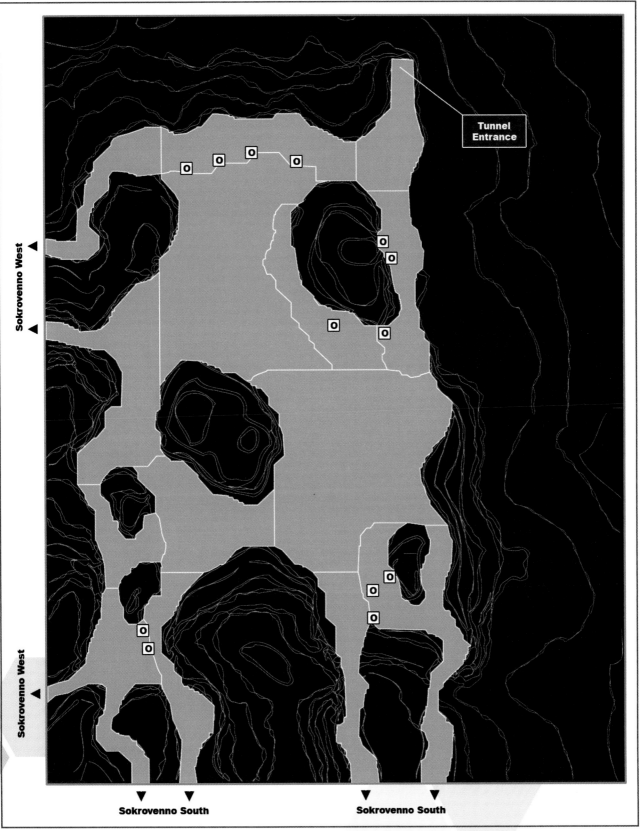

Tunnel
Entrance

Sokrovenno West

Sokrovenno West

Sokrovenno South

Sokrovenno South

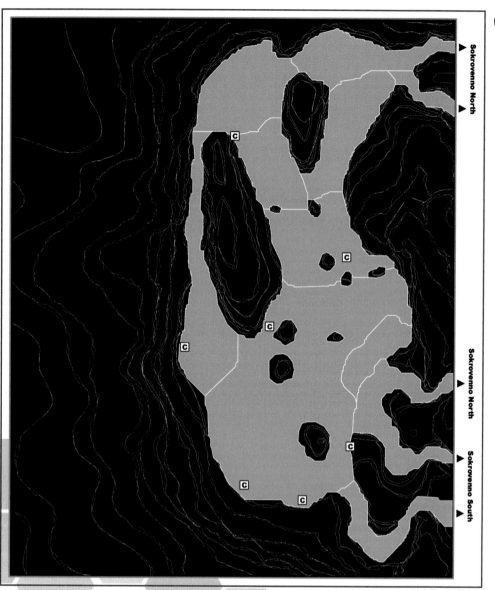

THE BOSSLESS BATTLE

Those who sniped The End on the dock outside the Ponizovje Warehouse aren't in the clear just yet. Although The End is no longer a part of this world, Snake is not alone in the Sokrovenno forests. A total of 20 GRU soldiers roam these woods in search of Snake. Snake encounters eight in Sokrovenno South, seven in Sokrovenno North, and five in Sokrovenno West. Some of the GRU try to attack in a group, but many of them are dispersed throughout the sniping locations that The End would have used. Follow the tips below to flush them out.

NON-LETHAL ALTERNATIVE

The End's Stamina gauge slowly decreases throughout the battle as he is forced to run from area to area. Continue chasing him until he is panting loudly, and then use the Mk22 to finish him off. Act fast, however, as The End is capable of calling to the forest for rejuvenation. Snake can find the **Moss Camouflage** after defeating The End in this manner.

THE END

BATTLE-SPECIFIC ITEMS

SVD Bullets x40

AMMO

XM16E1 Bullets x80

AMMO

M37 bullets x16

AMMO

TNT

Mk22 Bullets x24

AMMO

THE END

This battle takes place across three areas to the north of the starting position. The End is an expert sniper and a master of camouflage and positioning. As an energetic young solider, Snake must root him out of his hiding spots and keep the old man on the run.

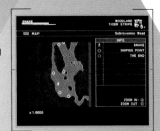

As Snake moves through the areas and more portions of the in-game maps are revealed, possible sniping locations are marked as white circles on the in-game map. Whenever The End fires from a sniping location, the marker representing his location turns red. Rather than risk further damage by looking around the environment for him, simply open the in-game map to see his position. Referral to the in-game map is an important part of winning.

Move northwest in the first area toward a munitions depot. As you head toward it, The End usually takes a sniping position on the cliff just northeast of the building. Avoid his shots and navigate to the depot. If you watched the previous cinema carefully, you might recognize The End's pet bird perched on the corner of the depot. Shoot it to obtain **BIRD A** type food— this is the only time in the entire game that this type of food can be obtained. The End sometimes becomes extremely angered at this and swears revenge. Go inside the depot, where all of the items in the list above are stored. If you missed obtaining the SVD earlier, it appears in the depot. Otherwise, additional SVD ammo appears. If you like, you can destroy the structure by setting TNT.

The End shoots tranquilizer darts instead of bullets. These special darts drain Snake's Stamina continuously until they're removed with the Survival Knife via the Cure screen. After removing the projectile, eat food to replenish strength. Maintaining Stamina is more important than Health in this battle, because The End is actually not interested in killing Snake. If Snake's Stamina falls to zero during the battle, a special scene occurs where The End captures Snake and leaves him in the jail cells of Graniny Gorki Lab B1. All enemies reappear in their respective areas, just to set you back that much further. Avoid this hassle to the best of your abilities by hunting and eating well throughout the battle.

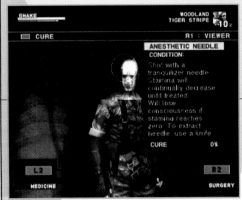

INTRODUCTION

CHARACTERS

SYSTEM

WEAPONS

ITEMS

FOOD

CURE

PROLOGUE: VIRTUOUS MISSION

OPERATION SNAKE EATER

SNAKE VS. MONKEY

BONUSES & EASTER EGGS

KEROTAN LOCATIONS

INTERVIEWS

METAL GEAR SOLID COMIC

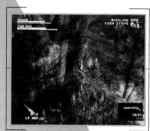

Exit the munitions depot and quickly head north to the Sokrovenno North area. Hook around to the southwest, and move toward the path that leads up to the cliff from which The End was just shooting. Either you will run into him as he tries to escape from that area, or he will have already moved into one of the sniping positions close to the southeast corner of the area. Root him out by running from sniping point to sniping point until you find him hiding in the brush. The End detects Snake immediately and usually fires a dart or sets off a stun grenade that momentarily blinds and deafens him. But these attacks inflict only minor damage as long as you remove the tranquilizer needle quickly. Blasting The End a few times with the shotgun is worth the risk, as long as Snake's Stamina is high.

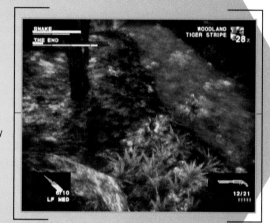

If The End moves through mud, he leaves footprints that make him easier to track. If ever you completely lose track of The End during a close-range shooting exchange, follow him through the closest exit into the next area, and search the closest sniping points to find him. If that fails, work your way around the area from sniping point to sniping point until you discover him.

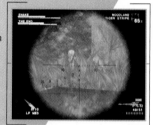

If The End manages to shoot Snake from a sniping point far across the area, quickly extract the dart. Crouch or go prone if possible and equip the Dragunov. Use the in-game map to help you aim toward the sniping point marked in red, and hold ∟1 to look through the scope to find The End. The scope of his rifle casts a glare in the sunlight that sometimes betrays his location. Blast him three or four times with the Dragunov, and then pursue him quickly to the next area.

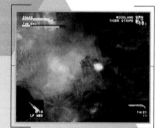

Occasionally it begins to rain, at which point The End might go to a sniping point and fall asleep. This is a great opportunity to run up on him and blast him without retaliation, assuming you can find and shoot him before he snaps awake.

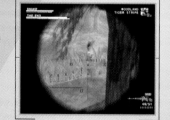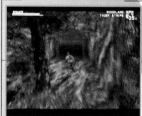

Because of his age and condition, The End's Stamina depletes. If his Stamina drops to almost nothing, he will eat to replenish his Stamina, but this also restores a majority of his Health! Try to win the battle before this happens.

After the battle, go to the northeast corner of Sokrovenno North and continue into a tunnel.

OPERATION
SNAKE
EATER

1 | ADAM AND EVA

2 | BEYOND THE FOREST BASE

3 | ESCAPE THE CAVE

4 | WAREHOUSE IN THE MANGROVE

5 | GRANINY GORKI LAB

6 | WOODLAND HUNT

| ALPINE ASCENT

| GROZNYJ GRAD

| SHAGOHOD

| THE BOSS

7 | MISSION OBJECTIVE SEVEN:
ALPINE ASCENT

Having defeated yet another bizarrely gifted member of the Cobras, Snake prepares to climb the impossibly tall Krasnogorje mountain range in the hope of meeting EVA to obtain her key to Grozynj Grad. Volgin has spent considerable time and funds fortifying the mountainside well enough to deter an invading army. Is there a shadow of a chance that Snake can sneak through enemy lines?

FOOD LIST: ALPINE ASCENT STAGE

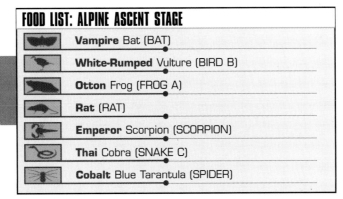	**Vampire** Bat (BAT)
	White-Rumped Vulture (BIRD B)
	Otton Frog (FROG A)
	Rat (RAT)
	Emperor Scorpion (SCORPION)
	Thai Cobra (SNAKE C)
	Cobalt Blue Tarantula (SPIDER)

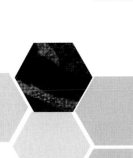

KRASNOGORJE TUNNEL

ITEMS FOUND

None

The Infinite Ladder

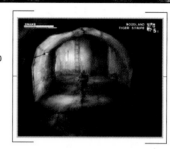

Head up the tunnel and climb a tall ladder that seems to ascend forever. Go out the top door.

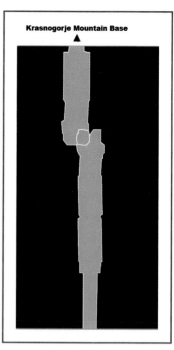

Krasnogorje Mountain Base

KRASNOGORJE MOUNTAIN BASE

ITEMS FOUND

Smoke Grenades (SMOKE G)

Serum (2 qty.)

SVD Bullets x40

Mk22 Bullets x24

Grenades

Chaff Grenades

OPERATION
SNAKE
EATER

1 | ADAM AND EVA

2 | BEYOND THE FOREST BASE

3 | ESCAPE THE CAVE

4 | WAREHOUSE IN THE MANGROVE

5 | GRANINY GORKI LAB

6 | WOODLAND HUNT

7 | ALPINE ASCENT

8 | GROZNYJ GRAD

9 | SHAGOHOD

10 | THE BOSS

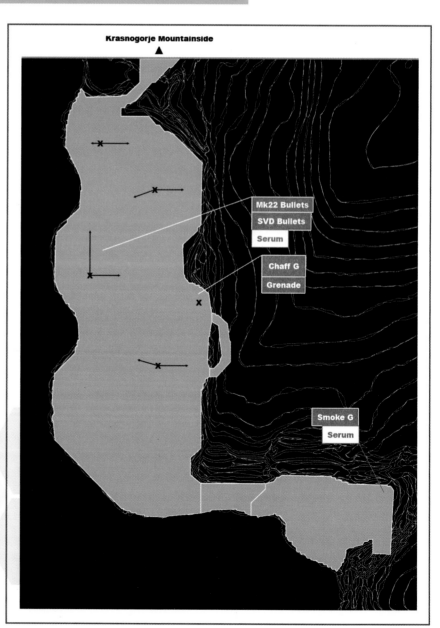

Krasnogorje Mountainside

Mk22 Bullets
SVD Bullets
Serum

Chaff G
Grenade

Smoke G
Serum

The Inhospitable Wastes

Equip the Choco Chip Camouflage and Desert Face Paint to better blend into the rocky environment. Run west and slide down the embankment. Once Snake is at the bottom of the slope, there is no going back to previous stages. Be extremely careful of the wildlife in this area, because much of it is poisonous. For example, a Thai Cobra in the path can strike almost without warning due to how well it blends into the ground. Emperor Scorpions are hard to spot, but they sting Snake and inflict poisoning if he steps near them. Keep a good supply of Serums on hand at all times, and cure poisoning immediately.

Sniper Assault

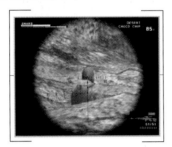

There are four guards in the next area. Move some distance into the section, following the west cliff along the left side to a light-colored rise that stands out above the rest. Lie on the embankment and wait for the closest guard to move to the easternmost end of his route. Use the Dragunov to take him down.

The idea is to shoot all the guards when they cannot see each other in order to avoid raising an alarm. Take each guard out at the furthest outside point of his patrol path. Allow the most distant guard patrolling the back area to come as far forward as possible before sniping him. Wait to shoot the guard holding the RPG on the high ledge until last. The fifth guard cannot be seen from this area.

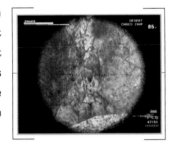

THEM'S GOOD VITTLES!

>> White-Rumped Vultures settle on dead guards and eat their flesh. Kill these buzzards to score some really good meat.

One Last Patrol

Two boulders lean on each other to form a triangular tunnel close to the west side of the area, just north of the map's middle. Crawl under the rocks to find various **ammunition** and **Serum**. Use this hiding spot to kill the fifth and final guard as he walks in front of the tunnel.

Just south of where the guard holding an RPG stood is a crawlspace-size tunnel leading up to his post. On this ledge you find **Grenades** and **Chaff Grenades**.

ITEMS FOUND

SVD Bullets x40 (2 qty.)

Stun Grenades (STUN G)

M37 Bullets x16 (2 qty.)

Antidote

M1911A1 Bullets x21 (2 qty.)

AK-47 Bullets x120

White Phosphorus Grenades (WP G)

XM16E1 Bullets x80 (2 qty.)

Styptic

Bandage

Russian Rations (RATIONS)

Calorie Mate (C. MATE)

Splint

Serum

Disinfectant

RPG-7

TNT

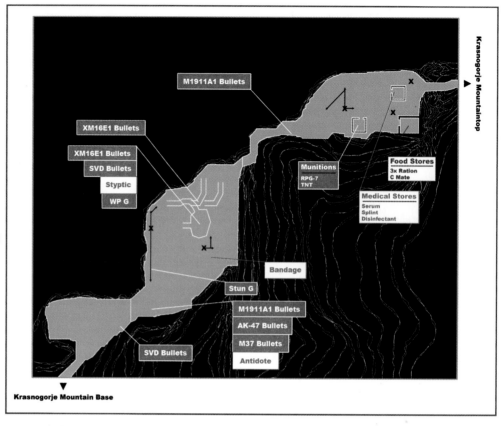

Krasnogorje Mountaintop

M1911A1 Bullets

XM16E1 Bullets

XM16E1 Bullets

SVD Bullets

Styptic

WP G

Munitions
RPG-7
TNT

Food Stores
3x Ration
C Mate

Medical Stores
Serum
Splint
Disinfectant

Bandage

Stun G

M1911A1 Bullets

AK-47 Bullets

M37 Bullets

Antidote

SVD Bullets

Krasnogorje Mountain Base

Charge the Cliffs

To get the drop on the first guard, race into the area and proceed a few feet up the slope. Hide in an alcove to Snake's right, and wait for the guard on the level above to cross down in front of the alcove. Then you can grab him, interrogate him, or dispose of him by your favorite means.

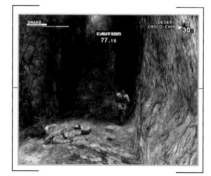

While collecting the many items to the right of the point where you attacked the guard, watch out for an Emperor Scorpion on the ground. Kill or capture the little beast, even though it does not supply much nourishment.

Variance in Security

Ascend the slope to the next level, and enter a small cave to find a Thai Cobra guarding several items. Then continue up the slopes, angling the camera upward and to the left to watch the guards on higher ledges.

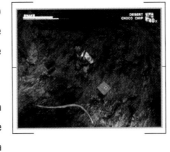

If you used TNT to destroy the helicopter parked at the Bolshaya Past Base, then no helicopter patrols this area. In a way, the area is more difficult without a circling Hind. This is because a

hovercraft guard takes the place of the Hind, and the guard is in a tricky location. Shooting the hovercraft guard is improbable until every other guard is subdued. If the hovercraft guard's vehicle explodes while guards remain in the area, the area breaks into alert. However, there is a way to sneak past the hovercraft guard.

HOLD YOUR FIRE

When you reach the anti-aircraft gun, avoid the temptation to mount it and blast the patrolling helicopter out of the air. Only a shoulder-mounted rocket launcher is capable of taking out a Hind in a single shot, and even then the explosion triggers a full-scale alert, including an air raid siren.

Sneaking Past the Hovercraft Guard

Find the alcove across from the anti-aircraft gun, where **XM16E1 Bullets** are located. Drop to your belly and crawl through the tunnel to a point where you can watch the hovercraft guard. The best time to crawl out and move is when the hovercraft guard is at

his lowest point, directly outside the tunnel exit. When the guard moves higher, his range of visibility is too great for Snake to move. Crawl just past his floating position, then stand and walk quietly to another crawlspace tunnel at the next corner between slopes. Quickly duck and crawl into this tunnel before the guard turns and rises in altitude. Continue through the tunnel and emerge to the other side.

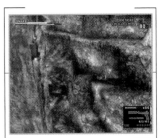

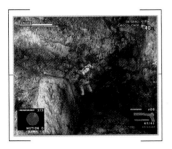

Now you must take down the guard patrolling the next rise without alerting the hovercraft guard. Press your back behind a boulder just below the guard's position so that the hovercraft guard is visible. Wait until the hovercraft guard descends in altitude and turns away, then dash up behind the guard in fatigues, take him out quietly, and hide behind the boulder atop the ridge. Wait for the hovercraft guard to rise and then descend, and make your way toward the right side of the screen. Move along this ledge, crawling and lying prone in plain sight when the guard raises his hovercraft.

Continue up to a sniper's perch where **M1911A1 Bullets** are located. With the hovercraft behind, it's impossible to snipe the guards in the next area. However, if a helicopter is patrolling then simply plug the patrols from up here and pass through the next area easily.

Outpost Assault

If a hovercraft guard is patrolling, use the lower ledge to sneak up to the outpost at the top of the area. Be sure to crawl or lie still when the hovercraft is raised in altitude. When the path widens out, stand and run behind the boulder on the lowest level. A guard that may not be visible right away emerges from behind the closest building on the right and patrols the lower area. When he moves nearby, step out to grab and silence him.

OPERATION
SNAKE
EATER

1 | ADAM AND EVA

2 | BEYOND THE FOREST BASE

3 | ESCAPE THE CAVE

4 | WAREHOUSE IN THE MANGROVE

5 | GRANINY GORKI LAB

6 | WOODLAND HUNT

7 | ALPINE ASCENT

8 | GROZNYJ GRAD

9 | GRAGOROD

10 | THE BOSS

Crawl up the lowest slope to a position just below the flat area. Watch the next-closest guard until he turns to face the left, then take him out with a suppressed weapon. The XM16E1 with a suppressor works great when it's set to single shot and aimed down the sights by holding L1.

That leaves only the guard positioned behind the upper left building. You can take him out with a CQC grab. Flank him by running around the building, and attack him from the side.

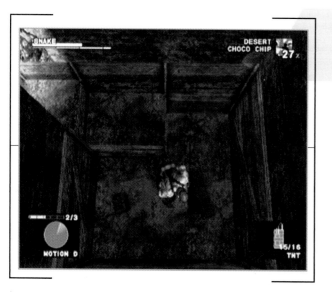

Inside the lowest building is the **RPG-7**, a weapon that is essential for the trials ahead. Collect the items in the other buildings and proceed to the next area. If you wish to blow up the provisions storehouse in this area, make sure to go back down the slope and take out the hovercraft guard first, if applicable.

ITEMS FOUND

Grenades

Smoke Grenades

M37 Bullets x16

AMMO

SVD Bullets x40

AMMO

RPG-7 Bullets x15

AMMO

TNT

Claymore

M63 Bullets x400

AMMO

Bandage

Ointment

Suture Kit

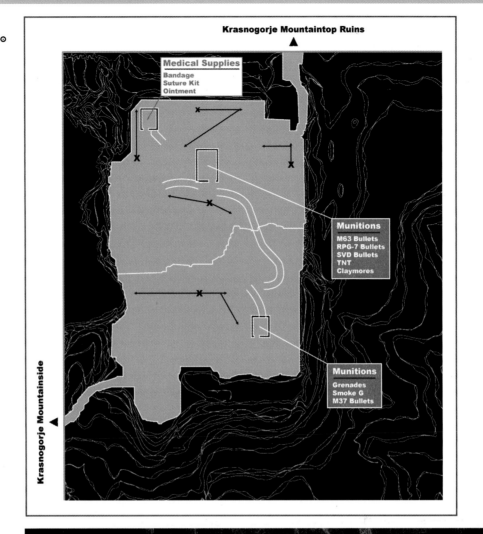

Krasnogorje Mountaintop Ruins

Medical Supplies
Bandage
Suture Kit
Ointment

Munitions
M63 Bullets
RPG-7 Bullets
SVD Bullets
TNT
Claymores

Krasnogorje Mountainside

Munitions
Grenades
Smoke G
M37 Bullets

Sniping

A helicopter definitely patrols this area. Because the aircraft is incapable of sighting Snake or sounding the alarm, Move when the chopper buzzes past to hide the sound of Snake's footsteps.

Hide behind the crates stacked near the entrance, wait for the closest guard to patrol nearby and turn his back, then run out and press the CQC button 🔘 to grab him. Hide the body if you like, and then return to the crates. Use the Dragunov to snipe the three guards patrolling near each of the anti-aircraft guns high up. Mask the sound of your weapon by firing as the helicopter passes overhead.

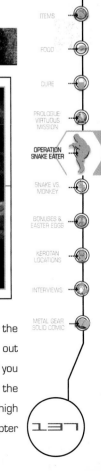

Trench Patrol

The last remaining guard patrols the middle trench in the circuit that runs back and forth down the slope. Ascend to a hiding point behind the brick wall. Drop into the trench, move just south of the corner, and lie flat on the ground. Wait for the guard to check the corner and turn, then attack him from behind. Collect the **provisions** and **ammunition** contained in the buildings in this area. Finally, go to the northeast building to meet EVA.

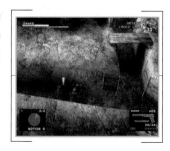

KRASNOGORJE MOUNTAINTOP: BEHIND RUINS

ITEMS FOUND

None

Overlooking Grozynj Grad

Standing at the edge overlooking Grozynj Grad, it is possible to spot a few guards patrolling areas in the base below. By all means, watch their patterns of movement to get a head start on infiltrating the fortress. However, avoid the temptation to take out any guards or exploding barrels with the sniper rifle. An air raid alarm sounds instantly, and Hind helicopters fly directly toward your position and attack with rockets.

KRAS MOUNTAINTOP RUINS

ITEMS FOUND

Instant Noodles (2 qty.)

XM16E1 Bullets x80

AMMO

Claymore

SVD Bullets x40

AMMO

M1911A1 Bullets x21

AMMO

AK-47 Bullets x120

AMMO

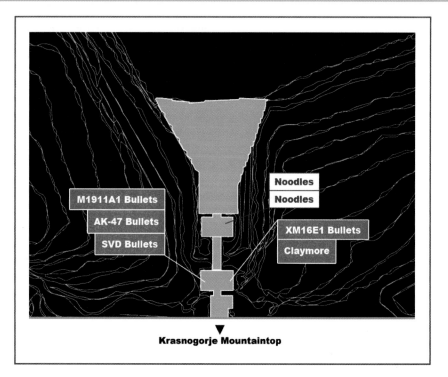

EVA's Meeting Point

After the cinematic, go back inside the building to the south of the ledge where the previous scene took place. Two packs of **Instant Noodles** rest by the door. Descend the steps to the bedroom to find other items under the bed, including **SVD Bullets**.

KRASNOGORJE MOUNTAINTOP

ITEMS FOUND

None (Previous items may still be available.)

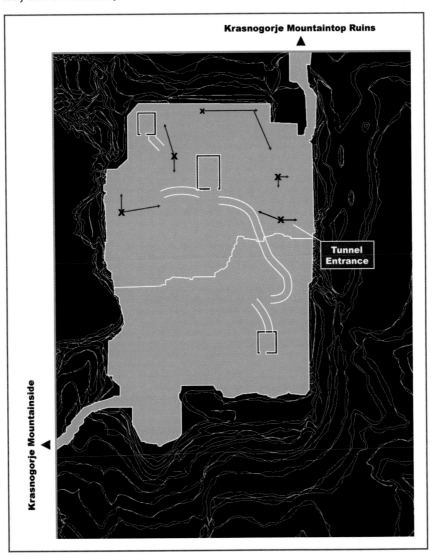

Krasnogorje Mountaintop Ruins

Tunnel Entrance

Krasnogorje Mountainside

INTRODUCTION

CHARACTERS

SYSTEM

WEAPONS

ITEMS

FOOD

CURE

PROLOGUE, VIRTUOUS MISSION

OPERATION SNAKE EATER

SNAKE VS. MONKEY

BONUSES & EASTER EGGS

KEROTAN LOCATIONS

INTERVIEWS

METAL GEAR SOLID COMIC

Retaking the Base

Additional guards patrolling near the anti-aircraft guns carry flamethrowers, and many guard routes have changed. The red door that **Key B** unlocks is almost directly south of the shack where Snake and EVA met up. Avoid detection and reduce game time by taking out only the guards standing between you and the door.

HUMAN TORCH

Shoot the flamethrower guard to the south near the anti-gun. However, be careful to shoot him in the head and not in the fuel tank he carries. If the guard bursts into flames and dies a screaming death, other guards certainly will be alerted.

Climb over the ridge, drop down, and take out the guard on the ledge below with a CQC grab from behind. Drop down another level and go through the red door with the key from EVA.

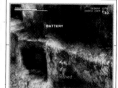

GROZYNJ GRAD UNDERGROUND TUNNEL

ITEMS FOUND

Grenades

M37 Bullets x16

AMMO

M1911A1 Bullets x 21

AMMO

XM16E1 Bullets x80

AMMO

Bandage

Ointment

Mk22 Bullets x24

AMMO

AK-47 Bullets x120

AMMO

Battery

BATT

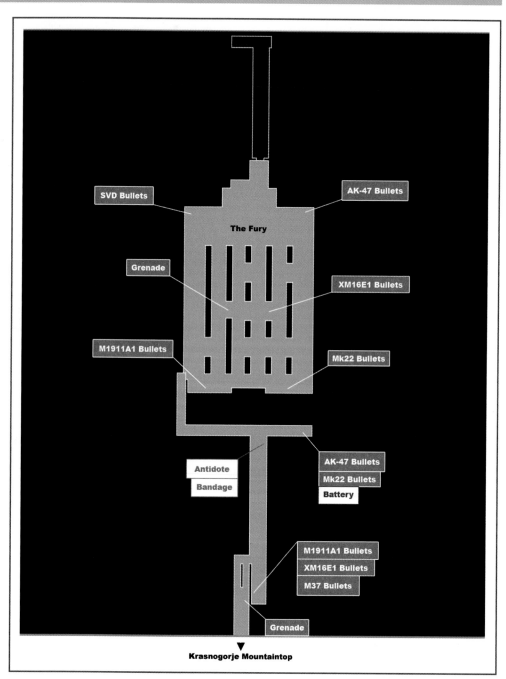

SVD Bullets

AK-47 Bullets

The Fury

Grenade

XM16E1 Bullets

M1911A1 Bullets

Mk22 Bullets

Antidote
Bandage

AK-47 Bullets
Mk22 Bullets
Battery

M1911A1 Bullets
XM16E1 Bullets
M37 Bullets

Grenade

▼
Krasnogorje Mountaintop

Descend the stairs to the bottom level. Starting with the **Grenades** in the corner below the stairs, work your way inward, collecting the items listed above. Follow the corridor out to a balcony overlooking a chasm, then head around the west side to a ladder. Drop to the level below to encounter The Fury.

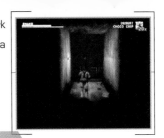

THE FURY

BATTLE-SPECIFIC ITEMS

SVD Bullet x120	M1911A1 Bullets x21	Mk22 Bullets x24	AK-47 Bullets
AMMO	AMMO	AMMO	AMMO
Russian Glowcaps	**Grenades**	XM16E1 Bullets x120	
		AMMO	

NON-LETHAL ALTERNATIVE

The Mk22 can be used exclusively during the battle against The Fury to deplete his Stamina in lieu of his Life gauge. Follow the same tactics outlined in the strategy but refrain from using more lethal weaponry. The **Fire Camouflage** can be found in the tunnel leading away from the battle after the victory cinematic.

Due to the weight of his spacesuit, The Fury plods slowly through the corridors looking for Snake. Use the Directional Microphone to listen for his heavy footsteps, which give away his location. Then lie on the raised north platform and snipe him with the Dragunov. Fire three or four shots at his head.

After giving your position away, stand up and get on the move. The Fury engages his rocket thrusters to pursue, but once he lands he is slow to turn. Run south in the area, and then north up another corridor. Avoid lingering near the south edge, because one of The Fury's goals in life is knock Snake off this ledge for an instant death. The idea is to stay away from the The Fury and attack from a great distance.

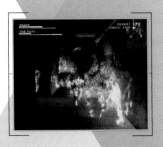

If you fail to outrun the flames, perform dive rolls to extinguish the fire on Snake's body. Treat burn wounds immediately so that your Health can recover while you set up your next sniper trap for The Fury.

If through your sniper scope you spot some exploding barrels near The Fury, shoot them to cause spaceboy some extra trouble.

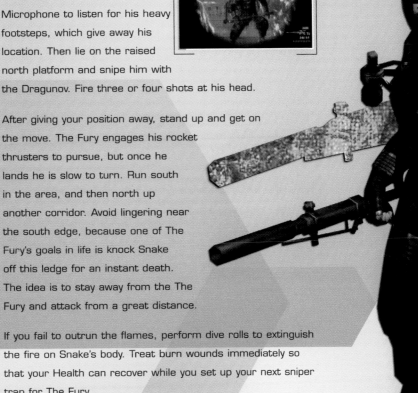

8 | MISSION OBJECTIVE EIGHT:
GROZNYJ GRAD

Finally, Snake penetrates Colonel Volgin's highly secured fortress of Groznyj Grad, the "Dreaded City." Security is tighter and more aware than in any area previously explored, and Snake's camouflage is weak throughout all areas. Snake enters the fortress through a maintenance hatch in the southwest quadrant. He must somehow penetrate the Weapons Lab's East Wing and locate Major Raikov. Once Snake identifies Raikov, he must follow the Major to a secluded location, overpower him, and steal his uniform. Wearing this convincing disguise, Snake should be able to fool the security guards posted at the entrance to the Weapons Lab's West Wing, where Doctor Sokolov is being held captive.

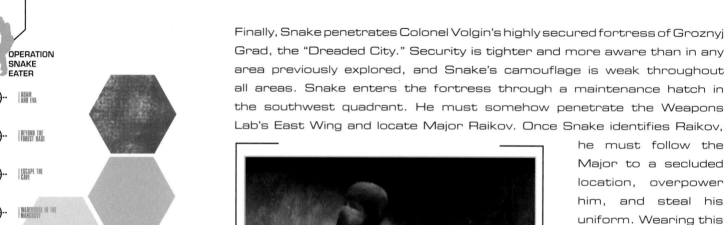

FOOD LIST: GROZNYJ GRAD

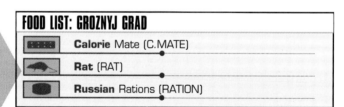

	Calorie Mate (C.MATE)
	Rat (RAT)
	Russian Rations (RATION)

GROZNYJ GRAD UNDERGROUND TUNNEL

ITEMS FOUND

Disinfectant

Mk22 Bullet x24

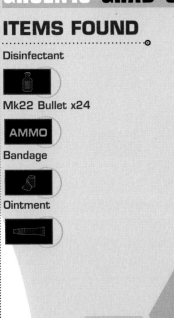

Bandage

Ointment

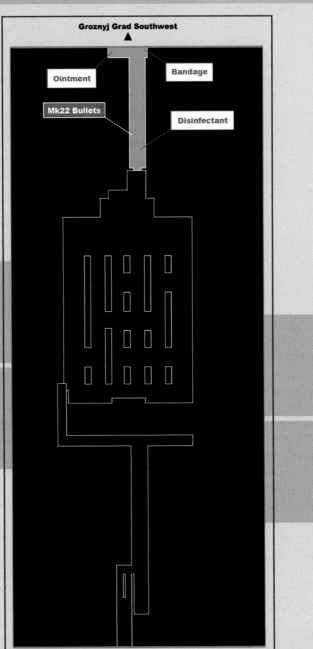

Groznyj Grad Southwest ▲

Ointment

Bandage

Mk22 Bullets

Disinfectant

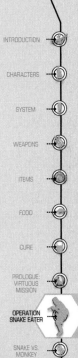

Below the Fortress

Proceed up the corridor from the collapsed wall and climb the ladder. Be sure to poach the rats before climbing up, because there are miniscule food resources in the fortress quadrants and interior areas. Groznyj Grad security is so tight that constant pest extermination is a major priority of all security staff.

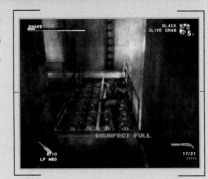

GROZNYJ GRAD SOUTHWEST

ITEMS FOUND

XM16E1 Bullets x80 (2 qty.)

Smoke Grenades (SMOKE G)

Grenades

M1911A1 Bullets x21

Mk22 Bullets x24

SVD Bullets x40

Styptic

Disinfectant

Bandage

Chaff Grenades (CHAFF G)

M1911A1 Suppressor (SP/M1911A1)

OPERATION
SNAKE
EATER

1 | ADAM AND EVA
2 | BEYOND THE FOREST BASE
3 | ESCAPE THE CAVE
4 | WAREHOUSE IN THE MANGROVE
5 | GRANINY GORKI LAB
6 | WOODLAND HUNT
7 | ALPINE ASCENT
8 | **GROZNYJ GRAD**
9 | SHAGOHOD
10 | THE BOSS

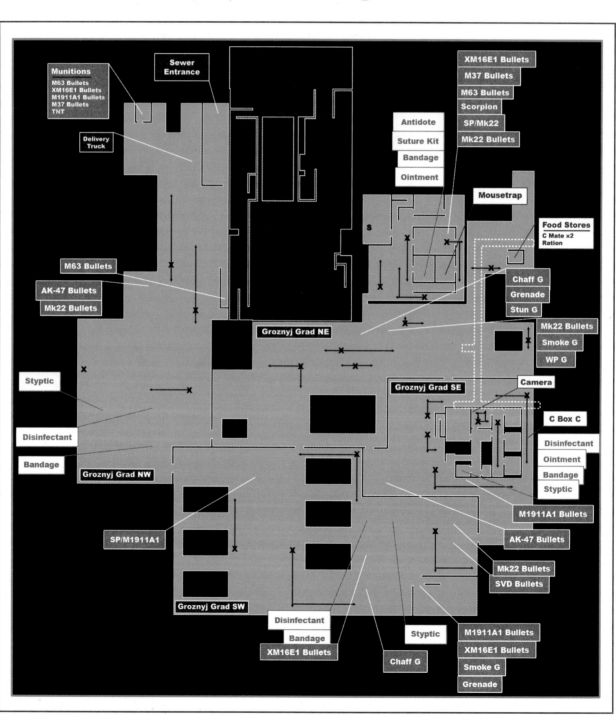

GROZNYJ GRAD SOUTHWEST

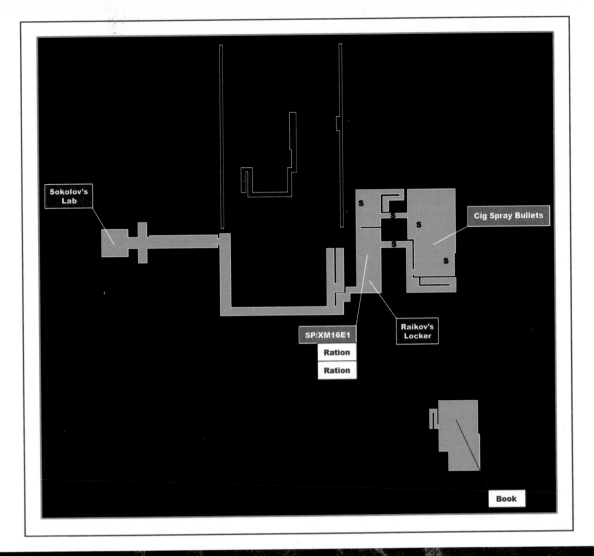

Sokolov's Lab

Cig Spray Bullets

SP/XM16E1

Ration

Ration

Raikov's Locker

S

Book

INTRODUCTION

CHARACTERS

SYSTEM

WEAPONS

ITEMS

FOOD

CURE

PROLOGUE: VIRTUOUS MISSION

OPERATION SNAKE EATER

SNAKE VS. MONKEY

BONUSES & EASTER EGGS

KEROTAN LOCATIONS

INTERVIEWS

METAL GEAR SOLID COMIC

Getting into the Yard

Ignore the items under the platform to the left of Snake's hiding spot, and focus on the guard patrolling the aisle between the nearby cargo containers. Set the XM16E1 with suppressor to single fire, and take out the guard from Snake's initial position. Hold L1 while aiming to sight down the barrel, and aim for the guard's head. This way, he is less likely to discover you when you collect the multiple items under the platform. Scattered **medical supplies** and **ammo** are also hidden under many of the cargo containers parked in this area.

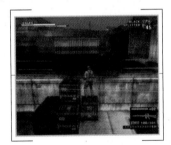 

Proceeding in Grozynj Grad

Groznyj Grad's yards are wide-open spaces where Snake has severe trouble hiding in plain sight, even with decent camouflage. The best he can do is equip the Splitter Camo and Face Paint, and crawl on his belly through every area until all guards are neutralized.

Speaking of guards, the best method of passing through zones without triggering an alert is to snipe all the guards from a distance with the suppressed XM16E1 set to single fire. Hold **L1** to aim down the barrel and also to gain a slight zoom on your target. Once all the guards and patrol dogs are eradicated, Snake can then blow up the food storage house and munitions depot. Then it's time to find a way to enter the Weapons Lab's East Wing.

Taking Down the Southwest

Crawl to the bottom corner of the northwest trailer and equip the suppressed XM16E1. Look northwest to spot a guard patrolling around the hangar building, and take him out by aiming down the barrel.

Move quietly to the southeast corner of the lowest hangar in the aisle's backside. Corner peek to see the status of the guards patrolling around the open-topped personnel truck. When you're able, crawl across the ground heading west, and creep under the truck. Continue belly creeping up to the front end of the vehicle. From this vantage point, use the suppressed XM16E1

to take out the two guards patrolling both sides of the roadway between the hangars. Do not overlook the **M1911A1 Suppressor** located on the armored transport parked just south of the north exit.

With the northwestern quad now firmly under your control, there are options as to how to proceed. You can either explore all four outer areas of Groznyj Grad and the detention facility to the east, or you can opt for a more direct route with less enemy contact by trying to make your way into the Weapons Lab's East Wing. Doors on the north and west walls lead to other areas. And you can crawl through a small hole in the east wall to reach the southeast quadrant, where the detention facility is located.

While this walkthrough explores the details of all areas, it is not necessary to navigate them all. In fact, there is less likelihood of detection when you take the more direct route.

Entering the Weapons Lab

Snake has two possible ways to enter the Weapons Lab's East Wing. One choice is to proceed north through the northeast quad and locate a small, orange door just to the right of the massive hangar doors.

A less direct route is to infiltrate the northwest quadrant and make your way north to a truck parked near the munitions depot. Climb into the back of the truck unseen and equip Cardboard Box A, which you procured way back in Rassvet. When a guard sees the box marked "Weapons Lab: East Wing," he drives off in the truck and delivers the box to one of the storage rooms in the East Wing. Snake is then inside the facility. Naturally, this option is not available if you overlooked Cardboard Box A at Rassvet.

GROZNYJ GRAD SOUTHEAST

ITEMS FOUND

M1911A1 Bullets x21

AMMO

Book

Cardboard Box C

Entering from the Southwest Quad

When entering from the crawl hole between the southwest and southeast quads, stay on your stomach and look north. Use the Motion Detector to help view the approach of a guard that patrols the south side of the detention building. Use the M1911A1 or Mk22 to take him down as he passes.

Grab the **M1911A1 Bullets** located near the stack of crates, and creep up to the southwest corner of the building. Peek around the corner and watch the patrol route of the guard watching the front of the building. When his back is turned, Snake can easily slip inside the detention center.

LEAVE THAT BOX ALONE!

As indicated on the map above, Cardboard Box C is located in the alleyway east of the detention center. Avoid acquiring the item at this time; if you take it now, you will not be able to obtain the item later...should you happen to be detained for a brief period.

Other Routes In

If you infiltrate this area from the northeast quad, enter via the southwest crawl hole and not the eastern door. If Snake steps through the eastern door in the north wall, two guards spot him almost instantaneously. Entering from the west, avoid detection by using the XM16E1 to take out the guards patrolling near the woodpile and along the south side of the detention building.

A series of storm drain ducts runs between the northeast and southeast quads. In the northeast quad's northeast corner, enter the storm drains via the open hatch on the provisions storehouse's north side. Crawl south, killing Rats for sustenance. Exit the duct via the opening on the north side of the prison building. Quickly take down the two guards patrolling to the north and east before you're detected.

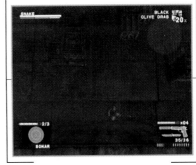

INTRODUCTION

CHARACTERS

SYSTEM

WEAPONS

ITEMS

FOOD

CURE

PROLOGUE
VIRTUOUS
MISSION

OPERATION
SNAKE EATER

SNAKE VS
MONKEY

BONUSES &
EASTER EGGS

KEROTAN
LOCATIONS

INTERVIEWS

METAL GEAR
SOLID COMIC

Exiting

To proceed to the northeast quad without being detected, climb the ladder on the south side of the building. From the north edge of the rooftop, look down and quietly snipe the guard below. Then take out the guard patrolling near the woodpile to the west. The western crawl hole into the northeast quadrant is the safest and least visible route into the area.

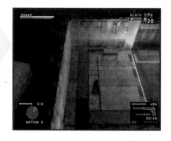

TREAD LIGHTLY!

When you're moving along the east wall, walk quietly to avoid detection by the guard posted on the other side of the wall. If Snake's footsteps are heard, the guard begins making his way to the door in the north wall. If he continues to hear sounds from within southeast quad, he eventually enters to investigate.

GROZNYJ GRAD TORTURE ROOM

ITEMS FOUND

Disinfectant

Styptic

Bandage

Ointment

Suture Kit

Camera

A Place of Obvious Sadism

Change into Olive Drab Camouflage and crawl as often as possible to avoid detection by the two guards currently posted in this area. Head south from the entrance, and enter the west door to find a bedroom full of **medical supplies**.

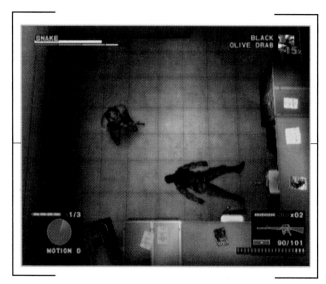

Exit the bedroom quietly, and crawl up the east side of the corridor to the corner. Through the bars on the window, snipe the guard inside the office with a headshot. Open the office door quietly by pressing the Action button, and collect the **Camera** in the north corner of the room. There are no other items in this area, so you can ignore the guard patrolling in front of the cells.

GROZNYJ GRAD NORTHEAST

ITEMS FOUND

Stun Grenades

Grenades

Chaff Grenades (CHAFF G)

Mk22 Bullet x24

Smoke Grenades (SMOKE G)

White Phosphorus Grenades (WP G)

Calorie Mate (C.MATE)(2 qty.)

Russian Ration

The Guards Around the Bunker

The Weapons Lab East Wing's entrance is an orange door partially hidden behind a large crate to the right of the massive hangar doors. To reach this door, you must take down several patrolling guards without letting them see each other fall. First, neutralize the two guards patrolling on either side of the area's south bunker, depending on your route of ingress.

You can easily take out the guard patrolling east of the bunker by using CQC grabbing tactics or a bullet in the back of his head. Just be sure to take him down as he leaves the south point of his route and is headed north up the alley.

The guard that checks the boxes stacked west of the bunker is trickier. The best method to deal with him seems to be lying flat at the southwest corner of the bunker and sniping him with the XM16E1 as he rounds the corner of the middle crate stack.

Guard by the Lab Entrance

One guard patrols the area around the armored cars parked just below the lab entrance. If you want to sneak straight into the lab without hesitation, then there really is no need to take him out. But if you intend to work your way northeast and take out the food storehouse located there, then eliminate this guard for safety. Also kill him if you want the freedom to jump into the armored transport vehicles to obtain numerous **grenades** and **ammunition** located there.

Destroying the Provisions Storehouse

More guards patrol near the crates and the bunker to the east. Remove them with a little XM16E1 sniping. The spotlights searching the path leading north cannot detect Snake, but they can reduce his camouflage enough to allow the guards to spot him easily. Shoot out the spotlight near the bunker. Then lie flat in the darkness you have created to snipe the guard patrolling in front of the food storage building.

INTRODUCTION

CHARACTERS

SYSTEM

WEAPONS

ITEMS

FOOD

CURE

PROLOGUE VIRTUOUS MISSION

OPERATION SNAKE EATER

SNAKE VS MONKEY

BONUSES & EASTER EGGS

KEROTAN LOCATIONS

INTERVIEWS

METAL GEAR SOLID COMIC

Collect the **Calorie Mates** and a **Russian Ration** in the storehouse, and set some TNT charges to blow the building. Hunger now drives the guards throughout Groznyj Grad to reveal their locations; it's easy to distract them by tossing food and rations into their paths. Hungry guards eat rotten and poisonous foods to their own detriment.

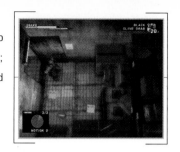

GROZNYJ GRAD NORTHWEST

ITEMS FOUND

Disinfectant 🫙	Mk22 Bullets x24 (2 qty.) AMMO	M63 Bullets x400 AMMO	TNT 🧰
Styptic 💉	AK-47 Bullets x120 AMMO	M1911A1 Bullets x21 AMMO	
Bandage 🧻	XM16E1 Bullets x80 AMMO	M37 Bullets x16 AMMO	

A Long Stretch North

The best way to enter this area is via the door between the northeast and northwest quadrants. With an armored truck parked just a foot away, Snake can easily drop to the ground and crawl under the truck without being noticed. The south entrance allows Snake to hide behind some boxes, but moving northward unseen is more difficult.

This area is actually quite easy to traverse. Simply run north along the east wall when guards are not looking. A patrol dog sleeps on an area surrounded by metal plates, but as long as you avoid stepping loudly on the metal you can easily bypass him.

However, the guard patrolling north-to-south near the sleeping dog's location is problematic. You must take him

SNAKE'S BEST FRIEND?

If you attempt to take the guard at close range or fire even a suppressed weapon anywhere near the dog, the animal awakens and leaps on you in a second.

The Ammo Dump

The guard patrolling near the munitions dump can be easily taken down by crawling under the parked truck and sniping him from the front end. Once all the guards in the north area are downed, enter the munitions dump and stock up on all sorts of **ammo** contained therein. Plant TNT charges and blow the munitions dump to reduce the enemy's combat capabilities. If guards remain in the south area, a Caution signal occurs and the guards come to check out the problem. Snipe them as they come your way, or jump into the nearby truck to hitch a ride.

Truck Ride

Climb into the back of the truck parked a few yards southeast of the ammo depot, and equip Cardboard Box A. A guard immediately notices the location marked on the box, and decides to return it to its proper area. Snake buys a ticket directly inside the Weapons Lab's East Wing.

GROZNYJ GRAD WEAPONS LAB: EAST WING

ITEMS FOUND

Suture Kit

Ointment

Antidote

Bandage

Book

M63 Bullets x400
AMMO

M37 Bullets x16
AMMO

XM16E1 Bullets x80
AMMO

Mk22 Suppressor (SP/Mk22)

Scorpion Sub Machinegun (SCORPION)

Russian Ration (2 qty.)

XM16E1 Suppressor (SP/XM16E1)

Cigar Spray-Bullets x5
AMMO

Disguised Inside the Weapons Lab

Whether you entered the area by hook or by crook, equip the Scientist Camouflage (and no face paint) for another spy mission in an enemy facility. Avoid the scientists in the northwest library on the first floor, as well as the team working in the lab on the second level.

Raikov's Path

the Colonel is weak against water.

Major Raikov's starting point is inside the weapons lab area on the upper level. Exiting there, he moves down the south stairs and then heads north up the center to the stairs at the north end. Ascending the other stairs, he moves through the file room south into the locker room. He basically waits there until you sneak up behind him—grab him and drag him south to the lockers.

151

INTRODUCTION

CHARACTERS

SYSTEM

WEAPONS

ITEMS

FOOD

CURE

PROLOGUE VIRTUOUS MISSION

OPERATION SNAKE EATER

SNAKE VS MONKEY

BONUSES & EASTER EGGS

KEROTAN LOCATIONS

INTERVIEWS

METAL GEAR SOLID COMIC

When you sneak up behind Raikov in the locker room, first check the area for a scientist that sometimes pokes around in this room. Because the scientist normally stands north behind Raikov, use a Cigar Gas-Spray on him first and then take down the Major.

IS THIS STALL TAKEN?

>> If an alert is sounded, Raikov hides in the bathroom stall in the northeast part of the lower level. If you enter his area, he may issue orders or punch you, motivated by his own sadistic impulses. Maintain your disguise around the Major until he is in the upstairs locker room and prime for a takedown.

Disguised As Raikov

After Snake secures Raikov in a locker, enter the Survival Viewer and equip the Mask and the Officer Camouflage. Dressed as Raikov, Snake can now go anywhere and be respected as a high-ranking officer. This means you can go downstairs and walk directly into the locked area containing **ammo** and the **Scorpion** sub machinegun.

Scientists ignore Raikov completely, but guards pause and salute. When a guard salutes, face him and press the Action button ⚠ to return the salute. The soldier continues to hold the salute until you leave his area. Failure to return a salute or holding a salute for too long causes guards to become suspicious.

Another Rescue Failed

When you're ready to proceed, head through the southwest door near the locker room on the upper level. Move through the next two corridors toward the sentries posted at the entrance to the West Wing. The sentries allow "Major Raikov" to pass into the area where Sokolov is held.

GROZNYJ GRAD TORTURE ROOM

ITEMS FOUND

Fork

Prison Breakout

Following some rather unfortunate events, Snake finds himself naked in a jail cell near the Torture Room area. A lone, inept guard patrols the corridor outside. Snake must find a way to outsmart the guard and break out of the detention area.

A **Fork** has been left in the lower corner of the cell. When the Fork is used to attack animals or other food sources, such as the Rat scurrying around the cell, Snake eats the rat instantly. The Fork can also be used to attack in a fashion similar to the Survival Knife.

Escape the Cell

The guard has a cold and a stomach virus, so Snake cannot remain here for very long without catching these ailments. The following paragraphs summarize your options for escape. Note that our preferred method is described under the next heading, "The Best Escape Method."

Although no red appears in Snake's health bar, open the Cure screen to view his status. A Fake Death Pill is lodged in Snake's leg. Dig it out with the Fork to obtain the pill. Additionally, Ocelot stabbed a transmitter into Snake's back during the scene. Remove the transmitter unless you wish for the guards to follow your every movement for the rest of the game.

Option 1: When the guard is nearby, use the Fake Death Pill to collapse. Although the continue screen appears, the item window can still be opened and you can use items. When the guard notices that Snake is "dead" and opens the cell door, take the Revival Pill implanted in Snake's tooth and overpower the guard.

Option 2: If you pressed R1 at a certain moment during the previous scenes, you may have glimpsed a bizarre individual waving a card bearing a number in the air. Dial that frequency on the radio to open the jail cell door. The guard rushes into the cell, and CQC is not available to Snake without the Survival Knife. Take him to the ground with punches or fork him to death.

With either of the two methods listed above, keep in mind that, unless Snake kills the guard, an alert is triggered that lasts throughout Groznyj Grad as Snake tries to escape.

Option 3: The guard tosses various food items into the cell after he comes out of his post across the hall. Position Snake in front of the window through which the guard throws the items, and toss the items out of Snake's cell in First Person View. When the guard spots the items on the ground, he consumes them. If he consumes rotten food, his stomach seizes up and he is driven to the bathroom. Now you can open the cell door by dialing the radio frequency as described above. Follow the guard into the restroom down the hall and take him out on the can—if you enjoy that kind of thing.

While you're incarcerated, there are several ways to mess with the guard's mind. When the guard patrols other areas, crawl under the bed and hide. At first, the guard freaks out when he cannot see Snake in his cell, but he then crouches and spots Snake under the bed. Performing any actions in the cell, such as punches or dive rolls, elicits an almost mocking response. Wherever the guard is patrolling, you can always draw him back to the cell and aggravate him by pressing your back against the bars and knocking [press [O]].

INTRODUCTION

CHARACTERS

SYSTEM

WEAPONS

ITEMS

FOOD

CURE

PROLOGUE, VIRTUOUS MISSION

OPERATION SNAKE EATER

SNAKE VS. MONKEY

BONUSES & EASTER EGGS

KEROTAN LOCATIONS

INTERVIEWS

METAL GEAR SOLID COMIC

The Best Escape Method

Another method is far more complex, but it allows you to view additional cinemas. Toss the food items into the corridor as described above. After the guard consumes three or four items, an additional scene between the guard and Snake occurs. During the scene, press [R1] when the icon appears to view the backside of the guard's photo. The radio frequency that opens the jail cell door is written on the back of the picture. This scene is additionally beneficial because the guard unknowingly passes Snake his Cigar Gas-Spray weapon.

After the scene, the guard stands outside the cell, staring in. Move close to the bars and use the Cigar Gas-Spray to knock him out. Then open the cell door using the radio frequency. Unlike other enemies and NPCs, the guard does not stay unconscious long. Either fork him until he's dead or beat him unconscious the next time he rises. You cwan shake the guard (if he's only unconscious) to obtain **Smoke Grenades** and **Instant Noodles**.

Sneaking Out of Groznyj Grad

With the Cigar Gas-Spray, Snake can now exit the building and knock out the guards surrounding the detention building. Without the spray, Snake must sneak from area to area unseen, which is extremely difficult. Be doubly sure to climb the ladder up to the rooftop, and knock out the new guard that keeps lookout from above. Remember to obtain the Cardboard Box C from behind the prison building. Also note that this item is available only in the back alley if you did not collect it previously. Other items are not available in their usual spots at this time, so don't waste time scavenging.

Use the crawl hole west of the prison building door to crawl through to the northeast area. Move quietly west, wait for the guard who patrols near the crates to come and go, and then dash to the western door that leads to the northwest area.

Make your way along the east wall to the north part of the area, being careful to tiptoe past the dozing patrol hound. Follow the wall directly north to an enclosed area. Crawl under the pipes to an open hatch.

ITEMS FOUND

Life Medicine (LF MED)

SAA Bullets x18 (2 qty.)

Russian Ration (2 qty.)

Styptic

Instant Noodles (NOODLES)

Wading in Muck

After a call from EVA, descend the stairs and collect the **Life Medicine**, **SAA Bullets** and **Russian Ration** before continuing north. Equip Snake with the SAA to protect him against patrol dogs throughout the sewers. Because Snake's backpack is still missing, throw out lesser food to obtain the better food sources in the area.

Proceed up the west wall of the tunnel until you reach a crawl hole. Creep through the hole and continue north until bars block the path. Then crawl back to the center tunnel, and jump into a deep section of water to obtain the remaining items in the list above.

Continue north, using the SAA to kill dogs that attack, and keep moving toward the sunlight at the end of the tunnel to escape Groznyj Grad.

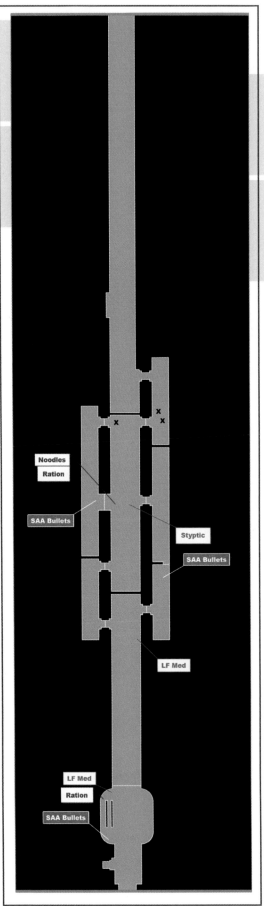

Noodles
Ration
SAA Bullets
Styptic
SAA Bullets
LF Med
LF Med
Ration
SAA Bullets

THE SORROW

BATTLE-SPECIFIC ITEMS

None

This "battle of wills" is unique in that there is no way to damage the boss. The encounter is mainly event driven, and your objective is to wade upstream continuously.

Every guard, boss and NPC you have killed appears during the battle. Therefore, this battle ostensibly will be longer or shorter depending on how many enemies you snuffed out. If the bosses are the only enemies you killed, then they appear one after another and that is all. If your body count is high, this event could prove to be quite a time-eater. Notice that The End's parrot appears if you blasted it during the previous boss fight.

Staggering past Snake, some of them notice his presence and attempt to retaliate from the spirit world. If a ghost manages to touch Snake, a small amount of his health is drained. Move left and right in the stream to outmaneuver ghosts and keep them from touching you. Use the SAA to shoot ghosts that get too close. While there is no way to kill a ghost, the blast serves as a disruption that causes the creature to pause. Use the opportunity to continue upstream out of harm's way.

Occasionally The Sorrow emits a translucent tendril in Snake's direction with the intent of knocking him down. The attack itself inflicts no damage, but if Snake is knocked down in an area crowded by the dead, then he may lose several wisps of life while rising. Do your best to walk around The Sorrow's tendrils as you outmaneuver the ghosts.

When Snake reaches the skeleton at the end of the stream, his remaining life is instantly drained and the continue screen appears. Do not be fooled; this is merely a ruse of The Sorrow. Open the item menu and use a Revive Pill to continue the game.

9 | MISSION OBJECTIVE NINE: SHAGOHOD

Although beaten, tortured and forced to make a desperate escape, Snake's resolve is only reaffirmed by the horrors he faced inside Groznyj Grad. After radio communication with EVA, he must proceed north along a stream to rendezvous with her at a waterfall. Ocelot Unit soldiers may be searching the falls area for him. Armed with only an SAA Colt Action Army revolver, Snake must make every shot count. After reuniting briefly with EVA, Snake reclaims his equipment and navigates through a tunnel back to Groznyj Grad. Following a much shorter infiltration route, Snake sneaks inside the Main Wing of the base. Somehow he must plant four C3 charges on the full tanks surrounding the Shagohod and destroy the monstrous weapon before Volgin can use it!

FOOD LIST: SHAGOHOD STAGE

	Maroon Shark (FISH B)
	Arowana (FISH C)
	Tree Frog (FROG B)
	Siberian Ink Cap (MUSHROOM C)
	Russian Glowcap (MUSHROOM E)
	Instant Noodles (NOODLES)
	Rat (RAT)
	Russian Ration (RATION)
	Vine Melon (VEGETABLE)

TIKHOGORNYJ

ITEMS FOUND

None

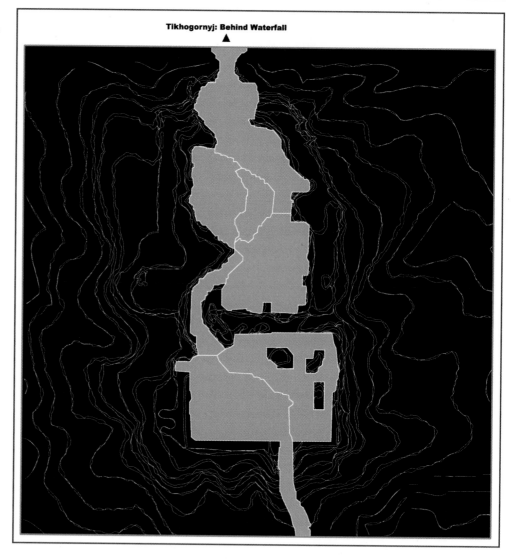

Tikhogornyj: Behind Waterfall

"Hunted" or "The Peaceful Woods"

If the transmitter was removed from Snake's body prior to this stage's opening, then Snake can proceed north toward the waterfall in peace. However, if the transmitter was never removed, Ocelot Unit soldiers continuously scour the gorgeous landscape, looking for Snake. Remove the transmitter as soon as possible. Hold L1 and aim the SAA at the soldiers' heads to kill them swiftly. Soldiers appear four at a time in the area near the waterfall as long as the transmitter remains lodged in Snake.

ITEMS FOUND

Disinfectant

M1911A1 Suppressor
(SP/M1911A1)

Styptic

Bandage

Mk22 Bullet x24

Cardboard Box B

M1911A1 Bullets x21

Mk22 Suppressor (SP/Mk22)

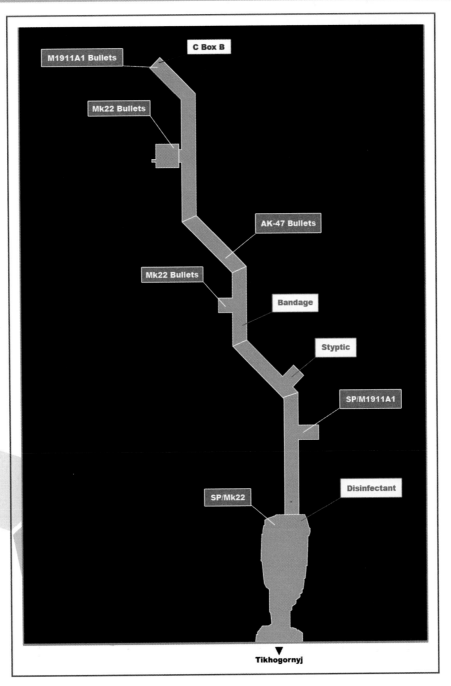

Reclaiming Equipment

At the waterfall, follow the path around the pond to the right side of the falls, and enter the cave behind the falls to meet EVA. She returns all of his equipment to him, and she hands over **C3** to use in Shagohod's hangar along with **Key C**, which unlocks the corridor door in Groznyj Grad's hangar area.

INTRODUCTION

CHARACTERS

SYSTEM

WEAPONS

ITEMS

FOOD

CURE

PROLOGUE,
VIRTUOUS
MISSION

OPERATION
SNAKE EATER

SNAKE VS.
MONKEY

BONUSES &
EASTER EGGS

KEROTAN
LOCATIONS

INTERVIEWS

METAL GEAR
SOLID COMIC

159

A Very Useful Box

Collect the **Mk22 Suppressor** and **Disinfectant** in the cave, and then proceed through the tunnel, collecting additional items along the way. When you arrive at a door, continue a little further up the corridor to obtain some **M1911A1 bullets** and **Cardboard Box C**. This box enables Snake to enter Groznyj Grad's Main Wing with little effort. Go through the door and climb the ladder.

SPIRIT CAMOUFLAGE

While equipping the proper camouflage, you might be surprised to see the Spirit Camouflage among the available options. This ghostly camo was awarded during the encounter with The Sorrow.

GROZNYJ GRAD NORTHWEST

ITEMS FOUND

None (Same items as previous stage)

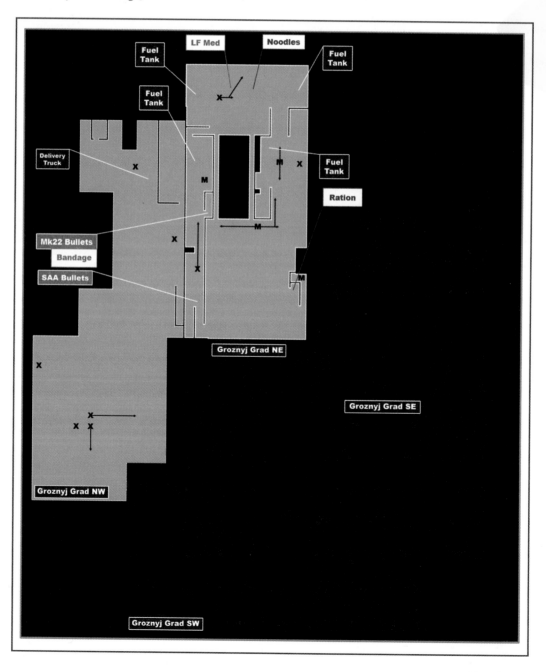

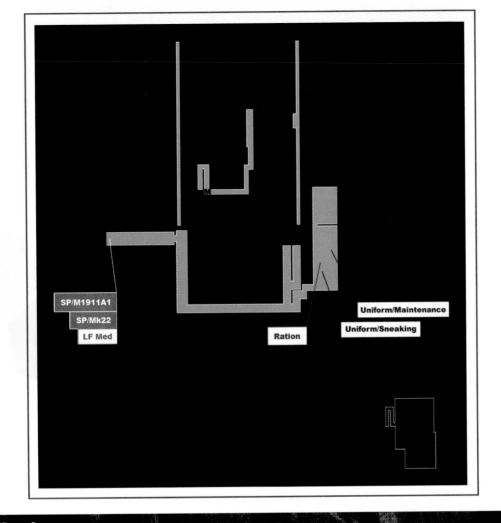

SP/M1911A1	
SP/Mk22	Uniform/Maintenance
LF Med	Uniform/Sneaking
	Ration

Greater Numbers

Additional soldiers patrol this area, including one guard that moves from tank to tank, checking under the treads. Navigating through this area becomes a little tricky and the threat of detection is slightly higher, but it's still possible to slip through unnoticed. Change back into the Splitter Camouflage and Face Paint to cloak yourself as much as possible. Move downward from Snake's initial hiding spot to the south wall, then head east to the door. Proceed north behind the armored truck transport. Following this wide path, Snake should be well out of the guards' sight range even though he runs in the open.

● DON'T MESS AROUND!

Due to increased troops patrolling every area, including a few performing some off-the-wall exercises, we recommend that you avoid exploring Grozynj Grad unless you badly need ammo or medical items that are in terribly short supply.

Get Back on the Truck

A guard posted on the nearby spotlight tower may spot Snake if he runs out in the open. Dash northward, hugging the east wall to avoid being seen. Upon reaching the corner behind a small stairway, crouch for a moment and check the position of the guard patrolling around the armored truck on the other side of the quad. If he is looking east, avoid moving until he turns and walks away.

Move onto the metallic area where the patrol dog is still dozing, drop to the ground, and crawl to avoid being seen or heard by the mutt. Crawl over to the cargo truck parked in the north section of the area, climb into the back, and equip Cardboard Box C for easy access to the Shagohod hangar.

GROZNYJ GRAD WEAPONS LAB: EAST WING

ITEMS FOUND

UNIFORM/SNEAKING

UNIFORM/MAINTENANCE

Snake Needs a New Pair of Shoes

Although Snake can easily infiltrate the Shagohod hangar, that doesn't mean he can move without being seen. The hangar's colors are like no other in the game, meaning Snake sticks out like a sore thumb no matter where he hides. Because the scientists are off duty today, Snake cannot rely on his usual disguise.

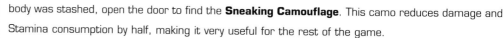

Either on your way through the building or after arriving in the hangar via cardboard box, head to the locker room on the second level of the East Wing to acquire new camouflage. Inside the locker where Raiden's...uh, *Raikov's* body was stashed, open the door to find the **Sneaking Camouflage**. This camo reduces damage and Stamina consumption by half, making it very useful for the rest of the game.

The items you previously found in this area have returned, just in case you wish to check the other lockers for items. The **Maintenance Camouflage** is in the second locker from the north, on the east side of the area. This uniform allows Snake to masquerade as one of the technicians currently working to prepare Shagohod for its final test.

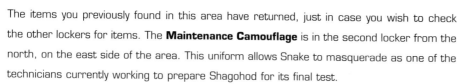

GROZNYJ GRAD WEAPONS LAB: WEST WING CORRIDOR

ITEMS FOUND

Life Medicine
(LF MED)

M1911A1 Suppressor
(SP/M1911A1)

XM16E1 Suppressor
(SP/XM16E1)

Discarded Items

Return to the crosswalk where Snake had to pose as Raikov to get past security. Someone has left several useful items at the west end of the corridor, including an always-useful **Life Medicine**.

GROZNYJ GRAD WEAPONS LAB: MAIN WING

ITEMS FOUND

SAA Bullets x18 (2 qty.)

Mk22 Bullets x24

Instant Noodles (NOODLES)

Russian Ration (RATION)

Life Medicine (LF MED)

Passing for a Tech

Wearing the Maintenance Camouflage and no face paint in the Shagohod's hangar, Snake can move unnoticed by the guards. Just avoid any hassles or beatings by trying not to bump into them. Maintenance workers, on the other hand, are a problem. Much like the scientists, all the technicians know each other and quickly recognize Snake as an impostor. The outcry they raise draws the attention of the guards. If ever a maintenance man is dangerously close to blowing your cover, quickly equip the Cigar Gas-Spray and tranquilize him. Otherwise, simply turn your back to him until he loses interest and walks away.

The only place where discovery might be a problem is where the maintenance man works very close to the fuel tank located directly west of the Shagohod. Be sure that the guard patrolling south of this location is not looking, and then tranquilize the technician before you apply the C3.

In all other cases, be sure that patrolling guards are not looking your direction when you attach C3 to the fuel tanks, or they trigger the alert status instantly. If guns are fired at the fuel tanks, it could result in an explosion that ends the game instantly. As with the TNT, press Snake's back against one end of each gas tank and press ⬤ to set the bomb. Set C3 charges on the four gas tanks, two on either side of the Shagohod.

CHECK UNDER THE TRUCKS

>> A Life Medicine and **Instant Noodles**, two powerful recovery aids, are hidden under the trucks parked at the north end of the hangar. In light of events about to occur, you cannot pass these up. Just be sure that no guards are looking when you lie prone and crawl under the trucks, or things could quickly get ugly.

INTRODUCTION

CHARACTERS

SYSTEM

WEAPONS

ITEMS

FOOD

CURE

PROLOGUE VIRTUOUS MISSION

OPERATION SNAKE EATER

SNAKE VS MONKEY

BONUSES & EASTER EGGS

KEROTAN LOCATIONS

INTERVIEWS

METAL GEAR SOLID COMIC

Volgin can be defeated using nothing but the Mk22. After each of his attacks, move into position behind him or off to his side, quickly equip the Mk22, and fire at him from the hip. Snake can often get in two hits before Volgin counters. Pick up the extra bullets from the northwest corner of the chamber to remain well armed. Snake acquires the invaluable **Cold War Camouflage** for his efforts.

VOLGIN

BATTLE-SPECIFIC ITEMS

XM16E1 Bullets x80	**AK-47 Bullets x120**
AMMO	AMMO
SAA Bullets x18	**M1911A1 Bullet x21**
AMMO	AMMO

First off, remove the Maintenance Camouflage so that Snake can equip weapons. Equip the M37, but only for a second. Equipping any weapon causes Volgin to prepare an electric attack in which he draws a bolt of lightning across the area. If the bolt contacts Snake, it delivers only a mild amount of shock damage. But if the bolt contacts Snake while he is equipped with a gun in hand, all the ammunition in the gun goes off, damaging Snake terribly.

Quickly equip and unequip the M37 to bait Volgin into performing an electric attack. Avoid his emission and run past him to face his back. Tap R2 again to equip the shotgun, and blast Volgin from behind. Quickly holster the weapon and run away before Volgin attempts a punching attack. This is one character you do not want to fight hand-to-hand. Repeat this strategy of baiting Volgin into performing his electric attack, and then run behind him to deliver a blast to his back.

When Volgin turns to draw energy from the electric panel in the corner, run up behind him and unload the shotgun into his back. That's what he gets for assuming too much of you. It should take only two or three shotgun blasts to his back to end the battle's first stage.

Whenever Volgin clasps both hands in the air, he is about to fire a rapid stream of bullets. To dodge his shots, run back and forth to Volgin's left or right. In the second half of the fight, Volgin gains a new attack in which he creates electric bolts between his hands and then fires bullets in all directions. This attack is simple to avoid simply by laying on the ground at an angle diagonal to Volgin. That is to say, if you and Volgin are facing each other head-on when he begins this attack, move a few feet left or right to a 45-degree angle to him and lie flat on the ground. Volgin's bullet attack should miss you completely.

Treat wounds as necessary so that your health continuously recharges. Volgin does a lot of posturing and electricity charging during the battle. Use the few seconds he allows to run to the other side of the area and take a knee.

Escape from Groznyj Grad

EVA and Snake jump on her motorcycle and attempt to escape. The amazing thing about this cinematic sequence is that you get to fire from the sidecar with unlimited ammo! Equip the M63 and blast the soldiers in all directions. Whenever EVA stops, enter First Person View and eliminate all the soldiers in the area. Release R1 whenever EVA continues driving, because you do not want to miss the chase sequences!

Barreling Down the Strip

As the action moves to the runway, equip the RPG-7 and use it to take out the majority of the motorcycle pursuers. Aim low toward the motorbikes' front wheels to blow the riders off their machines. As you aim, center the target motorcycle on your screen and then hold L1 to aim more accurately through the scope. The RPG fires a single rocket, and Snake reloads the weapon very slowly. Speed up the pace by double tapping R2 to perform a tactical reload after each shot.

Finally, the Shagohod itself plows through the last pursuers and tries to slam into the motorbike. Shoot the screw treads under the behemoth to slow it down. When Volgin fires rockets, toss a Chaff Grenade to confuse their tracking, and shoot them out of the sky with the M63.

Blowing the Bridge Struts

As the Shagohod plows across the bridge, look through the Dragunov's scope and find the charges EVA planted under the bridge. Thermal Goggles can help you locate them, but each charge bears a flashing red light that is hard to miss. Follow EVA's directions for aiming, and shoot the charge furthest out first. Then find the second charge in the scope and wait for EVA to give the order. A dangling beam swings back and forth in front of the second charge. When the beam swings away, fire!

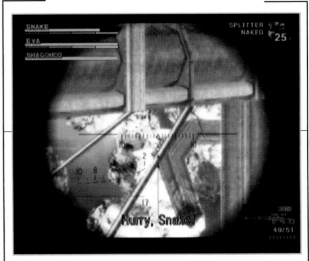

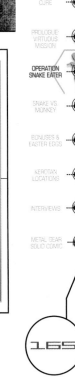

SHAGOHOD

SPECIFICATIONS

DESIGN:	Sololov / Granin Design Bureau
IN SERVICE:	Unknown
YEAR OF DEVELOPMENT:	1961
CREW:	2
COMBAT WEIGHT:	152.5 tons
OVERALL LENGTH:	22,800mm
HEIGHT:	8,200mm
WIDTH:	6,400mm

ARMAMENT

12.7-mm DShKM Heavy Machine Gun (300 rounds) x 2

12.7-mm DShKM AA Machine Gun (360 rounds) x 1

100-barrel Machine Gun pod x 1

9K112 Kobra Surface-to-Air-guided Missile x 6

SS-20 Saber-class nuclear missile x 1

Maximum speed: 80 kph

Range: 650 km

BATTLE-SPECIFIC ITEMS

None

EVA continues piloting the motorcycle in circles around the spinning Shagohod. Immobilize the machine by firing RPG-7 rockets at its treads. When Volgin complains that he cannot move, EVA then pilots the bike to the rear side of the Shagohod and stops. Aim for the damaged and smoking section at the back of the Shagohod's head, and fire one or two rockets. Use the scope to aim all of your shots, and use tactical reloads to prepare the weapon quickly, rather than waiting for Snake to do it manually. When the Shagohod fires a volley of missiles, quickly toss a Chaff Grenade to confuse their targeting, and switch to the M63 in an attempt to blow them from the sky.

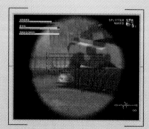
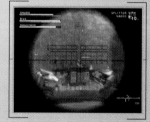

VOLGIN

BATTLE-SPECIFIC ITEMS

None

The final battle against the Shagohod begins with Volgin atop the metal hulk, chasing EVA around on her motorcycle. Run to the outside edge of the area and grab one of the mounted weapons. Fire a barrage of bullets with Volgin himself as your target. When the madman loses interest in EVA and comes after Snake, release the weapon and try to dodge roll out of the Shagohod's path.

Once Volgin's sights are trained on Snake, it's time to dodge a series of devastating attacks. Volgin fires two machine guns on the machine's front, which wave back and forth in consecutive arcs. Avoid this attack by running directly away from the Shagohod, even if it means dropping over the side of the cliff and hanging from the edge. At least the machineguns cannot hit you while you're hanging.

When the Shagohod's central rapid-fire flak gun emits a constant stream of fire, run to the left or right and don't stop for anything. Running in a circle around the Shagohod, Snake should be able to stay just a few steps ahead of the flak storm. So much running depletes quite a bit of Stamina, so eat when necessary.

Volgin may also fire missiles at Snake; start running and toss a Chaff Grenade to throw off the missiles' tracking. Continue running in a circle, and dive-roll as needed to avoid the explosions.

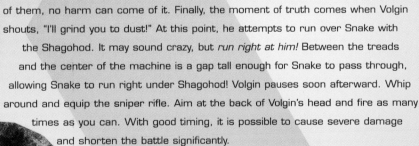

Volgin might repeat these attacks several times, but as long as you focus on dodging all of them, no harm can come of it. Finally, the moment of truth comes when Volgin shouts, "I'll grind you to dust!" At this point, he attempts to run over Snake with the Shagohod. It may sound crazy, but *run right at him!* Between the treads and the center of the machine is a gap tall enough for Snake to pass through, allowing Snake to run right under Shagohod! Volgin pauses soon afterward. Whip around and equip the sniper rifle. Aim at the back of Volgin's head and fire as many times as you can. With good timing, it is possible to cause severe damage and shorten the battle significantly.

Volgin then begins to chase EVA again. Man one of the turrets or machineguns and bring his focus back to Snake. Dodge all of the attacks and run under the Shagohod for another opportunity to snipe Volgin from of the world depends on it!

With the Shagohod destroyed, one objective remains. Snake must face the woman who trained him, raised him as a soldier, and then abandoned him. But first, Snake and EVA must escape yet more hounds from Groznyj Grad still nipping at their heels.

FOOD LIST: THE BOSS STAGE

Tree Frog (FROG B)	
Russian False Mango (FRUIT B)	
Siberian Ink Cap (MUSHROOM C)	
Russian Ration (RATION)	
Green Tree Python (SNAKE F)	
Reticulated Python (SNAKE H)	
Snake Liquid (SNAKE I)	
Snake Solid (SNAKE J)	
Snake Solidus (SNAKE K)	

GROZNYJ GRAD RAIL BRIDGE NORTH

ITEMS FOUND

None

The Chase Resumes

As in the previous chase sequences, equip the M63 and mow down the motorcyclists chasing EVA and Snake. Enter First Person View and aim shots more specifically whenever EVA skids to a halt at a roadblock or ambush zone.

LAZOREVO SOUTH

ITEMS FOUND

None

Through Tree and Woods

After escaping from the roadblock, EVA and Snake find a squad of hovercraft-riding guards hot on their tail. Equip the RPG-7 and blow each out of the sky before they do significant damage to Snake. When EVA starts shouting about a log in the path, turn around to face the front of the vehicle, and use scope sighting to destroy the tree trunk blocking the path.

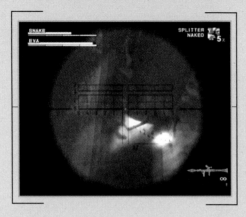 

LAZOREVO NORTH

ITEMS FOUND

None

Last of the Motorcycle Commandos

Use the RPG-7 to obliterate motorcycle squads in direct pursuit behind your vehicle. When motorcycles zip across the stream and fire from the right bank, switch to the M63 and fire across the river, aiming just slightly ahead of each motorcycle.

INTRODUCTION

CHARACTERS

SYSTEM

WEAPONS

ITEMS

FOOD

CURE

PROLOGUE: VIRTUOUS MISSION

OPERATION SNAKE EATER

SNAKE VS. MONKEY

BONUSES & EASTER EGGS

KEROTAN LOCATIONS

INTERVIEWS

METAL GEAR SOLID COMIC

ITEMS FOUND

Smoke Grenades (SMOKE G)

Grenade

Stun Grenade (STUN G)

Mk22 Bullet x24

Claymore

XM16E1 Bullets x80

AMMO

Russian Ration (2 qty.)

AK-47 Bullets x120

AMMO

SVD Bullets x40

AMMO

M1911A1 Bullets x21

AMMO

OPERATION SNAKE EATER

1 | ADAM AND EVA
2 | BEYOND THE FOREST BASE
3 | ESCAPE THE CAVE
4 | WAREHOUSE IN THE MANGROVE
5 | GRANINY GORKI LAB
6 | WOODLAND HUNT
7 | ALPINE ASCENT
8 | GROZYNJ GRAD
9 | SHAGOHOD
10 | THE BOSS

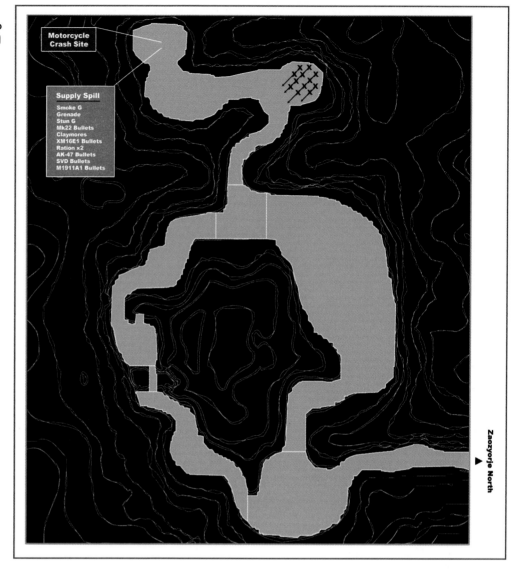

Motorcycle Crash Site

Supply Spill
Smoke G
Grenade
Stun G
Mk22 Bullets
Claymores
XM16E1 Bullets
Ration x2
AK-47 Bullets
SVD Bullets
M1911A1 Bullets

Zaozyorje North

HOLY COW, DOES THIS WOMAN EAT!

EVA's Stamina drops continuously the entire time you try to lead her through the woods. Her tastes for wildlife are as unrefined as Snake's were when the game first started, so she does not recover much Stamina from items like Siberian Ink Caps until she has eaten them several times. Collect every available food source to have it handy for EVA throughout this area.

Wounded EVA

What they say about motorbikes is true: it's always fun until someone gets hurt. When the Cure screen opens, treat the wounds of both Snake and EVA. The woman suffers from two cuts, both requiring the normal treatment of Disinfectant, Styptic, Suture Kit, and Bandage.

A treasure trove of **items** lies behind Snake and EVA. Collect what you need, then equip the Thermal Goggles and begin hunting for food immediately.

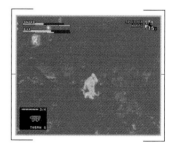

Leading EVA Out of the Woods

Guide EVA south from the starting point by pressing the Action button [tri] to wave a beckoning hand. EVA must be within Snake's line of sight in order to see the hand signal and obey. Take only about five to steps away from EVA, and then beckon for her. Repeat this pattern of movement and waving to guide her out of the woods as quickly as possible.

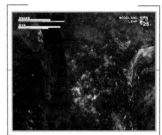

EVA moves and responds to Snake's commands quickly or slowly depending on her Stamina level. To make EVA get the lead out, make sure she is well fed.

Outrunning Search Parties

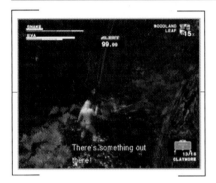

Proceed south until soldiers invade the woods looking for EVA and Snake. The path forks in two directions at this point. Lead EVA as quickly as possible down the narrower west route. While guiding EVA this direction, turn around occasionally, run back a few steps behind EVA, and set a Claymore on the ground, facing north. Creating a web of explosive traps to slow down the pursuing soldiers.

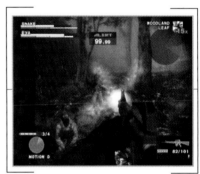

If the soldiers do catch up with Snake and EVA, which is more likely to occur at the start, EVA stays and fights until the last soldier is dead. Fire a sub machinegun and use Grenades to take out clusters of soldiers as quickly as possible. Try to get away as soon as the wave of enemies subsides.

If EVA is injured during combat, open the Cure screen and treat her wounds the same as you would Snake. You must be standing no more than roughly five feet from EVA in order to cure her.

Leaving the Soldiers Behind

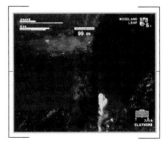

The western path leads southward, eventually arriving at a tree trunk that acts as bridge across a ravine. Lead EVA across the trunk, and then go back onto the limb and set at least two Claymores to slow down the soldiers further.

With enough Claymores set to the north, Snake should be able to hunt for food a little more in the area just before the exit. When both Snake and EVA stand near the tall embankment, he helps her climb up into the next area.

INTRODUCTION
CHARACTERS
SYSTEM
WEAPONS
ITEMS
FOOD
CURE
PROLOGUE: VIRTUOUS MISSION
OPERATION SNAKE EATER
SNAKE VS MONKEY
BONUSES & EASTER EGGS
KEROTAN LOCATIONS
INTERVIEWS
METAL GEAR SOLID COMIC

ZAOZYORJE NORTH

ITEMS FOUND

None

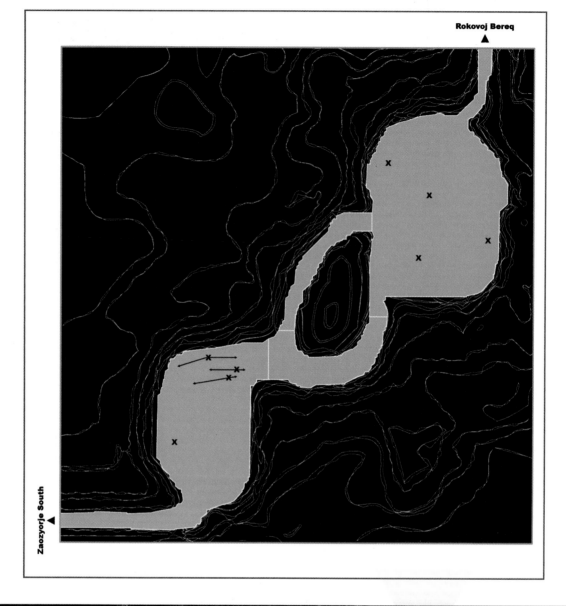

Rokovoj Bereq

Zaozyorje South

Ambushes Ahead

In this area, the soldiers are already set up in sniper positions and lying in wait. Leave EVA behind and crawl forward with the best possible camouflage. Use the Thermal Goggles to spot the soldiers crouched in the woods. Take them out with the sniper rifle. Avoid shooting them anywhere but in the head to avoid an all out firefight.

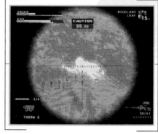

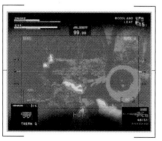

Lead EVA northeast with the Thermal Goggles equipped, looking carefully for snipers and patrolling guards the whole way. To get the drop on the soldiers lying in ambush in the final clearing, follow the extremely narrow northern path into the second area. Help EVA climb up the northwest embankment to proceed to the final battle.

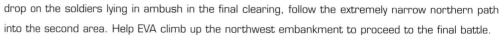

ROKOVOJ BEREG

ITEMS FOUND

Snake Liquid

Snake Solid

Snake Solidus

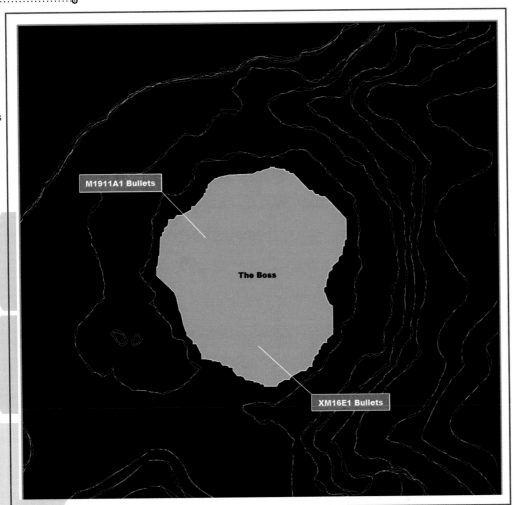

M1911A1 Bullets

The Boss

XM16E1 Bullets

NON-LETHAL ALTERNATIVE

It isn't easy, but it is possible to defeat The Boss by using nothing but the Mk22. Successfully depleting her Stamina gauge nets Snake the always-useful **Snake Camouflage** for subsequent play-throughs of Story Mode.

THE BOSS

BATTLE-SPECIFIC ITEMS

XXM16E1 Bullets x80

AMMO

M1911A1 Bullets x21

AMMO

Immediately open the menu and switch to the Snow Face Paint and Snow Camouflage. The Boss starts off by charging at Snake. When in range, she begins a complex series of take down moves. Tap the ⊙ button rapidly to try to break out of her grip. If Snake breaks free, punch and kick her until she groans and falls onto her back. Quickly equip the M37 shotgun, look down at her prone body and blast her. Even if The Boss wins the grappling match and tosses Snake to the ground, get up as soon as possible, and punch her until she falls. Getting her on her back is important so that you can get away and hide.

INTRODUCTION

CHARACTERS

SYSTEM

WEAPONS

ITEMS

FOOD

CURE

PROLOGUE: VIRTUOUS MISSION

OPERATION SNAKE EATER

SNAKE VS. MONKEY

BONUSES & EASTER EGGS

KEROTAN LOCATIONS

INTERVIEWS

METAL GEAR SOLID COMIC

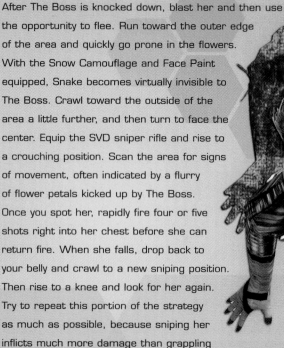

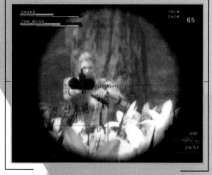

After The Boss is knocked down, blast her and then use the opportunity to flee. Run toward the outer edge of the area and quickly go prone in the flowers. With the Snow Camouflage and Face Paint equipped, Snake becomes virtually invisible to The Boss. Crawl toward the outside of the area a little further, and then turn to face the center. Equip the SVD sniper rifle and rise to a crouching position. Scan the area for signs of movement, often indicated by a flurry of flower petals kicked up by The Boss. Once you spot her, rapidly fire four or five shots right into her chest before she can return fire. When she falls, drop back to your belly and crawl to a new sniping position. Then rise to a knee and look for her again. Try to repeat this portion of the strategy as much as possible, because sniping her inflicts much more damage than grappling with her.

The main obstacle to winning this battle is the time limit. The Boss gleefully calls out a countdown to destruction. If battle times out, an additional cinema plays. If the battle continues into the last 30 seconds, work hard to snipe her one last time rather than rush into a grapple fight.

Avoid equipping a weapon while The Boss is about to grapple Snake, or she unloads the weapons and throws the ammo and weapon around the area.

During the battle, equip the Thermal Goggles occasionally to spot items to the north and south. Look for Snake Solid, Snake Liquid and Snake Solidus. Each of these unique snakes is near the logs scattered around the area.

Mission Accomplished

Provided you can beat The Boss within the ten-minute time limit, the mission is basically complete. There are a few odds and ends to take care of before the final credits roll, but to keep this guide's content spoiler-free, it's nothing you can't handle on your own. Enjoy taking in the end of the story!

SNAKE VS. MONKEY

Just when Snake thought his days of roaming the jungle were over, along comes Major Zero with a new mission. Much to Snake's dismay, he must revisit the Tselinoyarsk region and return dozens of monkeys to captivity. And no, neither Sam nor Gabe is available to take Snake's place.

MONKEY-SNAGGIN' BASICS

Despite Snake's obvious displeasure with being sent back into the jungle for such a lowbrow mission, chasing down those cheeky monkeys makes for a fun, lighthearted break from the life-or-death seriousness of Operation Snake Eater. This optional gameplay mode contains five unique missions, each taking place at a different locale visited in the main story. Only the first three missions are initially available. The final two "Snake Vs. Monkey" missions become unlocked after completing the main story mode.

Snake is equipped with state-of-the-art monkey catching gadgetry and has even gone through the trouble of donning the rare Banana Camouflage in hopes of luring the unsuspecting, butt-slapping, monkeys toward him with the sweet aroma of their favorite treat. Snake's full compliment of weapons and items include the following:

- EZ Gun
- Stun Grenades
- Directional Microphone
- Active Sonar
- Thermal Goggles
- Scope

Using the EZ Gun to zap the monkeys with a bolt of electricity stuns them and knocks them to the ground for roughly five seconds. Once a monkey is stunned, Snake must run up and snag it before it jumps back to its feet and runs away—or worse! Monkeys don't like being held in captivity and many will stand and fight if they feel they're cornered. Monkeys are surprisingly strong, and Snake's CQC tactics are no match for the agile creatures. Monkeys may run up to Snake and knock him down, but they might resort to tossing monkey-matter at him—and nobody wants that! Lastly, another monkey tactic involves holding up makeshift shields to block the EZ Gun darts. It's still possible to zap them in the head, but monkeys with shields are obviously harder to capture, as they present a much smaller target.

 MONKEYS ON ALERT

The beacon on each monkey's head is similar to the "!" that appears over the enemies in story mode. This light remains blue so long as the monkey is unaware of Snake's presence. The light turns yellow when it is in a state of caution, and it turns red when it sees Snake trying to capture it.

The goal of "Snake Vs. Monkey" isn't to just capture the monkeys, but to do it as quickly as possible. Although stealth tactics often take longer to employ than a run-and-gun approach in the main story mode, it is far more efficient to capture the monkeys as stealthily as possible. Unlike enemy guards, which run toward Snake and try to fight him, the vast majority of the monkeys try to run and hide once they're spotted. Even when the monkeys run away in plain sight, they are quite swift and can be very difficult to shoot with the EZ Gun while they're on the move. However, monkeys are not nearly as intelligent as humans, and together with his superior brainpower and Banana Camouflage, Snake can get surprisingly close to his quarry before they notice him.

Although the five missions each take place in different terrain, one proven strategy works in each of them. As soon as the mission begins, quickly equip the EZ Gun and the Active Sonar. Send out a Sonar beacon every five seconds or so to keep tabs on the monkeys' whereabouts and try to move into a position where Snake can stun and capture multiple monkeys simultaneously. Stun Grenades are very beneficial in a few instances, but Snake should ultimately rely on the EZ Gun almost exclusively.

 THOSE SILLY CLIMBING MONKEYS

Often, a blip appears on the Sonar yet no monkey is to be seen. When this happens, try looking up. Monkeys love to climb trees and buildings, so don't forget to glance skyward every now and then to spot stragglers. Once shot, the monkey tumbles down to Snake's feet.

THE MISSIONS

Each mission has three preset times that represent first, second, and third place. Follow the tips listed for each mission to finish it in gold medal time! Each monkey's initial location is shown on the maps, and they're numbered in the order in which we recommend capturing them. Monkeys move around a bit, especially if they're scared, so their locations may vary slightly from those shown on the maps. Nevertheless, the maps should prove useful in your quest to unlock the secret awards.

MISSION 1 ESCAPE FROM THE JUNGLE

CAPTURE 9 MONKEYS IN 1:30.

This first mission takes place in Dremuchij South, the first location in the main story mode. The key to achieving a gold medal performance is to move efficiently from monkey to monkey without alerting any of them. Capture the monkeys in the southern section first by moving in a counter-clockwise path from the starting point. Use the Active Sonar to locate the monkeys, and avoid moving forward without first checking the Sonar. This reduces the chance of blindly stumbling onto a monkey's hiding spot.

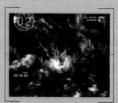

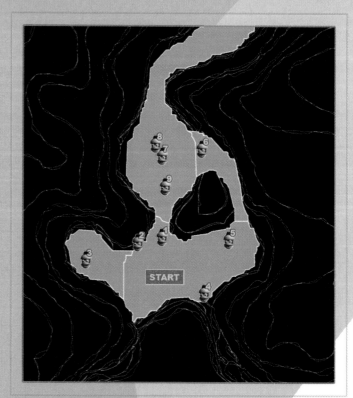

Climb the slope in the northeast corner and capture the monkey atop the ledge. Shoot the two monkeys in the tree from atop the ledge, and then drop down to snag them both at once. To save time, Snake can slide down the cliff face while the monkeys fall to the ground.

MISSION 2 DRAGNET OF THE APES

CAPTURE 15 MONKEYS IN 3:00.

This mission takes place in the main loop of Dremuchij North. This area contains some wide-open areas with grass nearly as tall as the monkeys, so the Active Sonar and Thermal Goggles are particularly useful. Some of the monkeys hide on tree branches, in hollowed-out tree stumps, and even on the inaccessible cliffs on the sides of the area.

Sweep across the map in a counter-clockwise loop. Shoot the three dancing monkeys from a safe distance, and then rush

in to capture them before they recover. A fourth monkey dangles from the tree overhead. Follow the edge of the map into the southeast area of the loop, and look for the monkeys in the grass and tree stump on the map's outer portion.

The two hardest monkeys to find are labeled #9 and #10 on the map. Monkey #9 is high in a tree near the center of the map. Monkey #10 is on the hill directly behind that tree and can be very difficult to see. It's possible to get a clean shot on monkey #10 from the north side of the hill, but beware that the monkey tumbles to the southeast and lands on the other side of the large tree.

Continue the counter-clockwise loop around the area to capture the remaining monkeys. The final monkey hides inside a tree stump to the west.

MISSION 3 DAWN OF THE APES

CAPTURE 21 MONKEYS IN 3:00.

Success in this mission at Rassvet is largely determined by your ability to capture nine monkeys with a single Stun Grenade. Capture the two monkeys in the yard to the southeast, and then turn to face the nine monkeys dancing in the corner of the bombed-out factory. Lob a Stun Grenade into the center of the area, wait for the blast to dissipate, and then rush in to collect the dazed monkeys—the dance floor is now closed!

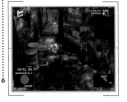

Exit to the east and shoot the monkey in the window, along with the one to the north. Use somersaults to cover ground quickly, and pick up both before the shock wears off. Quickly climb the ladder to the roof, and shoot the sunbathing monkey located there. He doesn't roll down to the ground, so shooting him from elsewhere is not an option.

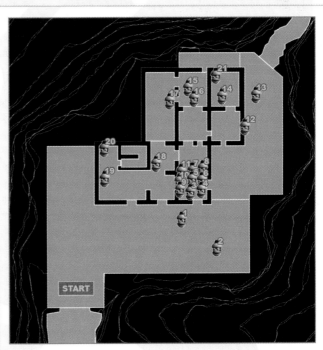

Shoot the two monkeys near the stack of crates in the center of the ruins while you're on the roof, and jump down and snag them. Exit to the grassy area to the west, and immediately turn to the left and shoot the monkey there. Three monkeys can be found near the stairs. One tiptoes across the beam above the ground, another sleeps on the upper platform, and yet another dangles from a piece of scrap metal. The final monkey is in the interior room of the factory, where Snake had to go during the "Virtuous Mission" to find Doctor Sokolov.

MISSION 4 APE FEAR

CAPTURE 18 MONKEYS IN 4:30.

The Bolshaya Past Base is a moderately large, sprawling complex, and there are numerous places for a cheeky monkey to hide. Snake must move fast to complete this mission in time.

Begin by turning to the east and shooting the monkey sprinting toward Snake. Turn and shoot the one in the tree near the starting point next—two down, sixteen to go!

Enter the base in the southwest corner, cross the ramp over the trench toward

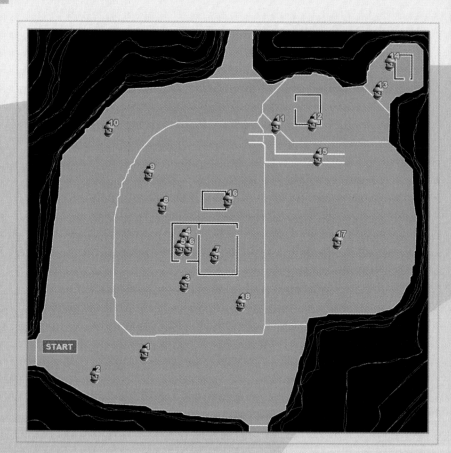

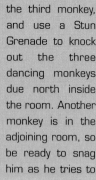

the third monkey, and use a Stun Grenade to knock out the three dancing monkeys due north inside the room. Another monkey is in the adjoining room, so be ready to snag him as he tries to make a run for it.

Exit the building to the west and capture the monkey in the trench. Next, crawl under the barbed wire to get the monkey in the northwest corner of the map. Head to the northeast corner of the area, and capture the monkeys near the two outposts in that area. Reenter the main base area on an angle to the southwest, and capture the monkey in the northeast trench and on the deck in front of the shed.

Now it's time to make the final push and go after the monkey leaping atop the Mesal Gear. Wait for the monkey to leap back to the Mesal Gear's head, and then fire the EZ Gun before it jumps back to the Mesal Gear's hand. The final monkey is in the trench near the southeast corner of the building.

MISSION 5 GONE WITH THE APES

CAPTURE 18 MONKEYS IN 4:30.

The final mission takes place at the Graniny Gorki laboratory facility. Monkeys are split between the first and second floor of the building, but there is no access to the basement. The only outdoor monkeys are on the second floor ledge and in the central courtyard outside the library.

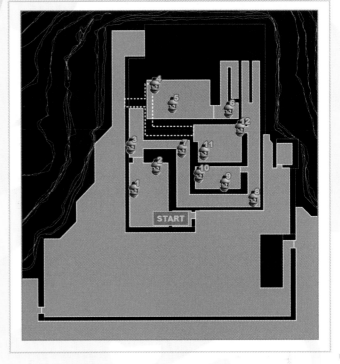

Run into the main reception area of the laboratory on the first floor to take out the three visible monkeys right away. Head north to the large atrium area and capture the three monkeys there. Spend a second to try to shoot the monkey down from the railing on the second floor balcony; he doesn't always fall to the first floor, so be ready to move on without him.

Return to the main hallway on the first floor and head east. Capture the two monkeys in the hall outside the library. There are two more monkeys in the library. Enter the small courtyard and shoot the monkey on the ground. Then turn and aim at the one on the ledge over the door. With twelve of the monkeys caught, it's time to head up the stairs.

There are two monkeys in the hall overlooking the downstairs atrium. Try to shoot the monkey on the railing at an angle from across the room so that the impact knocks him off the railing and onto the second floor hallway. If he happens to fall to the floor, simply ignore him and move on—he'll return to the railing soon enough.

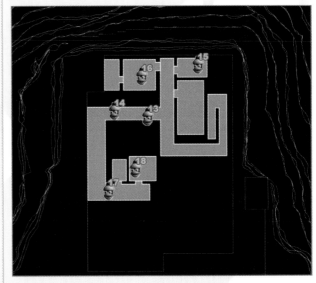

Run to the northeast corner of the second floor, and capture the monkey on the toilet in the bathroom. Another monkey is down the hall to the west. There are only two monkeys left, and they're in the south section of the second floor.

BONUSES

Earn the top-ranked time in each of the five missions to unlock the following secrets:

- Banana Camouflage
- Monkey Mask

The Banana Camouflage will appear in the Uniform menu the next time you start a new game in story mode. The Monkey Mask can be found in the Item portion of the Backpack menu. Be sure to head to the Survival Viewer to get a good look at Snake in his new monkey suit!

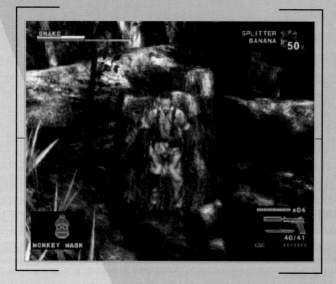

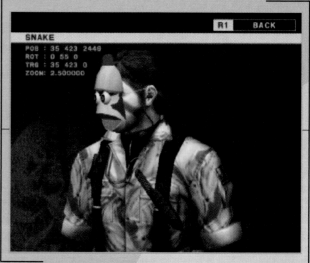

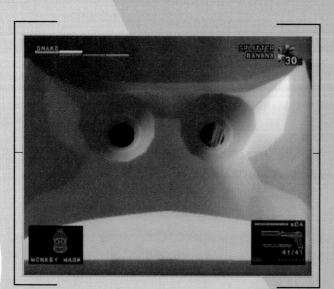

BONUSES AND EASTER EGGS

BONUS ITEMS

Clear the game and replay it to unlock additional Camouflage uniforms and Face Paints listed in the Systems chapter. Also, completing the game unlocks the Patriot, the Camera, the Single Action Army, and the Tuxedo camo. Additional stages become unlocked in Snake Vs. Monkey. Clear all stages of Snake Vs. Monkey with the number one record time to unlock the Monkey Mask and the Banana camouflage in the normal game.

EASTER EGGS

"Easter Eggs" refer to dialog, menu or environmental details that reference subjects that might be outside the game's scope. They tend to be relatively extraneous to the main story and progression of the game. Most Easter Eggs are humorous or curious, and the player might otherwise overlook them unless he or she knows what to look for and what it means. This section describes several Easter Eggs we've found in the game, including small bonus visuals and extra snippets of funny dialog.

TITLE MENU MANIPULATION

While Snake and the guard demonstrate CQC maneuvers, hold **L2** to make the two characters move at normal speed. Hold **R2** to slow the action to a crawl. The pressure applied to the buttons dictates the degree of slow or fast motion. Depress the Right Analog Stick **R3** or Left Analog Stick **L3** to change the color or camouflage displayed behind the characters. Move the Left Analog Stick to rotate the characters very slightly onscreen. Press △ to make the background black or another solid color with a single set of characters. The **L1** and **L2** buttons switch the colors of the foreground and background characters.

DEMO MOVIE SYMBOLISM

Once the title screen demo movie is unlocked (by completing the Prologue stage), have a little interactive fun by moving the Right Analog Stick during the movie to cause symbols to appear onscreen. The more the control is moved, the greater the number of symbols that appear. The symbols' movement can be controlled to some extent by moving the Right Analog Stick. Depress the Right Analog Stick **R3** to change the symbols as well as their direction. The demo alternates between solid-colored and camouflage-patterned symbols, depending on how many times the demo plays consecutively.

Rotate the Left Analog Stick to cause the credits to make waves as they cross the screen. Depress the Left Analog Stick **R3** to cycle the titles' language from English to Japananese to Chinese and then Russian, and then one more time to turn all the titles into Snake bones. Press **R1** to make the singer whisper "Snake Eaterrrrr" in time to the groovy beat.

OPENING QUESTION

When starting a new game, the first screen asks you to choose an option. The first two options start the game with the basic cinemas. However, choosing the third option, "I like MGS2!" starts the game with Snake wearing the Mask. There is an additional scene and radio conversation at the beginning of the game. This feature is a nod to the character of Raiden from *Metal Gear Solid 2: Sons of Liberty*.

VOMITING

Enter the Survival Viewer and press R1 to view Snake. Hold the Right Analog Stick left or right to make Snake spin. Allow him to spin for roughly 30 seconds, and then press START to exit the Survival Viewer while in mid-spin. After a second, Snake vomits onto the

ground. This is actually useful. In case you accidentally eat rotten food, make Snake vomit to cure a stomachache or food poisoning. Using a Digestive Medicine is better, because vomiting lowers Stamina. But keep this trick in mind in case Digestive Medicines are not available.

DRONE DECORATION

During Snake's reinsertion during Operation Snake Eater, press R1 during the cinema when the R1 icon appears onscreen. This changes the view to the inside of Snake's insertion drone. Move the Left Analog Stick upward to raise the viewpoint until Snake is staring at the capsule's door—a pretty girl accompanies Snake on his mission!

That's it?

SNAKE THE PERV

During EVA's introductory scenes, press R1 to view her from Snake's perspective. Snake seems a little...*distracted*...during their conversations.

IMPOSSIBLE AFFECT

After eating Russian Glowcaps for the first time, contact Para-Medic to discuss the battery-recharging affects of the food. She sets down her headset for a moment to discuss with Sigint the impossibility of such a thing occurring. The whole conversation is hysterically funny.

145.73

Yeah. There's no way eating a bioluminescent mushroom would cause your batteries to recharge.

RADIO MUSIC NETWORK

When interrogated CQC style, certain guards and scientists in the game divulge secret radio frequencies that serve special functions. For instance, the guard who patrols in and out of the Graniny Gorki B1 East Jail Cell level's security post divulges frequency 144.86. Tune to this frequency

141.85

DON'T BE AFRAID / RIKA MURANAKA

on the radio to hear rockabilly music. There are eight hidden frequencies in the game where music is played. Interrogate all the enemies in the game to determine them all!

RESEARCH READING

Magazines strewn throughout the Graniny Gorki Lab, and in a few other indoor locations, bear the covers of several popular videogame magazines that previewed *Metal Gear Solid 3: Snake Eater* before its release. Shoot the magazines to make them flop around. The

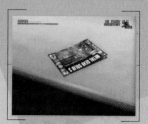

magazines may open to reveal the article contained in the specific issue. Other magazines feature *Zone of the Enders* articles.

SILENT HILL 3 ART

On the second floor of the Graniny Gorki Research Lab is a library decorated with paintings. The artwork is the same that hung in the final stage of Konami's chilling horror experience, *Silent Hill 3*.

GRANIN'S MODELS

Granin's room in the Graniny Gorki Lab stage contains a wealth of references to other *Metal Gear* games. The man in the picture with Granin, to whom Granin says he will send the Metal Gear designs, bears a striking resemblance to Hal Emmerich, a.k.a. "Otacon," the designer of Metal Gear Rex from

Because of him, I have been stripped of my authority.

Metal Gear Solid. Perhaps he is Otacon's father. When Granin hands Snake designs, press R1 to look them over. The sketch at the bottom is one of series artist Yoji Shinkawa's orginal design sketches for Rex. Models of Metal Gear Rex and Metal Gear Ray from *MGS* and *MGS2: Sons of Liberty/Substance* are displayed on Granin's shelf during the cinema. Furthermore, the model directly behind Granin's desk is Jehuty from the *Zone of the Enders* series.

BELLIGERENT DRUNK

After the scene where Snake meets Granin, stay in the room just outside the drunken scientist's office to hear him belt out some incoherent insults. After a while, he begins to snore. Try to open the door to hear more gruff talk.

RAIDEN'S LOCKER

During the scene in Groznyj Grad where Snake stuffs Major Raikov's body into a locker, a poster of Raiden from *Metal Gear Solid 2: Sons of Liberty* is posted on the inside of the locker door. Striking resemblance, don't you think?

SNAKE'S NIGHTMARE

A chance to create a data save occurs just after Snake is captured in Groznyj Grad. Save this data in a slot of its own and do not overwrite it! When the game is played through normally, Snake appears in a jail cell outside the Torture Room. However, if you load the game from this data save, you may think the wrong disk is in your game console!

A playable demo begins in which a dual-sword wielding character is attacked by incessant zombie cops. Press ⬜, △ and ⭕ to attack. Press ✖ to jump, and press R1 to dash. After killing enough consecutive enemies, the character enters a kind of overdrive state wherein the screen turns orange and he can slay enemies much easier.

After roughly two or three minutes, this strange demo times out and Snake awakens in his holding cell, as if the demo was his nightmare. This feature is available only by loading this particular data save!

EVA'S REWARD

After leading EVA safely out of the first woodland area subsequent to the Shagohod battles, enter the Survival Viewer and open the Cure screen. EVA appears only in her bathing suit, as a reward for getting her out of trouble.

EXPOSED EVA

While leading EVA through the forest area toward the lake, open the Cure menu and press R1 to view her in X-Ray mode. After a moment, EVA begins to look around self-consciously, wondering where her clothes went.

EVA'S REQUEST

While leading EVA through the Zaozyorje areas, feed her Instant Noodles to increase her Stamina. Each time she gets really hungry again, EVA moans for Instant Noodles by name.

METAL GEAR ACID

Interrogating enemy forces doesn't just yield information about the immediate area. Sometimes it even reveals information on upcoming games! Try interrogating the guards at Groznyj Grad—one of them reveals a password for Konami's upcoming *Metal Gear Acid* game for the PSP game system.

GAME RANKING

Ranking is determined by play time, number of saves, number of continues, how many times you got into ALERT PHASE, how many humans killed, how many major injuries you have suffered, how much damage you have taken, how much life medicine you have used, and how many special items you have obtained. There are 55 ranks:

FOXHOUND	HAWK	KOALA
FOX	FALCON	HIPPOPOTAMUS
DOBERMAN	SWALLOW	ZEBRA
HOUND	WHALE	DEER
OSTRICH	MAMMOTH	CAT
RABBIT	ELEPHANT	SCORPION
MOUSE	PIG	JAGUAR
CHICKEN	COW	IGUANA
KEROTAN	ORCA	TARANTULA
MARKHOR	JAWS	PANTHER
TSUCHINOKO	SHARK	CROCODILE
CHAMELEON	PIRANHA	CENTIPEDE
LEECH	TASMANIAN DEVIL	LEOPARD
PIGEON	JACKAL	KOMODO DRAGON
NIGHT OWL	HYENA	SPIDER
FLYING FOX	MONGOOSE	PUMA
BAT	GIANT PANDA	ALLIGATOR
FLYING SQUIRREL	SLOTH	
EAGLE	CAPYBARA	

INTRODUCTION

CHARACTERS

SYSTEM

WEAPONS

ITEMS

FOOD

CURE

PROLOGUE VIRTUOUS MISSION

OPERATION SNAKE EATER

SNAKE VS. MONKEY

BONUSES & EASTER EGGS

KEROTAN LOCATIONS

INTERVIEWS

METAL GEAR SOLID COMIC

KEROTAN
LOCATIONS

A frog-like toy coin bank named Kerotan is located somewhere in every area of the game. Find the hidden Kerotan and shoot it with a gun or detonate a grenade very near to it. In some areas, Kerotans are located on shelves where Snake can shake them by punching them instead of shooting. This is called "shaking" the Kerotan. A shaken Kerotan emits a series of weird giggles. You can use this noise to strategically lure nearby guards toward the Kerotan, if you wish. Wait until the giggles subside, and then attack Kerotan again to trigger another series of brays. Attacking Kerotan three times causes it to break. Locate and shoot all the Kerotans to unlock bonuses.

We've listed the Kerotan locations in the order in which you visit the areas in the game. Certain notes and warnings indicate special circumstances that may prevent you from shooting Kerotans for a while. You need shoot any given Kerotan only once. If you find and shoot every Kerotan in the game, you'll unlock a special camouflage upon completion.

If the Kerotan is located too far from your sniping position to be heard, shoot it and then equip the Directional Microphone. Point the Mic toward the Kerotan and listen to the noises to determine when they end, then shoot the Kerotan again if necessary.

"VIRTUOUS MISSION" LOCATIONS

DREMUCHIJ SOUTH

Stand on the tree branch, look south in First Person View, atop the bank slightly to the left.

DREMUCHIJ SWAMPLAND

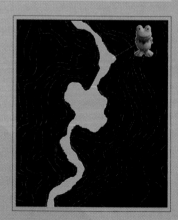

Move to the north section of the area past the quicksand. Stand in front of the tree cluster near the area's east wall and look south to spot Kerotan on top of the rise.

DREMUCHIJ NORTH

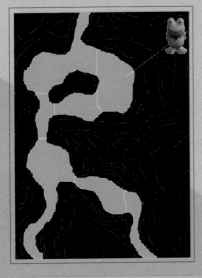

Move to the area's northeast portion and look at the hollow stump to the south. The Kerotan is on top of the stump.

DOLINOVODNO

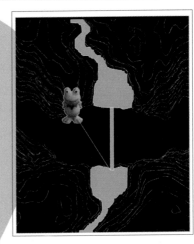

The Kerotan is perched atop the post to the left of the rope bridge's entrance.

RASSVET

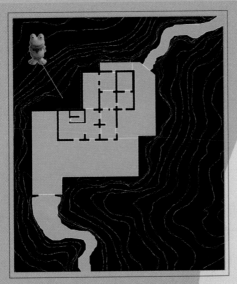

Move inside the building ruins and navigate to the northwest corner. Underneath the platform where the XM16E1 Bullets are located, there is a hole in the brick wall. Look through the hole in First Person View to spot the Kerotan.

"OPERATION SNAKE EATER" LOCATIONS

DREMUCHIJ EAST

In the north section of the area, move west and look south toward a small, ground-level alcove made out of collapsed trees. The Kerotan is on the ground inside the alcove.

MUST GET A GUN!

Snake is without a gun at this point in the game. The next weapon Snake can procure is the AK-47 assault rifle in the ruins at Rassvet. Head to Rassvet first, and before or after the battle with the eight Ocelot Unit soldiers, work your way south, shooting all the Kerotans before heading to Chyornyj Prud. When you're shooting Kerotans with the AK, be sure to first take out all nearby enemies because there is no suppressor for the assault rifle. Set the mode to single-shot, aim in First Person View, and hold L1 to aim down the sights.

RASSVET

After you obtain the AK-47 from the raised northwest platform inside the ruins, descend the stairs and drop off the mid-level landing. Turn around and look under the stairs to spot the Kerotan.

DOLINOVODNO

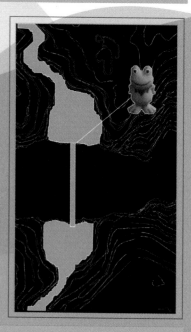

The Kerotan stands atop the post at the northeast corner of the rope bridge.

DREMUCHIJ NORTH

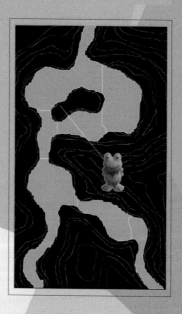

Climb the tree and look northwest to spot the Kerotan on the central embankment.

DREMUCHIJ SWAMPLAND

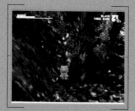

Move through the quicksand to the west bank, and go to the area's north end. Look east and down at the ground behind the tree cluster to spot the Kerotan. Detonating Grenades near this particular Kerotan can cause it to giggle.

DREMUCHIJ SOUTH

Navigate to the southern section, move west, and climb on top of the fallen tree trunk. Look west above the Chaff Grenade location to spot the Kerotan high up on the embankment.

CHYORNYJ PRUD

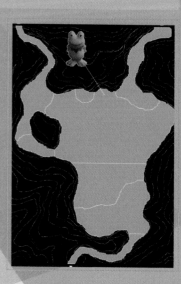

Swim directly north up the center of the lake into a tight underwater area. The Kerotan is underwater to the left of center. Shoot it with an underwater-friendly weapon, and then surface while the noises emanate.

BOLSHAYA PAST SOUTH

While you're still on the south side of the northernmost electric fence, move to the northeast corner and look east to spot the Kerotan on the ground behind some trees. Tossing Grenades can set off this Kerotan.

BOLSHAYA PAST BASE

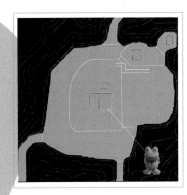

Enter the barracks area of the central building and look under the chair at the desk. Tossing Grenades can set off this Kerotan.

BOLSHAYA PAST CREVICE

During the Ocelot boss fight, move to the lower area's southeast corner, and look south across the gorge. The Kerotan is high up on the embankment.

CHYORNAYA PESCHERA CAVE BRANCH

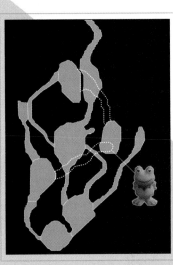

Navigate to the cave where the Night Vision Goggles (N.V.G.) are located. Standing at the floor pit's north edge, look south to spot the Kerotan stuck high up on the wall.

CHYORNAYA PESCHERA CAVE

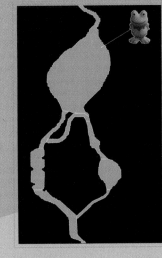

After you defeat The Pain, swim to the rock islet in the chamber's southwest portion, where the battle took place. Climb out of the water and look northeast. The Kerotan is perched on the lower ledge of the largest brightly lit opening high up in the cave. Use the Binoculars to pinpoint the Kerotan's location, then set the AK-47 on single-shot and hold L1 to aim down the sights.

CHYORNAYA PESCHERA CAVE ENTRANCE

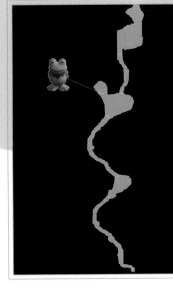

Follow the narrow path until a small cave appears on the left. Enter the cave, but watch out for Claymores. Standing at the back of the cave, face southeast and look in First Person View at the ledge overhead.

PONIZOVJE SOUTH

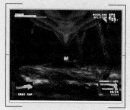

From the entrance, move up the stream's left side and occasionally look to the left. The Kerotan is behind the rocks to the left, but only his head pokes out.

PONIZOVJE WEST

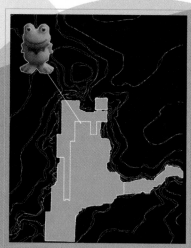

Swim toward the concrete portion of the dock and dive underwater. The Kerotan is behind the bars blocking the drainage tunnel. You can shoot this Kerotan twice: once when the setting is dusk and a second time after visiting the docks area to the north.

PONIZOVJE WAREHOUSE: EXTERIOR

The Kerotan is perched atop the canal gate's left column in the area's southeast corner.

PONIZOVJE WAREHOUSE

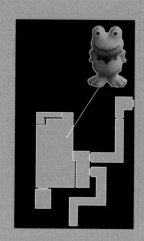

Climb onto the tall stack of crates at the south end of the open floor space. Then look north toward the ceiling. The Kerotan is on top of a ceiling pipe, and this is the only position that allows you to see it. Use the SVD (after slaying all the guards) to shoot the Kerotan.

GRANINY GORKI SOUTH

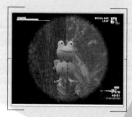

The Kerotan is perched on the tree branch to the left of the north exit. Climb the next-closest tree and use the SVD to shoot it.

GRANINY GORKI LAB EXTERIOR: OUTSIDE WALL

Penetrate the electrified fence and move to the wall's southwest corner. Look west to spot Kerotan atop the rise.

GRANINY GORKI LAB EXTERIOR: INSIDE WALLS

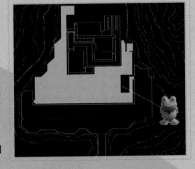

Move toward the small building on the courtyard's east side, and look through the window. Shoot the Kerotan through the glass.

GRANINY GORKI LAB 1F

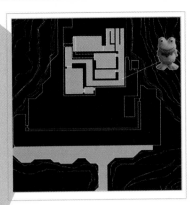

Follow the corridor behind the lobby to the building's southeast corner. The Kerotan is atop the lockers on the east wall, in the south corner. Don't shoot the Kerotan until you're ready to exit the lab after meeting Granin.

GRANINY GORKI LAB B1 WEST

Head west past the guard's station and enter the break room. The Kerotan is resting on the table. To avoid drawing suspicion, tranquilize the scientist in this room before you punch the Kerotan.

GRANINY GORKI LAB B1 EAST

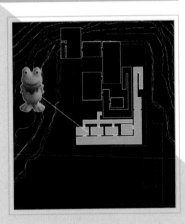

The Kerotan is prominently displayed on the table inside the west prison cell. You can punch the Kerotan to trigger a noise. Just don't strike it while a guard is looking, or Snake is discovered even if he's wearing the scientist disguise.

SVYATOGORNYJ SOUTH

Move a dozen steps into the area, turn around and look above the entrance to the right. The Kerotan is perched atop the concrete slab poured around the entrance.

SVYATOGORNYJ WEST

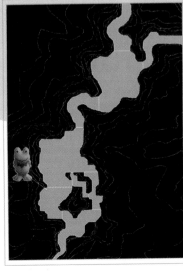

The Kerotan is near the climbable tree and fallen log features on the area's west side.

SVYATOGORNYJ EAST

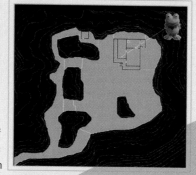

In the bedroom inside the cabin, stand south of the shelves in the room's lower part and look north to spot Kerotan.

SOKROVENNO SOUTH

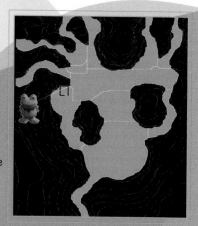

The Kerotan rests on the side of the cliff behind the munitions depot in this area.

SOKROVENNO WEST

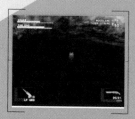

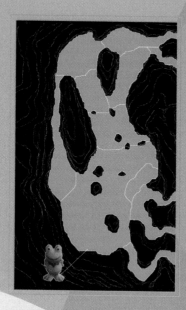

Move to the rock wall with an opening into which the waters from the stream flow. Crouch and look into the opening to spot Kerotan.

SOKROVENNO NORTH

FIND ME!

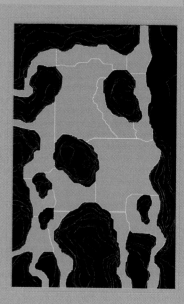

KRASNOGORJE TUNNEL

Head to the north end of the tunnel, turn around and look south. Kerotan should be easy to spot behind the arch leg on the right.

KRASNOGORJE MOUNTAIN BASE

Kerotan is located atop the northwestern rock, to the left of the area's exit.

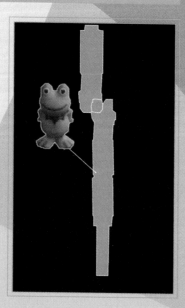

KRASNOGORJE MOUNTAINSIDE

The Kerotan figure is atop the food storage building.

KRASNOGORJE MOUNTAINTOP

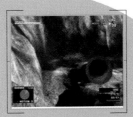
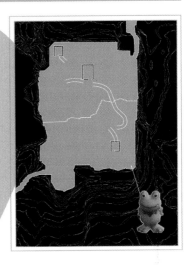

Kerotan appears on a cliff in the southeast corner. Shoot him from beside the lowest building.

KRASNOGORJE MOUNTAINTOP: BEHIND RUINS

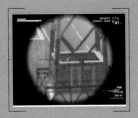

Kerotan is on the radio tower at the base's southeast corner, just above the lights. Use the Dragunov to shoot it, and then listen with the Directional Microphone.

KRASNOGORJE MOUNTAINTOP: RUINS

Kerotan is in the bedroom area's southwest corner, on a shelf above the bed.

GROZNYJ GRAD UNDERGROUND TUNNEL

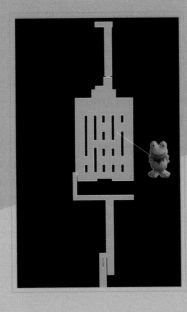

While fighting The Fury, climb onto the north platform and look south down the passage just east of center. Kerotan sits on the corner of a red pipe high over the floor.

GROZNYJ GRAD SOUTHWEST

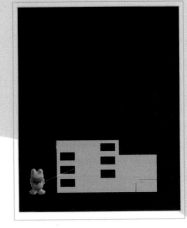

In the western aisle of hangars, move to the middle hangar's east side and look through the partially open hangar door to spot Kerotan.

GROZNYJ GRAD SOUTHEAST

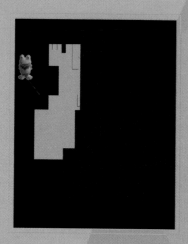

Climb the ladder on the south side of the detention center. Look east to spot Kerotan on the roof's southeast corner.

GROZNYJ GRAD NORTHEAST

Drop into the trench and crawl under the tarmac to the spur leading off to the west. Kerotan is beyond a metal grate.

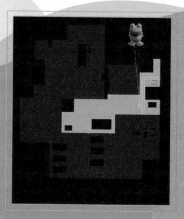

GROZNYJ GRAD NORTHWEST

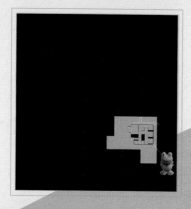

Move to the westernmost building's southeast corner, and look west over the top of the fence surrounding the spotlight tower. Kerotan is behind the fence, resting on a stair platform.

GROZNYJ GRAD TORTURE ROOM

Kerotan is located under the desk in the office area. Enter the Torture Room area before you proceed to the Weapons Lab: East Wing area to be sure you can shake Kerotan, because Snake's weapons are stolen later.

GROZNYJ GRAD WEAPONS LAB: EAST WING

Kerotan is perched atop the file shelves running along the upper level's northwest wall.

TIKHOGORNYJ

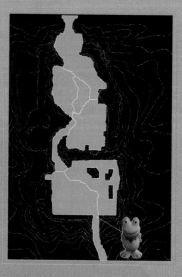

At Snake's starting point, turn and look south at the branch lying over the flowing stream. Kerotan appears on the east side of the water.

TIKHOGORNYJ: BEHIND WATERFALL

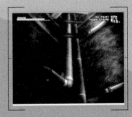

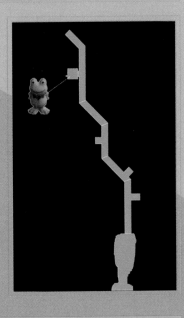

In the room with the ladder leading up to Groznyj Grad's northwest quadrant, stand to the right of the ladder and look at the pipes in the corner to find Kerotan.

GROZNYJ GRAD: RUNWAY SOUTH

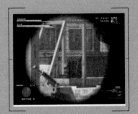

During the escape sequence, EVA pulls into a courtyard full of soldiers. Look for Kerotan on the distant forklift on the left after she stops the motorcycle.

GROZNYJ GRAD RAIL BRIDGE

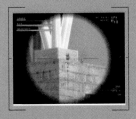

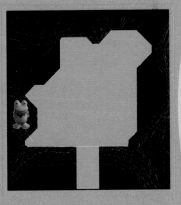

A Kerotan is located at the base of the radio tower on the building to the southwest. Shoot it during the first boss fight against Shagohod.

GROZNYJ GRAD WEAPONS LAB: MAIN WING

Kerotan is between the eastern fuel tank and the Shagohod. Peer over the railing down toward the Shagohod to the right of the fuel tank to find it.

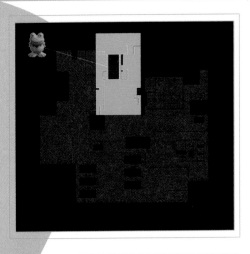

GROZNYJ GRAD RUNWAY

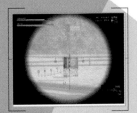

Look back off the motorcycle and continue to look toward the right with the sniper rifle. Kerotan is atop one of the signs off to the side of the runway.

GROZNYJ GRAD RAIL BRIDGE NORTH

When EVA skids to a halt in front of a roadblock, a Kerotan sits on the ground between two of the barricades.

INTRODUCTION

CHARACTERS

SYSTEM

WEAPONS

ITEMS

FOOD

CURE

PROLOGUE
VIRTUOUS
MISSION

OPERATION
SNAKE EATER

SNAKE VS
MONKEY

BONUSES &
EASTER EGGS

KEROTAN
LOCATIONS

INTERVIEWS

METAL GEAR
SOLID COMIC

LAZOREVO SOUTH

FIND ME!

LAZOREVO NORTH

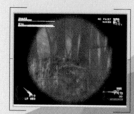

Kerotan stands on the east side of the path. Equip the Dragunov and look forward and to the left of the direction you're traveling as soon as you enter the area. Scan the ground off the road and fire when you spot the Kerotan.

ZAOZYORJE NORTH

FIND ME!

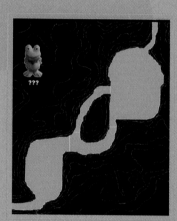

???

ZAOZYORJE SOUTH

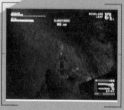

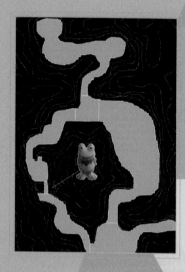

Lead EVA southward down the area's western path. Stand on the fallen tree trunk that acts as a bridge across the stream. Look east and down to spot Kerotan on a ledge far below the tree.

ROKOVOJ BEREG

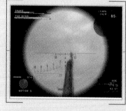

Kerotan is perched on the very top of a tree just south of the area's center.

INTERVIEWS

AN INTERVIEW WITH MR. MOTOSADA MORI, MILITARY ADVISOR TO THE METAL GEAR SOLID SERIES

PROFILE

Motosada Mori

Born in Hiroshima, Japan, 1964, Motosada Mori roamed around the world at the age of 19. After battle experience in regional conflicts, he participated in SWAT training instruction and the protection of the Dalai Lama 14th (Nobel Peace Prize winner). He then became a writer. He established "Mori International," which specializes in the prediction of violent crimes, threat assessment, and countermeasures, and has since given advice as a specialist to corporations and security organizations. He also teaches self-defense and gives advice to the public on how to deal with stalkers and domestic violence. He participated in the development of *Metal Gear Solid 3: Snake Eater* as military advisor, just as he did in the previous installments of the series.

GLOSSARY

CQC: Abbreviation for Close Quarter Combat, the newest hand-to-hand fighting technique focusing on close combat, performed while equipped with guns and knives.

"In *MGS3*, we focused on the 'handgun and knife' style, which is a characteristic form of CQC. When you have a handgun and a CQC knife equipped in the game, CQC is used."

ABOUT CQC

What is CQC?

Motosada Mori: It is the abbreviation for Close Quarter Combat. In actual battle, it is used in the jungle, bushes, and indoors when you cannot use a gun. It is also used when terrorists with hostages are in a facility or an airplane. The technique has been developed for when you have to fight multiple enemies that are very close to you, or when you don't know from where you will be attacked. It is a total combat technique used when you are close to enemies and you have to be able to fight with your bare hands, knife, and gun accordingly.

In *MGS3*, we have kept in mind at all times the use of CQC. The posture of the character and how you throw the enemy is based on CQC, as is how you walk and keep an eye on things around you. I think fans will enjoy this.

Where did you learn this technique?

Mori: When I was a SWAT instructor about 10 years ago, I realized the necessity of this kind of battle and learned it then. Only after reaching a certain level in the use of guns, knives, and my bare hands was I able to practice CQC.

How is CQC an advantage over regular knife battle and gun battle?

Mori: CQC is a high-level professional tactic. It doesn't necessarily work to everyone's advantage. Only when you have mastered fighting with knives and guns does it become an advantageous tactic. Someone who has no experience with weapons will injure him- or herself if he or she uses this kind of knife. Only special forces personnel in the real world and Snake in MGS3, who are "amazing," can use this technique.

Can you name any actual police forces or militaries that use this technique?

How do you think this tactic will evolve in the future?

Mori: I cannot reveal actual organization names. It seems as though European organizations are more aggressive when it comes to adopting new fighting techniques than American organizations. I'm sure terrorist organizations, which are aggressive when it comes to adopting new fighting techniques, will be using CQC soon. It is always a cat-and-mouse game.

Countermeasure-type fighting techniques I think have reached the final stage in terms of the physical aspect. What is becoming more important is psychological warfare—making the first move to affect the enemy's psychology so that the enemy does not attack you.

The knife used in CQC is very distinctive. Can you please talk about the shape?

Mori: Although the shapes of knives used by police forces and militaries do vary, what you see in the photos is the most basic and popular shape. The serration (saw-like edge on the back) is really unique. This, you hook onto the enemy. In other words, with this side, you fix the enemy so that he or she does not move. With a knife of this shape, you can hook it onto an enemy and control him or her, and you can also use the bottom of the handle as an impact weapon. So, you can "cut," "hit," and "fix" an enemy with this knife.

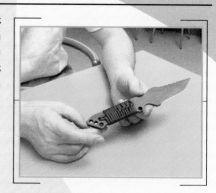

DESCRIPTIONS OF CQC TECHNIQUES

Basic Posture

- Relax when standing. Do not have unnecessary tension in your body so that you can move quickly.

- When putting away weapons, do so one by one. Look around and make sure you don't hurt anyone in the process.

Stun by a Blow—When You Are too Close and Cannot Fire a Gun

- Determine where the attack is coming from, and shift the focus of the enemy attack off you.

- If the enemy comes punching at you, move to the right and dodge the enemy hand with your left hand.

- Then hook the serration of your knife onto the enemy's left arm and pull the enemy toward you.

- Due to reflex, the enemy will pull back and try to stay in position.

- Utilize the enemy's pulling back by moving forward. Hook your left leg onto the enemy's right leg and put the enemy off balance.

- While using your momentum of moving forward, stun the enemy with a blow to his or her chin.

- With the leg hooked, the enemy cannot pull back further. And with his or her chin being pushed against, he or she cannot move forward. The enemy is off balance and defenseless.

THROW (from the Front)—When Near an Enemy with a Rifle

- To shift the focus of the enemy attack off you, take a slanted pose and approach the enemy quickly.

- Hold the enemy's right hand (mainly the fingers) with your own gun's handguard.

- Push it up so that the enemy gun points the other direction. At the same time, hook your left leg onto the enemy's right leg.

Push and the enemy will lose balance easily.

THROW (from Behind)—When Near an Enemy with a Rifle

- The enemy suddenly attacks you from behind.

- Your arms are held, and you cannot use your weapon.

- Do not move forward to try to get the enemy off you. Lean back toward the enemy by shifting your center of gravity to the back.

- Seek an opening and tilt yourself diagonally, and pull out your right leg. Press your elbow against the enemy's chest.

- Hook your right leg (which you pulled out) onto the enemy's leg. And at the same time, turn your body and push the enemy backward.

Strangle Enemy's Neck and Use Enemy as Shield

- One piece of advice: in real combat, do not show your face like in the photo (laughs).

- At most, only your left eye should be showing.

Caution When the Enemy has Surrendered

- Do not drop your guard, even when the enemy has surrendered. Be prepared for when the enemy decides to attack. While remaining relaxed, maintain a position that allows you to attack immediately. The gun should be pointed at the enemy at all times.

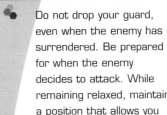

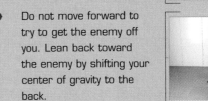
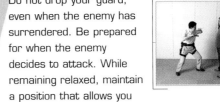
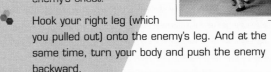
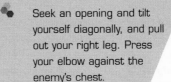

MOTION CAPTURE ACTOR INTERVIEWS

The motion capture and voice actors that appear in the Japanese version of MGS3 were kind enough to give interviews. Here is what they had to say.

YUMIKO DAIKOKU

Please introduce yourself to *Metal Gear Solid* fans.

Daikoku: I am Yumiko Daikoku. I played EVA. I do voiceovers and narrating.

How did you become an actress?

Daikoku: I became an actress for a very silly reason. I thought I could purchase MANGA (comic books) even as an adult if I was in this business. When I as small, I believed that it was embarrassing for adults to buy MANGA (laughs).

What were your first impressions when you first read the *MGS3* script?

Daikoku: I was like, "Wow, there are a lot of love scenes." Like, "Really? This much?" That really was my first impression. I had been told by Mr. Kojima before the sessions that there would be love scenes. But then I got the script and found a love scene here and a love scene there.

And the whole thing is really like a film. Reading the script was like seeing a 007 movie. The role I played is a really cool woman, and that's something that stuck to my mind while reading the script.

Any similarities between EVA and yourself?

Daikoku: We are total opposites (laughs). I could never move like she does in everyday life. In that sense, it was easy for me to develop her character within myself. Since she was so different from me, I could come up with ideas saying, "EVA would be doing this."

There was a lot of rigorous action, wasn't there?

Daikoku: Yes, I remember all those scenes. I've done many flips, and I was hung with cables. I was allowed to play a bit and fly around like Peter Pan (laughs).

Have you experienced wire action before?

Daikoku: There was this one scene where I lean forward at a big angle. That was so scary I was laughing (laughs). When watching someone else doing it, it didn't look that scary, but when I did it myself, I was like, "I'm going to fall!"

How was doing the motion capturing for *MGS3* different from the other acting roles you work on?

Daikoku: This is the second time I've done motion capturing. But the first time was not this long. I've never spoken or moved this much in any other acting job (laughs). And most of the people in the studio are men. When I occasionally saw other women, I was relieved—not that I'm any different when there are only men around me (laughs). It was a comfortable atmosphere.

The sessions went on for about six months. Any tough or fun moments?

Daikoku: The commuting was tough. I live far away, and I took the first train in the morning and the last train when going home. That was pretty much every day. Every day was a small trip for me (laughs). Everything else was really fun.

What I enjoyed the most was that there were always snacks in the studio (laughs). It's great to have a lot of food near you in the studio. And talking with everyone was fun. Of course the actual sessions were fun too (laughs). What was tough was getting up early in the morning.

How were the action scenes?

Daikoku: The wire action was great! That's a once-in-a-lifetime experience. That's why I chose to be hung. The back flips were very difficult, but I did not want to give up. I didn't want the staff to hand-draw the back flips in the game without my doing them myself. Thanks to everyone's support, I was able to do the action scenes without feeling much fear.

What did you think when you saw your own motions implemented in the E3 trailer?

Daikoku: Embarrassing! EVA isn't in the trailer that much, but I was embarrassed from the little I saw. I thought I couldn't watch the whole thing. Watching the walking of EVA made me think, "Oh my God, that's how I walk..."

Were there any jargon or customs at the motion capturing sessions that you found strange?

Daikoku: When people were shouting "air mat," I thought they were saying, "EVA mat." I thought they were calling me (laughs). There were many words I'd never heard before. And putting on the motion capture suit was a unique experience.

Was it difficult to move around in one of those suits?

Daikoku: The suit itself was okay, but it was the points (white ping pong ball-like things) that made moving around a bit tough. Everything was fine in the rehearsals, but when you put on the suit with the points, the points bump into the other actors. That's something I had to be careful with. Another thing was how tall characters are. Colonel Volgin is about two meters (6' 7"), but Mark (the actor who played Volgin) is not that tall. I was not supposed to look at his eyes when speaking to him. I had to look above his head, but I often looked at his eyes. That was difficult.

Anything about your scenes that you want fans to pay special attention to?

Daikoku: I've got to say the back flips. Those were really tough to do. Please watch for them in the game to see if I did them well. The staff really helped me when doing them.

How did you feel when the sessions were over?

Daikoku: I was like, "We're all done... There are so many scenes I'd love to redo." "We're...done..."

What kind of role do you want to play if there is another *MGS*?

Daikoku: A dual-personality character. It's a buy-one-get-one-free deal. I'd love to play a good and evil role together (laughs).

ERIKO HIRATA

Please introduce yourself to *Metal Gear Solid* fans.

Hirata: I am Eriko Hirata. I played The Boss.

How did you become an actress?

Hirata: When I was in junior high school, I was listening to the radio, and I heard this radio drama—probably anime-based. I was really impressed by their acting, and that's when I thought of doing what they were doing.

What were your first impressions when you first read the *MGS3* script?

Hirata: When I was given her role, I read the script—mainly her scenes. I thought from the bottom of my heart that The Boss is an incredible person.

It seems a difficult role to play. Was it tough?

Hirata: Yes, but I personally enjoyed it very much. I never had to force doing it. She is someone who leads a cool life. I did not want to make her too feminine. But I did not want to make her too masculine either. I paid special attention to keep her between those extremes.

Any similarities between The Boss and yourself?

Hirata: Hard to say. I'm not as physically powerful as she is (laughs). Maybe the fact that neither of us is that feminine (laughs).

The sessions went on for about six months. Any tough or fun moments?

Hirata: The cap I had to wear during the motion capturing was tight, and it was painful (laughs). Once you wear the cap and start shooting, you cannot take it off 'til the end of the day. That sucked. And the CQC and horseback riding scenes were difficult.

The fun moments were when Daikoku-san (actress playing EVA) and I ate cake on Christmas and when the crew went cherry-blossom-viewing. On Valentine's Day, Daikoku-san and I went out and bought sweets to give to the men on the set. I've never done that kind of thing like giving out chocolate on Valentine's Day, so that was really fun.

What did you think when you saw your own motions implemented in the E3 trailer?

Hirata: The Boss did not make that much of an appearance in the trailer. All she does is point her gun. But I thought she looked really cool, and I was really happy to see her. I cannot wait to see more of her in the final game.

What did you think of the scenes of the other characters you watched in the studio?

Hirata: I was like, "Oh, that's how the story goes..." I enjoyed watching Ocelot. I saw so much of Kanazawa-san (actor playing Ocelot) acting in the studio, but obviously he was not wearing a military uniform, and his face was not that of Ocelot's. Then I saw the trailer, and his motions matched Ocelot's visuals totally. Ocelot's conceited way of moving and talking and Kanazawa-san's acting matched perfectly. I was really surprised.

How was doing the motion capturing for *MGS3* different from performing on stage?

Hirata: With plays, you spend about two to three months rehearsing. It is during this period that all of us work on character development and stage directions. And when we finally perform in front of an audience, that is when we get to see the final results. With motion capturing, the rehearsing period is much shorter, and solidifying the character in that short period of time is quite difficult. We sort of have to visualize in our minds the character before rehearsing. It is more like recording episodes of TV drama. That's how I think it is.

How about acting using CQC?

Hirata: Mr. Mori (military advisor and CQC advisor) did demonstrations for us, but he does these sequences of multiple moves in like half a second (laughs). Then Mr. Abe (action coordinator from AAC STUNTS) explains the sequence to us piece by piece. While other actors did their shooting, Mark (actor playing Colonel Volgin) and I kept on practicing our CQC.

Any scenes of other characters that you look forward to seeing?

Hirata: The love scene (laughs). I did not get to see the actual shooting of it. Daikoku-san said to me, "Don't dare come into the studio that day!" The shooting of that scene was kept 'til the very last day. All actors including myself wanted to be there when the shooting wrapped up, but Daikoku-san insisted that we don't come (laughs). But I do understand her feelings. Love scenes are embarrassing, and I did not want to humiliate her. That's why I really look forward to seeing that.

If you were to appear in the sequel if there is one, what kind of role do you want?

Hirata: Someone who falls between the EVA type and The Boss type (laughs). I do want to try doing a sexy role, but not as sexy as EVA.

What are your future plans?

Hirata: I am working on a role called "Sanako Chiba" in an anime called *Shura no Koku*. And I do the narrations in the newest TV ad for the sports drink "Aquarius." If you watch the TV ad after watching my acting as The Boss, you'll definitely think that they're done by two different people (laughs).

INTRODUCTION

CHARACTERS

SYSTEM

WEAPONS

ITEMS

FOOD

CURE

PROLOGUE:
VIRTUOUS
MISSION

OPERATION
SNAKE EATER

SNAKE VS
MONKEY

BONUSES &
EASTER EGGS

KEROTAN
LOCATIONS

INTERVIEWS

METAL GEAR
SOLID COMIC

TARO KANAZAWA

Please introduce yourself to *Metal Gear Solid* fans.

Kanazawa: I am Taro Kanazawa. I was the motion capture actor for Ocelot.

You belong to Napalm Films, led by film director Ryuhei Kitamura, right? How did you become an actor?

Kanazawa: I was in a band in high school, and I found out that I enjoyed doing things like that. I know all professions are tough. Actors are commodities themselves. While there are all kinds of professions, I wanted to use my "self." I had to make up my mind between becoming a musician and an actor, and I chose acting.

How did you meet Mr. Kitamura?

Kanazawa: A friend (girl) of a friend of mine was in Tokyo working as a hair stylist. We became close friends. I told her that I was soon moving to Tokyo. She told me that I should contact her if I were going to act in Tokyo.

Seven or eight months after I moved to Tokyo, she called me saying, "We are now shooting a film. You should come over." That film happened to be Mr. Kitamura's *VERSUS*. The film was to be completed in another week. I had no idea what was going on, but I helped them do things as ordered. On the final day of shooting, we were shown something like a trailer—something still under editing. I was like "This is so cool!" I said to myself, "This is where I belong." The first shooting site was the best site ever.

What were your first impressions when you first read the *MGS3* script?

Kanazawa: When I first received the script, I got the lines for Ocelot only. Then halfway through the sessions I received the entire script with all the lines. When I read it, I almost cried. Even now if I think about the final scene, I get really emotional. I was so touched, "What a privilege to be part of this game!"

What do you think about your role as Ocelot?

Kanazawa: I like his being cool. Unlike me, he is cool, and I like that. While he is cool, he can be careless, and that's something I share. We both act before we think.

Any favorite lines of his?

Kanazawa: I like it when he says, "This time XXXXX." (hidden) You can figure out just from this line what is going to happen next. Just like the film *My Darling Clementine*. I love it when he takes out his XXXXX (hidden) and points it. I would love to see this scene in the game as soon as possible.

How was doing the motion capturing for *MGS3* different from shooting other films?

Kanazawa: They are completely different. First of all, (in motion capturing), there are no costumes or sets. But there are many cameras around you, and they can shoot you from all angles. That's the biggest difference. And I had to imagine for each scene a forest or house around me.

One thing that was similar with film was that the atmosphere was great. When I work with film director Ryuhei Kitamura, the entire staff works as one in unity. Mr. Kitamura is powerful, and everyone is like "Hell yeah!" trying to do what Mr. Kitamura envisions. Mr. Kojima and his staff are very friendly, and they all seem to be having fun at the sessions. It was really easy for me to work with them. And it was really fun too.

With motion capturing, you don't see the actual actor on the screen. You don't hear his voice. All you see is the game character. So what you really see of me in the game is my motion. I couldn't believe this at the very beginning of the sessions.

What did you think when you saw your own motions implemented in the E3 trailer?

Kanazawa: I was really impressed. Obviously, the character's appearance and voice are not mine, but I could tell that it was me. That definitely is me. I was like, "Hey, that's me!" I was very much surprised.

Mr. Yoshida, who plays Snake, had trouble imagining Ocelot as a young man before the sessions. But when the sessions started and he saw you in action and then saw your motion implemented in the game, he was surprised to see that your motion suited young Ocelot really well.

Kanazawa: That's pleasant to hear. Mr. Yoshida is way superior to me, and for such a person to commend me for my motion is an honor. Mr. Yoshida has been doing Snake for a long time, and his actions are sharp. The way he points his gun is as if he is in the military. So, I am really happy that he likes what I did.

The sessions went on for a long period of time. What was tough about the sessions?

Kanazawa: When Mr. Kojima points the gun, he looked very cool. But when I did, I did not look cool at all. Keeping in mind to lower my shoulders when acting was tough.

Any other tough moments?

Kanazawa: Actually no. On the contrary. Everything was great. I learned so much—how to point a gun correctly, how to point a gun cool. Everything was so positive.

If I ever have to act in the future with a gun, I'm sure I can act with a lot more variation than other people. I look forward to that moment. I know where to stare when pointing the gun. Mr. Mori (MGS military advisor) has really tormented me (laughs).

Anything about your acting that you want fans to pay special attention to?

Kanazawa: I acted as Ocelot. But I am not the only one who acted as Ocelot. People like Mr. Tornado Yoshida and Mr. Bill Yokoyama—professionals in gun action—handled that kind of action for Ocelot. So there are scenes where I do Ocelot's body and these men do his hands. I look forward to seeing this in the game.

There are scenes where you twirl the gun yourself, aren't there?

Kanazawa: Yes, there are, but I'm no match. Their twirling is incredibly faster.

Did you keep in mind what Ocelot was like in *MGS2*?

Kanazawa: I saw Ocelot from *MGS2* once, but I did not want to be influenced by Ocelot's motion from *MGS2*. There were only two specific actions that I used from what I saw. But from there on, I stopped watching Ocelot in *MGS2*. I did not listen to his voice anymore. I focused on the new script.

What are the two specific actions?

Kanazawa: Spinning the revolver's magazine with his hand applied to it, and taking the gun off-aim after pointing the gun. I imagined that he probably did those things even when he was young. The spinning of the magazine shows that Ocelot is a guy who enjoys showing off. Taking the gun off-aim shows that he has composure to not shoot right away. Other than that, I simply tried not to see or hear Ocelot from *MGS2*.

What kind of image of Ocelot did you have in mind when acting?

Kanazawa: At the audition, I already constructed this image of Ocelot in my mind. Then I was chosen and when the time came for me to act, I already knew what I wanted to do as Ocelot. I have not experienced too many auditions. I was more nervous at the audition than during the sessions.

What kind of role do you want to assume if there is another *MGS*?

Kanazawa: If Ocelots appears in it, I would like to be him again.

What are your plans for the future?

Kanazawa: We are now shooting *Godzilla*—the very final Godzilla film. I have a role in this film that our president Ryuhei Kitamura is directing. The film is going to come out in December. So if *MGS3* is released around the same time, we can enjoy some healthy competition.

INTRODUCTION

CHARACTERS

SYSTEM

WEAPONS

ITEMS

FOOD

CURE

PROLOGUE-
VIRTUOUS
MISSION

OPERATION
SNAKE EATER

SNAKE VS
MONKEY

BONUSES &
EASTER EGGS

KEROTAN
LOCATIONS

INTERVIEWS

METAL GEAR
SOLID COMIC

TAKASHI KUBO

Please introduce yourself to *Metal Gear Solid* fans.

Kubo: I am Takashi Kubo. I played Sokolov.

How did you become an actor?

Kubo: Please don't get me wrong, but there was this point in my life when I was bored with life itself. When I wasn't enjoying life, I decided to take on something that seemed difficult—something from which I kept a distance but at the same time had interest in. That was acting. That's how it happened. I wanted to do it some time in my life. Becoming an actor was one of the reasons why I move to Tokyo. I am not the type of person who is filled with enthusiasm. I wasn't like "I'm going to make it big!" I thought I'd be able to meet celebrities. Life has to be fun, and I thought acting would add to it.

Was acting as Sokolov easy?

Kubo: I really enjoyed playing him. I thought I might have overdone my acting, but Mr. Kojima said I was doing so when I was indeed overacting. His likes and dislikes were very obvious, and that made it easy for me to act. There are some directors that don't say "no." They say, "You're doing great, but..." They don't have the guts to say "no." I'm a tough one. I like it when a director tells me "no."

Any actors or works you have used as references when playing this role?

Kubo: I try not to refer to something else when I'm acting. I don't want to end up imitating something. All I can do is what I can do. I'd rather express the most out of how I have felt when reading the script.

The sessions went on for about six months. Any tough or fun moments?

Kubo: What was tough was wearing this tight motion capture suit. I also had to wear this cap. You sweat with that cap on, and you get itchy on your forehead (laughs). That's about it. What was fun were the lunches. All of us in the studio thanked the crew every day for the gorgeous lunchboxes. I've never worked together with stuntmen before. It was a valuable experience. Stuntmen usually spend more time on the set, and they know all of the behind-the-scene stuff. They told me some very interesting stories. Spending time with them not only during acting but also during breaks and waiting time is when you learn some great things from them. Some of the things that they tell you end up relieving you of your fears and make you relax. It really was a great learning experience.

What did you think when you saw your own motions implemented in the E3 trailer?

Kubo: From what I have seen, I remember Sokolov appearing for a second. He was running across the screen. His running was so animation-like. I was like "that's no product of motion capturing!" (laughs). I haven't seen much of Sololov in action yet. I look forward to playing the final game to see more of him.

How about other people's scenes?

Kubo: One of the scenes that I happened to see on set that are in the trailer, there is a scene with Ocelot where an enemy soldier is shot and falls from above. When I saw the trailer, I recognized that scene.

Acting done by humans is flexible and fluid. That's what makes it great. You can't really imitate an individual's motions. Motion capturing is really a form of acting. I hope it becomes more established as an acting form.

Motion capturing data is a collection of dots in motion. When you watch the dots moving, you don't see the face or body of the actor. This makes it easier for you to concentrate on the acting itself. You can really tell that different people move in different ways.

Anything about your acting that you want fans to pay special attention to?

Kubo: After discussing it with Mr. Kojima, the motions of Sokolov that I had in my mind had gone through this explosion. I can say that all of Sokolov's motions are worth paying attention to. Please keep your eye on the smallest details such has his finger movement. Oops, we did not capture any finger movements (laughs). But the "weaselness" you see in his posture is actually calculated. People in Russia might complain, "We Russians never walk like this!" (laughs)

The joy of a video game I think is the betrayal of people's expectations. That betrayal results in the player's surprise, and it is this element of surprise that makes the player enjoy the game. That's why I believe we must make the player say, "What the hell is going on?" or "I've never seen anything like this before!" When this is done in a way that the player knows that the game creator is trying to surprise the player at that particular point, the experience gets spoiled. It's trying to surprise the player in a way the player thinks it was done unintentionally that makes it work. And at the end, we want the player to say that *MGS3* was a really fun game.

All I could contribute was my motions. In that sense, I was able to go back to the basics of acting. For example, when turning around, I had to make sure I moved my shoulders. If I simply moved my eyeballs in a different direction, you couldn't tell in the game that I was staring in a different direction. It was such basics of acting that helped me perform. Sometimes I thought I moved enough, but I ended up being told that my motion was not big enough. With motion capturing, you have to move more than you think is enough, and it looks normal in the game.

Since we act without actually speaking the lines, our movements tend to be smaller than necessary. That's why we had to pay extra attention to expressing everything with our movements and not with words or facial expressions. A little bit of exaggeration in my movements was key. That's something I was able to realize.

If there were a *MGS4*, what kind of character would you like to play?

Kubo: I would like to do another Sokolov-like character. Or maybe a very military kind of guy. Someone who makes militaristic movements—pointing a machine gun, crawling, .etc. Or how about a dying part? I'd love to do five of those parts. Let's say there is a scene in which five soldiers get killed. I would love to do the motions for all five of them. That would be fun (laughs).

MARK MUSASHI

Please introduce yourself to *Metal Gear Solid* fans.

Mark: I am Mark Musashi. I played Colonel Volgin. I was Liquid Snake for "Twin Snakes."

How did you become an actor?

Mark: I first started out because I simply loved film. If you see American films, you can tell that actors go through all kinds of training—from horseback riding to SWAT training. I thought that I'd be able to experience a lot of things if I became an actor. And I thought that would be really fun.

Now, I am mainly a stuntman. I practiced martial arts in college, and I always hoped I could make use of that.

Have you played the *MGS* series so far?

Mark: When I was in college, a friend recommended *MGS* to me saying, "There's this game that's really cool!" I bought the game and a PlayStation together to play *MGS*, and I really enjoyed it.

When *MGS2* came out, I was not part of AAC (the action group that Mr. Yoshida, who plays Snake, belongs to as well) yet. So I did not do any of the motion capturing for *MGS*. However, I did play the game and enjoy it.

Finally for *Twin Snakes*, I was able to act as Liquid Snake. I never thought I'd be part of the series that I enjoyed playing as a college student (laughs). I was so happy, and I had such a great time. So I really look forward to playing *MGS3* for which I did the motion capturing. When I saw the E3 trailer and playable demo, I was like, "Man, I really want to play the final game!" (laughs)

INTRODUCTION

CHARACTERS

SYSTEM

WEAPONS

ITEMS

FOOD

CURE

PROLOGUE:
VIRTUOUS
MISSION

OPERATION
SNAKE EATER

SNAKE VS.
MONKEY

BONUSES &
EASTER EGGS

KEROTAN
LOCATIONS

INTERVIEWS

METAL GEAR
SOLID COMIC

What were your first impressions when you first read the *MGS3* script?

Mark: Hmmm... "Japanese is a tough language." (laughs) With *Twin Snakes*, the story was the same as *MGS1*, and I knew it really well. Reading the script was not a problem. But with *MGS3*, the script was thicker, and just reading through it was tough.

The storyline has the '60s spy film flavor while still maintaining the *MGS* atmosphere. It is really interesting.

What do you think about your role as Volgin?

Mark: In the beginning, it was like, "Who's going to play Volgin?" There really was no actor who seemed to fit the role. When I heard such discussions that no actor would be suitable, I was like, "I can do it! I will do it!" (laughs)

Volgin is a character that does whatever he wants to do in his own way, but just doing that does not comprise a good character. Volgin is a physically big guy with a lot of power as a colonel. He must be tough physically and position-wise. That's why I thought that not only does he do things as he wishes but he's also allowed to do so. I tried to make him this invincible character who fears nothing.

There's a Volgin line in the E3 trailer, "Welcome to my country—and to my unit." Volgin's motion there in the game (not revealed yet) is really cool. Did you come up with that yourself?

Mark: Initially, there was less movement to that scene. Then Mr. Kojima asked me if I could add arm movements. Then I came up with natural arm-spreading. I don't really think about what I want to do for each scene. They come about naturally.

Sometimes I intentionally throw in movements that are cliché-type movements so that one can tell what kind of emotional state the character is in, even without words. There may be certain things in the overall flow that I wish to highlight. For example, in a dynamic scene, it will stand out if I turn back very slowly. Varying the speed or strength of movements to add personality to that character is fun to do.

Are there any specific lines that you remember or like in particular?

Mark: "Kuwabara, kuwabara." (laughs) When I first read the script, I had no idea what it meant. It said, "He comes into the room while chanting 'Kuwabara...'" I still didn't get the feel of the chanting. I ended up asking people in my office. They gave me explanations, but I was still like, "Hmmm..."

An editor who was asked the same question by the foreign press told him that it was something like "God bless you."

Mark: I see...But that's not what it is. I understand why he said that, though. There really is no equivalent in America. I believe the English subtitles for that in the game will be "Kuwabara, kuwabara." (laughs) You just can't translate that. But that line ends up being the most memorable line for me.

How was doing the motion capturing for *MGS3* different from the other things you do as an actor?

Mark: I work on films and TV ads, but I do stuff for a lot of games too—opening movies and basic motions in particular. So I'm used to doing motion capturing. But I enjoy working on *MGS* the most. I feel like I am friends with the Konami people. With other projects, they ask me to do something, and I do it. With *MGS*, I feel this bond during the shooting and even during breaks. We talk about a lot of things. There is chemistry there. It's really fun working with them.

Any scenes of other characters that you look forward to seeing?

Mark: I haven't seen any of the scenes of the other boss characters. I also look forward to the CQC scenes. While I know how my own scenes go, I have no idea how the other scenes go.

What did you think when you saw your own motions implemented in the E3 trailer?

Mark: I'm always deeply touched and astonished—every single time I watch it. With film, you can figure out what the finished product will look like because there are actual sets and costumes. But with motion capturing, you into a studio with no sets or costumes that appear in the game. We carry a plastic gun or wooden sword. There are no special effects. But the final product (the game) has the lighting, effects, etc. It ends up looking incredibly cool.

One thing that is easy to catch is other people's motions. You don't see yourself acting, but you do remember how other people acted. Let's take the running of Mr. Yoshida (actor for Snake). You can tell from the trailer that it is Mr. Yoshida's running (laughs). There definitely is an element of peculiarity. You see him acting in the rehearsals. Then you see the character in the trailer. The CG character is running exactly the way he runs. This is awesome.

MIZUHO YOSHIDA

Please introduce yourself to *Metal Gear Solid* fans.

Yoshida: I am Mizuho Yoshida. I have been the motion actor for Snake since *MGS2*, which was four years ago. This is the third game for me as Snake (*MGS2*, *Twin Snakes*, *MGS3*).

How did you become an actor?

Yoshida: I first started acting as hero characters in attraction shows held on the roof floor of department stores. I was doing my best acting while wearing masks that showed none of my facial expressions. What turned things around was my appearance in *Mirai Ninja* by director Keita Amamiya. The staff were from the Eiji Tsuburaya ("Ultraman") era. As someone who was pretty much an amateur, I was really nervous. But I enjoyed working with them. But it was this spirit as a professional that I learned from them and experience I gained that enabled me to do what I am still doing.

Have you played the *MGS* series so far?

Yoshida: I am not good at playing games, and I always get stuck in the beginning (laughs). I know it's an infiltration game, but I end up shooting anyone in sight. I soon run out of tranquilizer shots and I suck at close combat... I've tried many times, you know (laughs).

But I think I will enjoy *MGS3* because of the new gameplay elements.

What elements specifically?

Yoshida: Food capturing. It is really fun. I have heard a lot about it from Mr. Kojima. When I saw it for myself, it was great. I'll probably do a lot of walking around in the game—probably throughout the entire map and get excited every time I spot a snake or frog.

What were your first impressions when you first read the *MGS3* script?

Yoshida: I knew I was going to be tossed around a lot. In the previous *MGS* games I performed for, I was always this sharp guy. This time, I was thrown around like trash (laughs).

What do you think about your role as Snake?

Yoshida: He does not talk that much. I tried to be cool in my acting when he simply stands, sits down, looks at something, etc. And Snake in *MGS3* is more "original" genetically, right? While doing my usual Snake acting, I tried to think of how he could or should be different from what I did before.

DUCTION

CHARACTERS

SYSTEM

WEAPONS

ITEMS

FOOD

CURE

PROLOGUE:
VIRTUOUS
MISSION

OPERATION
SNAKE EATER

SNAKE VS.
MONKEY

BONUSES &
EASTER EGGS

KEROTAN
LOCATIONS

INTERVIEWS

METAL GEAR
SOLID COMIC

Are there any specific lines that you remember or like in particular?

Yoshida: The lines about the weapons were really long and difficult. But those who are interested in weapons will enjoy it because you get to hear Snake's detailed appreciation for his weapons.

How was doing the motion capturing for *MGS3* different from shooting other films?

Yoshida: In film, you really don't have to care about what is not shot by the camera. What is used is only stuff that gets within the frame. But with motion capturing, you really don't know where the cameras are shooting you from. So you have to keep in mind that the cameras are shooting you all the time from all angles.

The sessions went on for about six months. Any tough or fun moments?

Yoshida: What was tough was maintaining my physical health. I did get hurt when there were dynamic action scenes. But I healed myself with my strong will (laughs). I was never seriously injured, but I got stepped on my feet during the CQC scenes. My thumbs were bleeding internally during CQC. But I found CQC action very fun. I ended up learning a whole new set of actions. However, I don't think I'll ever get to use them in real life (laughs).

What I enjoyed was that I was able to act with actors other than those who belong to where I do (AAC). I learned a lot from Mr. Kanazawa (actor for young Ocelot), as he really got into his acting.

Ocelot was always this old guy in the other games, and I thought it would be tough to do a young Ocelot. He's really got character, and maybe fans would like to see him more than Snake. Snake is pretty much an established character. I was like, "What? Ocelot is young this time?" (laughs) But it was done really well. I was surprised in a positive way.

As Snake, you have interacted with pretty much every character. With whom did you enjoy interacting?

Yoshida: It was fun working with everyone, but I really enjoyed working with Mr. Kubo (Sokolov). Back when we did the auditions, I was hoping that he got chosen. Sokolov is a character that is hard to figure out, but thanks to Mr. Kubo's acting, Sokolov ended up being a very interesting character. I hope you look forward to seeing Sokolov in the final game.

What did you think when you saw your own motions implemented in the E3 trailer?

Yoshida: I thought the lighting in this game looks really cool. Inside the plane at the very beginning, and the sun light you see on the mask before jumping looked very different from what we had seen in the past. They were beautiful.

Anything about your acting that you want fans to pay special attention to?

Yoshida: (laughs) When I get grabbed in my crotch (laughs). I wonder how many fans picked that up. It's from *MGS2* where the President...(laughs)

How did the love scene go?

Yoshida: No matter what scene I was acting for, I always had in mind that the love scene had to be done (laughs). It was a lot of pressure. Up until when we actually did that scene, there was so much thinking I did, but when the time came, I just did it. Doing the scene well was one of my biggest goals, and I thought of it as part of growing up (laughs). When it was over, Daikoku-san (actress for EVA) said, "You were not gentle." I was hurt a bit (lots of laughs).

The story of *MGS3* is about a tragedy during the Cold War era. What did you think of it?

Yoshida: It's very tough and complicated. It is not only a Cold War thing. We seem to understand the feelings of those who go to war, but we don't in actuality. We can read about this subject. I think we Japanese have in our heart the spirit of "doing something for a cause." We pray to God, depend on some form of support—not exactly because we are weak. I guess we are relieved by being able to depend on something.

Artwork by
Ashley Wood

Written by
Kris Oprisko

Lettered by
Robbie Robbins

Edited by
Chris Ryall

KONAMI
www.idwpublishing.com
Special thanks to Hideo Kojima, Scott Dolph, and the entire Metal Gear Solid team at Konami.